WARRIOR

Also by Peter Hathaway Capstick

Peter Capstick's books are available from St. Martin's Press.
His videos may be obtained by writing to:
Sportsmen on Film
P.O. Box 1818
Kerrville, Texas 78029

THE PETER CAPSTICK LIBRARY

Peter Capstick, Series Editor

WARRIOR

THE LEGEND OF
COLONEL RICHARD MEINERTZHAGEN

Peter Hathaway Capstick

St. Martin's Press

New York

A THOMAS DUNNE BOOK.
An imprint of St. Martin's Press.

WARRIOR: THE LEGEND OF COLONEL RICHARD
MEINERTZHAGEN. Copyright © 1998 by Peter Hathaway
Capstick. All rights reserved. Printed in the United States of
America. No part of this book may be used or reproduced in any
manner whatsoever without written permission except in the case
of brief quotations embodied in critical articles or reviews. For
information, address St. Martin's Press, 175 Fifth Avenue,
New York, N.Y. 10010.

Design by Jennifer Ann Daddio

Library of Congress Cataloguing-in-Publication Data

Capstick, Peter Hathaway.
    Warrior : the legend of Colonel Richard Meinertzhagen   /
by Peter Hathaway Capstick. — 1st ed.
        p.   cm.
    Includes bibliographical references and index.
    ISBN 0-312-18271-6
    1. Meinertzhagen, Richard, 1878–1967.   2. Great Britain—
History, Military—20th century.   3. Great Britain. Army—
Biography. 4. Soldiers—Great Britain—Biography.   I. Title.
DA69.3.M4C36   1998
355'.0092—dc21
[B]   97-31884
                                                              CIP

10   9   8

FOR GENERAL NORMAN SCHWARZKOPF
SOLDIER, HUNTER, HERO

In Admiration and Gratitude

Contents

List of Maps

Foreword

Peter died in South Africa on March 13, 1996, after cardiac surgery and a valiant fight. He had been working on this, his thirteenth manuscript, when he fell ill, and it has been my task to complete his book and see it safely delivered to the publishers in New York.

Colonel Richard Meinertzhagen first came to Peter's attention in 1983, when Peter found a reprint of the colonel's *Kenya Diary, 1902–1906* at one of our favorite antiquarian book dealers in South Africa. This led to the tracking down and purchase of all the first editions of Meinertzhagen's books, which Peter considered relevant to his interests in hunting, African exploration, and military history and adventure. These books occupy a special niche in Peter's wonderful library of Africana.

Over the years, Peter shared his thoughts with me about Dick Meinertzhagen in many a discussion about that unique and memorable man. Peter searched through his works for clues as to his personality and hidden impulses, and he concluded that Meinertzhagen remained an enigma, a remarkable one at that, worthy of introduction to a new generation of readers who enjoy reading about people who lived bold and daring lives.

In an age of globalized sameness where the senses are often

bludgeoned by the banal, the extraordinary life and adventures of Meinertzhagen are refreshing in their diversity, in their challenges and triumphs. And it is easy to see why Peter, a man who lived for the open spaces, who had known combat and who was a seasoned hunter with very wide-ranging and cultivated interests, was attracted by Meinertzhagen's life and decided to write about him.

Peter had lived in several African countries before settling in South Africa in 1982. He had a natural empathy with the bush, with rural Africans and the world they inhabited. His library is testimony to a voracious reader with an abiding interest in hunting, natural history, military engagements, weaponry, and exploration, Africa being the focus. Meinertzhagen's experiences acted as a magnet to Peter's mind as he tried to uncover some of the layers making up that complex man.

Although Meinertzhagen gained international fame as an ornithologist, this memoir is not about birds. It is about hunting and pioneering military adventure, about political intrigue and clandestine activities, about the pitting of wits against humans and animals as Meinertzhagen takes us through his long and remarkable life. It is a book of anecdotes of high adventure on a vibrant Indian, African, and Middle Eastern canvas. It is the story of a man who truly marched to his own drum, a striking individualist, a pioneer, someone who made a difference. Peter shied away from the mundane and the predictable. He, too, marched to his own drum, and he recognized a kindred spirit in Meinertzhagen. He often remarked on how fortunate it was that Meinertzhagen had decided to go public with some of his diaries, so making accessible something of the spirit and challenges of his times. Peter was a retrospective soul who was very conscious of the transient nature of human life and of the importance of conserving the past in some form for later generations.

Today would have been Peter's fifty-seventh birthday. As I

look back over his adventure-filled life and the entertainment and escape his books have afforded legions of readers, I recall one of his favorite quotations. It is by Franklin Delano Roosevelt, who, in addressing the American Booksellers Association on April 23, 1942, had the following to say:

"Books cannot be killed by fire. People die but books never die. No man and no force can abolish memory. . . . In this war, we know books are weapons."

FIONA CLAIRE CAPSTICK
Waterkloof, Pretoria
Republic of South Africa
JANUARY 11, 1997

Acknowledgments

I should like to express my profound gratitude at the outset to Ran Meinertzhagen, son of the late Colonel Richard Meinertzhagen, for so graciously agreeing to read the entire manuscript of this book when it was in its "raw" stage and for facilitating the granting of permission by the Rhodes House Library in Oxford for certain photographs and for the extensive quotations from the Colonel's diaries to be reproduced. I am also indebted to Mr. Meinertzhagen for his advice concerning the manuscript. His goodwill and wonderful cooperation have been crucial for the publication of this book.

In this context, my thanks are also extended to the following people for their invaluable assistance.

Mr. J. R. Pinfold of the Rhodes House Library in Oxford, the repository of Colonel Meinertzhagen's diaries and photographs, for his outstanding efficiency and cooperation and permission to make use of certain photographs and to quote from the colonel's published diaries.

General Norman Schwarzkopf, U.S. Army (retired), the epitome of the modern–day warrior, for according the memory of my late husband the unique honor in accepting the dedication of this, his final book.

Richard Curtis, my late husband's literary agent, who placed unwavering faith in me and whose patience, kindness, and fortitude towards me will be treasured for all time.

Matt Walker, Peter Wolverton, and all at St. Martin's Press of New York for unparalleled understanding and competence.

Mr. R. Carr of the Bodleian Library in Oxford who was responsible for putting me in touch with Mr Pinfold of the Rhodes House Library, thereby facilitating the entire process.

Robin Fryde of Frank R. Thorold (Pty) Ltd. of Johannesburg and Paul Mills of Clarke's Bookshop of Cape Town, both pivots of the antiquarian book market in South Africa and esteemed friends who, together with their respective members of staff, were of great assistance to me.

Jill Lake, Rights Manager of Macmillan Press Limited for permission to quote from *Kenya Chronicles* by Lord Cranworth, the book having been published in 1939 by Macmillan and Company Limited of London.

Sara Jillings, permissions manager of Prentice Hall Europe, for her advice concerning permission to quote from Charles Miller's book, *The Lunatic Express*. As Prentice Hall Europe does not appear to have a record of this book as being one of the titles purchased from Macmillan, recourse is hereby made to fair use in order to cover permission to make use of the brief quotation from the book in question.

Ms. Anne Peacock of Random House for her assistance.

Ms. Janet Sykes of Addison Wesley Longman for putting me onto the right track

Mr. Nicholas Combrinck of Johannesburg for his advice concerning the brief quotation from *They Fought for King and Kaiser* by James Ambrose Brown, published by Ashanti Publishing (Pty) Ltd of South Africa, the company no longer being in business. The practice of fair use holds true in this instance.

Ms. Natasha Steinberg of Random House UK Limited for putting me in touch with M. V. Carey Esq. of the "Seven Pillars of Wisdom Trust" in London concerning permission to use the brief quotation from T. E. Lawrence's *Seven Pillars of Wisdom*. As of this date, no reply has been received from Mr. Carey. The quotation is fully identified in the text and my gratitude is expressed here to the Trust for its understanding in this regard.

My special thanks to Magda van Staden, the noted artist, of Pretoria, South Africa, for her superb sketch maps and her unfailing good humor and hospitality as the pressure mounted.

Bernard Clark of Pretoria, South Africa, for the professional preparation of photographic material.

Marisa Fenderl of Pretoria, South Africa, a great friend of very long standing, who knew Peter well and who stood by me through difficult days immediately after Peter's death and during the months that followed as I completed this manuscript. Her steadfast belief in my abilities and optimism can never be adequately repaid but the publication of this book is every bit her triumph too.

My sister, Laurian Coughlan, of Pietermaritzburg, South Africa, for her research into the Indian Mutiny, for her incisive advice and for giving so generously of her time and talent in reading the manuscript. Peter always had the greatest regard for her abilities.

His Excellency Ambassador Uri Oren, Ambassador Extraordinary and Plenipotentiary of the State of Israel to the Republic of South Africa, for his time and valuable insights into Jewish history and for his advice and comments concerning relevant sections of the manuscript. This book is appearing in the golden jubilee year of the founding of the State of Israel for which Meinertzhagen fought so hard for so long. *Harbeh todot lekha, Adoni Hashagrir.*

To Safari Club International and the international hunting

community for their outstanding support and encouragement and for providing the best possible venue for the book launch at their annual convention in Reno, Nevada, in January 1998. Peter was always deeply appreciative of the support, friendship and camaraderie of fellow hunters and readers of his books with whom he conducted a lively correspondence until shortly before his death.

Finally, to Adelino Serras Pires, veteran hunter of Africa and esteemed friend of many years of both Peter and myself, and to his extended family, my profound appreciation for their continued love and support, for their wonderful hospitality and unwavering belief in my ability to complete this daunting task and to bring honor to the memory of a fellow hunter and friend whose writings brought so much pleasure to so many for almost thirty years.

The warrior merely carries the sword on behalf of others.

His task is a lordly one because the warrior still agrees to die

for the mistakes of others.

—ALEXANDRE SANGUINETTI

WARRIOR

Introduction

Evening had already sulked up with a dark, tawdry look when the seventeen Allied soldiers slipped through the unprotected perimeter of the Imperial German camp. There were two white officers and fifteen black East African askaris, and they had all fastened bayonets to their .303-caliber rifles, the standard bolt-action issue firearm of World War I. The taller of the two British officers had already sniped three enemy from the German positions, rolling to one side to deny the Huns return fire. Even though he had fired at the first silhouettes of dusk, the barrel of his rifle was still vaguely warm. He later commented that although the German strength was roughly 500 men, hardly a shot came near him as he coolly spattered brains backlighted against the sliding sun, ignoring the return fire. He noted that he considered the almost suicidal show "exciting," as the enemy had fired what he thought must be well over "several thousand rounds at me," which is hardly an inconsiderable amount of firepower. Curiously, his commanding officer had declined to counterattack the German forces those few days before Christmas, but the aging British officer wasn't finished yet.

He and his men arrived back in the area, a place called Karungu, near the shore of Lake Victoria, the very tenuous British

East Africa, on the December 22, 1915, each man carrying 150 rounds of .303 ammunition, some water, weevily food, and a considerable amount of courage.

On the basis that it would be somewhat socially unreasonable to call an officer born on March 3, 1878, a young man in 1915—although an extremely dangerous one—the thirty-seven-year-old was fully up to the task before him. He left with his black scouts and Major J. J. Drought, no casual hand with a bayonet himself. It was Christmas when they crossed the German lines, and they were traveling light and fast, with only their canteens, rucksacks, and rifles; in harm's way, for sure. And harm was there to greet them. The enemy was found just before five that afternoon.

They first got word from tribesmen of an enemy patrol—not nearly as big as the one they had shot up a few days before—at a place called Kitambi Hill. In superb shape, they continued their march and found the Germans and their black allies just before dusk. It was a perfect setup: no sentries, no alarm, unarmed soldiers lounging around in the flickering firelight. There were four tents that Christmas Day of 1915, and the attacking party counted fourteen German askaris. At about dusk—and it falls like a lead-lined shade into the blackest night in East Africa—they discerned the lantern-lit canvas. For Baby Jesus' birthday, at least from the German point of view, it was not a very successful show. The British silently twisted and locked on their well-greased bayonets and charged the Germans and their black askaris. They killed fifteen, took seven unwounded prisoners as well as two wounded who were well winged. Major Drought had himself killed three men with the icy steel, an event that impressed even the other officer as "a great effort."

The bloodletting among the thoughtless enlisted troops was over; the dark gore had flowed and the officer went among the enemy tents. To this time, there had not been a shot fired. Kitambi Hill was quiet, quite literally deathly quiet. Yet there was a bulbous shape showing through the shadow of the interior light, obviously that of a white man. Blacks did not have tents during the Great War, to "Make Civilization Safe for further Colonization." The young officer charged; and found a stout German Offizier sitting, somewhat amazed, on a camp bed with a definitely sumptuous Christmas dinner spread before him. He rather foolishly snatched for a Luger or Mauser under his pillow, necessitating the only shot of the encounter as the Briton fired and killed him with a single black-edged round in the approximate area of his solar plexus, which bounced him off the edge of the canvas and once again onto the bed.

He turned out to be, however, a rather high-ranking fool. The British officer, rifling his pockets, found that he was referred to as Graf, which he interpreted as "duke," an error as that term in German refers to a count or earl. Actually, this is a curious error as the British officer was educated in Germany. In any case, he reckoned that he must have shot his first duke, although it by no means ruined his Christmas appetite, or that of Major Drought, who shared the feed with substantial enthusiasm. Waste not, want not, especially during a major war in the bush of East Africa. Ignoring the cooling corpse when they had finished the plum pudding, they decided to take the silverware and the hallmarked, family-crested plates. They used the term *purloined*, that the dishes and cutlery might not be "looted" by the natives. Spoils of war.

The British were unable, through lack of manpower and tools—and possibly enthusiasm—to bury the enemy dead, leaving them to the hyenas, which are most efficient in the disposal of enemy personnel—or even close friends, for that matter. The small assault party marched with their prisoners until midnight and left the area on Boxing Day, December 26, 1915. Placing sentries out, they slept late and reached home base on the afternoon of the same day.

It was most interesting that some years later, the officer met the brother of the "duke" when he was in Amsterdam. When the brother heard that the officer had been in German East Africa during the war and inquired whether he could advise the circumstances of the "duke's" death, the Briton had not the heart to tell the truth that he had killed him personally.

The British officer's name, incidentally, was Richard Meinertzhagen.

Although he lived until 1967, Dick Meinertzhagen was a professional Victorian, a source of controversy, both physical and political, for eighty-nine years. Yet what actual niche in life did he occupy? This is a good question, to which there is no easy answer. He was a soldier, a big-game hunter and discoverer of a hitherto unknown species, an ornithologist of world repute specializing in migrating birds (of whose skins he accumulated more than 20,000), chief of intelligence against the Germans in World War I in the East African campaign and head political intelligence officer in the Mesopotamian theater, close friend of Lawrence of Arabia, adviser to the British throne, a founding force in modern guerrilla warfare, a Gentile who became one of the driving forces behind the birth of the modern State of Israel, a spy of great personal talent, and an intellectual whose personality and perspicacity shone like a new sovereign in a world known for bright men largely responsible for the fact that English was even then *the* world language. Dick was tricky, shifty, wealthy, well-connected, and absolutely ruthless. Although he did not coin the term that the ends justify the means, it was his personal dictum.

But if there was a single facet of Dick Meinertzhagen's character that truly set him apart, it was that he was a killer, an amber-eyed, unblinking, hand-to-hand killer with the soul of a paladin and the stroke of a headsman. In later years, especially since his death in June of 1967, several people of note have made and printed personal comments as to Dick's talent in this regard. This includes Elspeth Huxley of Kenya fame, in her reintroduction to Meinertz-hagen's *Kenya Diary (1902–1906)* (London, 1984), a rather scathing view of Dick Meinertzhagen that dwells largely on his "bloodlust" for hunting as well as killing fellow humans, many of whom needed killing. Well, as far as the second observation is concerned, what else would be wished of a professional soldier who ended up as a full colonel in the British army? Killing was what he was taught to do. Should there be an implied moral penalty if he learned to do it well?

We now live in an ever-greening world where hunting in any form is misperceived as well as ill-received by watchers of networks who declare virtually any and every species "endangered," often on tenuous biological evidence. The very essence of hunting as a conservation tool is misrepresented. Note, however, that little is said as to the threat of the black widow or the scorpion or the deadly poisonous stone fish becoming endangered. "Greening" is the classic exercise in fund-raising, in selling the electronic charm of furry creatures. It has extremely little to do with the actual facts of life and death in the wild. If you've ever watched anything die "naturally," you realize that nothing is nastier or less forgiving than Mother Nature. What do you think these fund-raisers for various "greening" organizations eat? Spinach?

Meinertzhagen has been alternately smeared as a racist, a mind-less killer, and a homicidal freak, not necessarily in that order. He was none of these. He killed people with a purely catholic lack of prejudice: Indian officers on his own team, whole villages of blacks in East Africa in punitive campaigns for their own outrages, and, in just one morning, twenty-three-plus assorted enemy troops on Europe's Western Front who, presumably, were white (there being notably few blacks in the German army), trying to crush the skull of the last one with his African war club. He also killed his own Indian horse-handler for maltreating one of the animals in his care. Yet, although he was by definition most competent at killing, as he did so much of it, this was the same man who refused to kill an elephant for rather unfathomable emotional reasons and the same man who rescued a little girl from a brothel in the Near East.

Richard Meinertzhagen was an enigma, an anomalous personality, a human non sequitur, a seeming jangle of contradictions. He was one of the most prolific diarists for one of the longest periods in the English language, having written the first words in 1884 at the age of six of what would become more than seventy volumes of typescript. He makes a curious statement, typical of him, however, saying that the diary he now keeps was begun in March 1899. This is a reference, possibly, to the fact that he destroyed large portions of his diaries in 1942, for reasons unknown. He may have done this so that they would not be found when he was considering publication. Most of his work appeared later in his life, and he may not have wanted to appear so politically preinformed as some statements would indicate, such as predicting Mau-Mau half a century before the eruption of the movement among, primarily, the Kikuyu tribe of Kenya, East Africa. Many Kikuyu scalps figuratively hung at his Sam Browne belt, although he appeared to have liked and respected the people.

Dick Meinertzhagen wrote in longhand and transcribed his material whenever he had the chance, perhaps, to think it over. We can only guess at what has been eradicated and why (although that might be interesting!), and it would be an injustice to draw conclusions when the man no longer exists to defend himself and his writings. I long ago decided to take him as he is, or at least as he seems to be through his writings, and to leave the hair-splitting and mind-numbing archival comparisons to others. I write to relax, to entertain, and, hopefully, to enlighten. In the case of Meinertz-hagen, I have tried to show the way things were in the African bush and elsewhere in his extraordinary life. This book is anecdotal in character as it attempts to highlight the hunting adventures, military daring, mayhem, travel, political intrigue, exploration, and espionage coups of a man who left his mark as few have on the events of his time. Meinertzhagen was the classic human inconsistent, which will come to light as his experiences are examined. He was, on one hand, an officer who would give orders to absolutely wipe out an African village during warfare, a man who killed dozens of people personally with the bayonet alone, who carried an African knobkerrie—war club—as commonly as he wore his socks. Yet the same man showed many unusual aspects of kindness to the same African tribesmen he fought. There is little confirmation, however, that he was terribly generous to Imperial German forces, black or white, in East Africa, although he was of German heritage himself.

I have always felt that T. E. Lawrence (of Arabia) caught Meinertzhagen's personality well, if not perfectly, in the first edition of his *Seven Pillars of Wisdom*. Meinertzhagen was horrified at the description by Lawrence of Arabia, his close friend, and the reference only appears in the first several printings of Lawrence's first edition work, having been later expunged. Lawrence said, speaking of Meinertzhagen's disinformation exercises against the enemy as well as of his personal character:

> This ally was Meinertzhagen, a student of migrating birds
> drifted into soldiering, whose hot immoral hatred of the
> enemy expressed itself as readily in trickery as in violence
> . . . Meinertzhagen knew no half measures. He was logical,

an idealist of the deepest, and so possessed by his convictions that he was willing to harness evil to the chariot of good. He was a strategist, a geographer, a silent laughing masterful man; who took as blithe a pleasure in deceiving his enemy (or his friend) by some unscrupulous jest, as in spattering the brains of a cornered mob of Germans one by one with his African knob-kerri. His instincts were abetted by an immensely powerful body and a savage brain, which chose the best way to its purpose, unhampered by doubt or habit.[1]

Let's take a look at Dick's Victorian background to understand something of the forces that molded him into this "silent laughing masterful man." I hope you enjoy him as much as I have over the years.

Chapter 1

Born in London on March 3, 1878, just fifteen months shy of Queen Victoria's Diamond Jubilee, Dick entered that halcyon age of empire where high-born privilege, spit, polish, tiffin, pigsticking, boiled beef, cold showers, and God Save the Queen would form part of the intricate tapestry of his long life. It was the height of the Victorian era, and the gas-lit streets and horse-drawn transport were a lifetime away from the supersonic aircraft, submarines, electric light, wireless telegraphy, world wars, atomic bombs, and space exploration Dick would live to witness.

Britain ruled the oceans unchallenged. The sun quite literally never set on her empire. There were still vast areas of the world virtually unknown to outsiders waiting to be explored and animals still to be discovered. Our Camel Man wouldn't have known where to begin, such were the challenges still open, the wilds untouched. It was a man's world in every sense.

Meinertzhagen was destined to survive many an encounter with big game, bloody warfare in the African bush and elsewhere, train crashes, shipwrecks, pistol duels and exploding shells, espionage missions, and fearsome personality clashes. And all the while he kept a daily diary that has left a unique record of this adventurer.

He had the immense good sense to be born into the wealthy

North Sea

Scotland

Ireland

Irish Sea

Wales

England
London
•Aldershot
HAMPSHIRE
•Southhampton

ENGLAND

and influential Huth banking family, who could trace their origins back to the late fourteenth century in Germany. Dick liked to believe he was of Danish Viking stock, basing this on his family crest, which featured a hag berry or bird cherry bush. One presumes it wasn't rampant. The family could boast centuries-old ecclesiastical connections in Cologne and a tradition of the firstborn sons always being named Daniel. One such Daniel had been mayor of Bremen, and Dick notes that the major's diary was as dull as third-hand wit, although he admired his ancestor's business acumen.

Dick's family became established in England in 1826, and his father, Daniel VI, married into the eccentric, highly controversial, and atypical Potter family of nine daughters, "that monstrous regiment of women," as one of the nine husbands put it. All the Potter girls married wealthily well, Dick's parents going on to have ten children in good old Victorian tradition. This was the most practical form of life insurance. It certainly insured the bloodline!

Dick was the second son. Throughout his life, until just before his father died and his mother had a change of heart, he had a troubled relationship with her. She was an icy, domineering woman capable of incredible rudeness and hurtful comment to anyone within firing range, starting with Dick, for unfathomable reasons. His father, on the other hand, was kind, tolerant, and generous. Quite obviously, the marriage was a disaster, and Dick felt shunned and unloved from a very early age. His mother's verbal cruelty bred in him a "horror of hurting other people's feelings,"[1] an interesting statement from someone who, in adult life, would not hesitate to bayonet, club to death, or shoot anyone perceived as being the enemy in a conflict situation.

And Dick would encounter many, many conflict situations.

Dick Meinertzhagen was the product of a family studded with purported Gypsies and Spanish grandees who at one time were entrusted with the Spanish royal jewels in exile. As a young boy, he met such luminaries as Henry Morton Stanley, Florence Nightingale, Charles Darwin, Cecil John Rhodes, Oscar Wilde, and Richard Burton of "source of the Nile" fame. He was at school with Winston Churchill, whom he attempted to knock off a sidewalk; he saw and heard Tchaikovsky play and conduct his own compositions; and grew up to become generally conversant with and considered the mental contemporary and equal of just about anybody of repute—either good or evil—of his times. Meinertzhagen was deadly, therapeutically tough despite his velvet-glove upbringing. Lord forbid that his family had not become anglicized generations ago. The Germans could have used him.

As a boy of ten, Meinertzhagen met Harry Johnston, one of Africa's greatest pioneers and the discoverer of the okapi. He says of that meeting, during which Johnston described East and West Africa:

> From that moment I had a tremendous desire to visit the Dark Continent and see for myself the big game, the huge tropical lakes and all the wonders of what was then an unknown continent.[2]

This proved to be one of those life-changing experiences.

As I read those words, I thought back on one of my own life-changing experiences when, as a little boy, younger than Dick at this time, I was taken to see the Carl Akeley lion-spearing bronzes in the American Museum of Natural History in New York. Little Peter was never the same after that, thank God!

Young Dick had already shown an interest in the outdoors when, as a kid of six, he "stole" some ducks at a pond in Hyde Park. He killed his first bird, a cock grouse, in that same year and quickly became a seasoned rabbit hunter before he reached double-digit age.

Meinertzhagen's schooling had certain lifelong effects on his character. His first years were spent very happily at school with his adored elder brother, Dan, in his mother's native Yorkshire, where the much-loved head, the Reverend Hales, would drum into the boys, "Don't just stand there, do something!" This may as well have been Dick's motto. The school's motto, in fact, was "Ex Quercu non ex Salice," that is, "Out of oak, not willow." In other words, be tough, do not bend. Dick's adult six-foot, twelve-stone frame and fearless nature would carry him through a lifetime of situations where, had he stood and done nothing, had he bent and not resisted, he would have had no more chance of living to eighty-nine than most mortals have of obtaining easy credit.

After this grand start in life, Dick was to endure a bitter interlude at another school, where he suffered horrendous physical and mental abuse by one of the two brothers who ran the place. Such was this maltreatment, with its homosexual and sadistic undertones, that Dick literally broke down when he revisited the site of his youthful torment as an old man. He freely admitted that this period of his life left permanent scars on his psyche that made it difficult for him to express emotion and be close to people.

Dick went on to Harrow, one of the most illustrious schools in Britain, where he poached partridge and hares and generally enjoyed life again with Dan. Once, when out with the school band, he slipped off to poach a rabbit to feed to the eagles he and Dan were allowed to keep at Harrow. This occurred on the property of one Lord Salisbury, who just happened to be prime minister and foreign secretary, and who saw the critter dangling from Dick's belt.

"And how did you kill it?" asked Lord Salisbury.

"With a stone," I said, a bit reassured.

"Well done, are you going to eat it?"

"No," said I, "it's for our eagles at Harrow."[3]

Dick then had Lord Salisbury and his staff officers engrossed with his story of the eagles and other birds the Meinertzhagen boys were allowed to keep, already being serious and gifted ornithologists. What really enthralled Dick was the chance to speak with this symbol of Empire and conservative values. Young Dick was all fired up about "getting out to the Colonies." He'd get there, all right. More's the miracle he survived.

But it was the family estate at a place called Mottisfont, in Hampshire, just seventy miles southwest of London, that really molded Dick's character. It was a sporting boy's dreamland. Meaning "meeting place" and referring to a central spring, Mottisfont was built in 1201, making it just barely thirteenth century. It had originally been an Augustinian priory founded by one William Briwere. Ninety years later, the income for the whole abbey was only fifty-eight pounds, but it must be borne in mind that at that period a full-grown pig brought only a few pennies at market. In 1536, the abbey, with its 2,000-odd acres of land, was seized from the Church under Henry VIII, and tradition has it that a curse was attached to Mottisfont because of this decision, a curse that would come back to haunt the Meinertzhagen family.

When Dick was about seven years old, his father managed to secure a very interesting and strange agreement with the owner of Mottisfont, one Mrs. Vaudrey, who had become stinking rich on railway leases and investments. A widow, she had the habit of striding about dressed in her late husband's boots and clothes. And the terms of the agreement with the Meinertzhagens were equally eccentric.

She forbade the installation of electric lighting or a heating system, but this didn't slow down Dick's mother, who went ahead anyway and even saw to the introduction of parquet flooring. Of course, when the Meinertzhagens left, fifteen years later, the old girl disemboweled these modern impositions, ripping out the pipes and tearing up the flooring.

The lease ran for periods of seven years, at the end of which Mrs. Vaudrey could not cancel it but the tenant could, by giving a year's notice. However odd the arrangement may have been, this magical estate would turn out to be Dick's spiritual home for the rest of his life, an idyllic domain supporting a battalion of gardeners and gamekeepers, grooms, servants, butlers, cooks, kitchen maids, and footmen. In a word, Mottisfont was Victorian society in miniature, an upper-class fiefdom secured for the princely sum of 320 pounds per annum. Dick and Dan got to know almost every tree and mistletoe bush on the estate. In fact, in 1897, they left some tins of food and cooking utensils in a favorite spot they called the "duck-ground." Dick returned to the exact place some forty-five years later and found these objects exactly where he and Dan had left them, somewhat rusted but still usable.

Mottisfont could never be called a "place." It was more of a "location," and to have grown up there must have been an experience few will ever know who do not own Monte Carlo, a chunk of Luxembourg, or parts of Inner Mongolia. Its vast woodlands and marshes bordered several miles of the quicksilver Test River, one of the finest trout waters in England, where snaggletoothed pike and swarms of duck and snipe certainly nurtured young Dick's hunting instincts. Acres of lawn, kitchen gardens, and hothouses blended with parks and marshland. Sweet and gentle beeches, heron rookeries, and elegant mayfly hatches embroidered the baronial landscape where the Meinertzhagens kept horses and hounds and an ever-increasing number of birds.

Daniel Sr. was a ballerina of a fly fisherman, one of the best in the realm, and Dick's whole existence was dependent on the ancient abbey and sprawling estate where he and Dan Jr. hunted, fished, rode horses, wing shot, kept aviaries of birds, and generally led the life of honest-to-God professional Victorians.

They were members of the upper class, the leaders, the soldiers, and the scholars. They picked no 'taties, and God help anybody who picked a succulent brown trout out of season, which, being landed Victorians, they owned.

Many, many decades later, as an old man, Meinertzhagen was once confronted at a dinner party about his shooting birds. His antagonist was a lady of some standing, chronologically and socially as well as self-appointedly ornithologically. She asked in rather a shrill voice if he were still thumping the general ranks of avia. He ignored her, probably feigning deafness. She tried again with the same result. Then, cocking her thumb in the classic manner, she said, "Bang! Bang!"

"No—bang," he replied without the slightest glimmer of a smile, and retired behind his chicken Kiev. As Lieutenant General Sir Gerald Lathbury, former commander of troops in East Africa, put it in his preface to the first edition of *Kenya Diary*: "Colonel Meinertzhagen has seldom found it necessary to use a second shot, whether killing an enemy, stopping a charging lion or expressing an opinion or contrary point of view."[4]

In any case, back to Mottisfont. Dick and Dan trained truffle dogs, using a torn tennis ball stuffed with the expensive fungus and burying it ever deeper under the roots of natural truffle trees. Of course, Dick was a poacher made in heaven, a point he would often prove.

Dick and Dan were particularly accomplished at the "wiring" or snaring of trout and pike, using copper wire, of all things, dangled like nooses from twenty-foot poles. They once had a contest with their father where the old boy agreed to put up a pound sterling per pound of trout by which his sons were able to exceed his skills. Old Daniel did well, too, but not well enough. He lost five pounds, not an inconsiderable sum for the times (a gamekeeper or gardener made that amount per month), although he was certainly good for it. He became a disgusted believer when his sons took him out one night for pike. Dick also routinely speared trout, but his all-time favorite was eel, the cooked result being a delicacy he loved into his frail old age. Dick once made the mistake of bringing his old man a number of game birds without a mark of any shotgun pellets on them. His father asked him, of course, if he had been poaching. Dick does not record the answer.

An estate like Mottisfont had its staff problems, as illustrated by the following: Dick was well aware that a large truck came from nearby Romsey twice a week to collect fruit, vegetables, and sometimes flowers from the head gardener, a Mr. Reid, as well as about the same amount of game from Mr. Watts, the head gamekeeper, ho, ho, ho. Dick later found out that Reid was making roughly 1,000 pounds a year and Watts three to four hundred. The village was understandably horrified, possibly on two bases: first, that they were not invited to share in the proceedings, although this is pure presumption, and, secondly, that, as the major tenants, the Meinertzhagens were too important to the status of the local economy to be treated poorly. In any case, the letter of protest was never sent, and it took from approximately 1897 until 1935 before Dick was even shown a draft of the note to the lord of the manor, his father. Obviously, Neighborhood Watch was not yet in place.

To give an idea of the contemporary extent of the perfidy, the damage was rather like stealing Yankee Stadium every twenty minutes, or nearly so.

It was some few days before Christmas 1893, the whip of wind and the wet iron smell of snow in the air. It would be the Day soon, and there were few Christmases such as existed at Mottisfont. Owing to their father's importance, a wealth of delicacies poured through the gray stone gates of the ancient abbey, which had

twenty fireplaces: Mallosol beluga caviar by the literal barrel from
Russia; Dutch turkeys; a trundle of candy from Riga, Latvia; a slug
of marzipan from Bremen as big as a boy's leg; and, always, Dick's
favorite, a box of Spanish turrón from Madrid, a mixture of al-
monds, sugar, and honey that made Christmas worth waiting for.
Apparently, BB guns had just come out but had not reached Mottisfont. At least his mother would have had cooked the usual twin
geese she presented through some quirk of imagined humor on her
and her husband's anniversary. Daniel Sr. thought it not funny.

Christmas Day was, however, only an overloading of the normal Meinertzhagen fare, which may explain why Dick was almost
180 pounds and over six feet by the time he was eighteen. With
the exception of the twenty-foot spruce and the 200 candles (why
Mottisfont hadn't burned down is in itself purely astonishing; it had
had 700 Christmases), there was little difference in the daily bill of
fare in the Victorian Meinertzhagens' home. In addition to the
gifted goodies, Dick records that during the festivities alone en-
compassing 1897, for example, the dinner featured such items
as two twenty-pound turkeys (one, of course boiled, the other
broiled; both stuffed with Mottisfont chestnuts); eleven separate
plum puddings for the children, varying in size and succulence
depending on the age of the intended end consumer; a big pudding
for the adults accompanied by a most impressive bowl of semi-
clotted Devonshire cream; mince pies by the presumed regiment
or cohort; the whole saturnalia topped off by an "enormous" box
of candy from Charbonel, courtesy and Sweet Holiday Greetings
from Aunt Alice. God only knows what they did for an appetizer.
Perhaps a partridge in a pear tree. Maybe a dozen?

Things were far from the same, however, at Harrow, Richard's
ultraprestigious prep school. At Hance's Tuck Shop, Dick records
that breakfasts cost sixpence a shot and included either two sausages
and mashed potatoes on toast, fried fish and chips, deviled kidneys,

or mushrooms and liver and bacon, or three boiled eggs, including their grease-proof bag (presumably patented). Lunch at Harrow included beer. (After all, it builds strong bones and a tooth.) Dinner included bread, butter, cheese, and more beer. Sweaty athletes had a bath in a cold pint of water in an eighteen-inch tub, which is likely why so many Britons turned to missionarism: The concept of being eaten by generally unreconstructed cannibals *had* to be a more cheerful culinary prospect than the food served at obviously less cheerful Harrow.

Matters were different, however, at the Meinertzhagen home. A normal breakfast alone consisted of four courses with perhaps seconds interspersed. There would be kidneys; liver; bacon; four kinds of eggs of various degrees of rarity; kippered herring; stewed, broiled, and fried tomatoes; bacon; sausage of various types; as well as a raft of preserves, marmalades, jams, and similar stomach-stuffers. But, remember, there were no Rolaids, Tums, or Zantac in those days, although it is easy to understand why they were invented. It's a wonder Dick wasn't eight feet tall and 400 pounds.

Unfortunately, one Christmas, nobody had remembered Dick, which must have hurt. He commented that there were presents for everyone except for him and wrote about how much he yearned for his mother's love.

Ah, but the Meinertzhagen kids had an aunt and uncle by the names of Ernie and Gwavas Carlyon to make up for such childhood setbacks. Their gifts were always generous and tended to come at unexpected moments. Take, for example, the punt, a low-profile waterfowl stalking boat, and the punt gun that went with it, which arrived with Father Christmas in 1893. As Dick wrote to Dan, "Glory be to God! Uncle Ernie and Aunt Gwavas have written to say that they want to give us a real good joint Christmas present. . . . Don't you think we might ask for that punt and a nice Holland swivel gun with a hundred rounds. . . . Let me know at once before they change their minds."[5]

Now what exactly is a punt gun? you may ask. Well, it's a minicannon expressly designed to clear the sky of a cloud of waterfowl, ducks, geese, reasonably low-flying aircraft, and, perhaps, out-of-orbit satellites, if such had been around at the time. It was so called because it was mounted on a punt or shallow-draft oar-propelled small boat until it came within range and a literal sleet of lead was fired, the charge depending upon the bore size of the gun. The punt gun was usually fired above the flock of waterfowl—often handling as much as two pounds of shot—as the sound of the round would usually wash over the flock and they would flush before the lead got there. Results were usually impressive or bad news, especially if you happened to be a duck or a goose.

Some of these literal smooth-bore cannons could run up to two inches in bore size. Unfortunately, as usual, Dick Meinertzhagen does not tell us the caliber of his and his brother's brute, but it certainly worked well and was less than conservative. Recoil was normally handled by a rope-pulley system or the punt itself would have been smashed asunder and sunk by the recoil of what would now be called the firearm equivalent of *T. rex*. In no way could it possibly be fired from the shoulder by a lesser entity than King Kong.

Punt guns were professional weapons, normally used by full-time wildfowlers shooting for the market. It sounds a heavy-handed one, but it was actually a delicate art to smoothly paddle/scull into range on the big flowages to within ideal shot range of where the huge flotillas of ducks were loafing in calm weather. After all, they were skittish geese that saved Corinth in Greece in ancient times from attack by their warnings. There are easier items to approach than waterfowl, a thing that Dick and Dan soon learned. Their first day proved nothing—naught. It was enough to make one take up Parcheesi on a professional basis.

The cost of a punt gun, including the boat that carried it, was about 200 pounds sterling—less ammunition. This gesture by Uncle Ernie and Aunt Gwavas would be tantamount to giving a couple of teenagers a nuclear submarine. Two hundred pounds sterling was sufficient to buy most of northern Scotland, which might well have been overpriced at that, considering the weather. But punt guns sure were hell on rafted-up ducks, especially when they flushed. The punt-gun incidents are mentioned as they well show Dick's and Dan's characters as outdoorsmen. There are things *I* would rather do than take a 200-pound gun in a kayak with only an inch or so freeboard into the freezing flowages of England for the sake of a couple of duck or goose breasts.

Actually, this might be a very precise place to point out that in those days, waterfowl were a most important source of British protein and relatively inexpensive. There was no bag limit such as we know it in North America today; there wasn't the gunning pressure and there was no shortage of birds. Of course, anybody who knows his nuts about ducks and geese is well aware that since outfits such as Ducks Unlimited got involved in acquiring and managing wetlands, the only problem has been natural, as in weather. *If* wetlands dry up, so do ducks and geese. My own late brother, Tom, founded and funded the American Brant Association, Inc., which, if you're not aware of the critter, now I'm sure pronounced "endangered" by those who have never seen one or surely cannot spell the name of the species, is sort of a trial-sized goose. Wildfowling was an industry as much as oystering or clamming or commercial fishing was and still is. These were all renewable natural resources and were handled as such. They still should be. Even the wood duck, once among the rarest as well as the most handsome of American wa-

terfowl, is likely the most common of "puddle"—shallow water—
ducks today, given the efforts of hunters to resurrect the breed.
Common sense. It works if game is permitted to pay its own way.
And, it does. If it can't or doesn't, it's gone: Now you see it, now
you don't.

At this point in his life, Dick was a tremendously strong, ropy
fifteen-year-old worshiping his elder brother. He pounced postally
on Dan about the concept of asking for the punt gun from Uncle
Ernie. Astonishingly, the boys got their Holland & Holland of un-
determined bore size, but you can bet it was a whopper! Dick was
cunning enough to ask also for just over 200 shells—each probably
big enough to anchor a reasonable yacht. Punt guns are not powder
puffs.

The 1912 Holland & Holland catalog explains that these hor-
rifiers were generally made from 1 ½ to 2 inches of excellent proof-
steel. For example, the measurement of decibels, increments of
sound intensity, are figured on the concept of a logarimithic scale,
the basis of human hearing being about one decibel. To make it
simple, the punt guns shot one hell of a lot more lead with a small
increase of bore (barrel) size than common sense would suggest,
not that punt gunners had any common sense to start with or they
wouldn't have been punt gunners in the first place. To use an
example, the 2-inch 200-pound London model that fired a full two
pounds of lead shot from a steam launch was only ⅛" bigger in
bore yet fifty pounds heavier and fired a charge of half a pound
more than the slightly smaller London 1 ⅞" model. I don't want
to teach you to fly; I want to explain *why* you can fly if you are
sufficiently foolish to attempt it.

The 2-inch-bore barrel weighed 200 pounds and used 5.5
ounces of powder in one mighty, tide-moving *Boom!* that was generally bad news for ducks and geese as well as UFOs, had there
been any. That charge, over chilled water, must have sounded like

a hailstorm with an intestinal blockage suddenly coming free. But there was no such item as overkill in punt gunning, one of the few instances where bigger was definitely, without question, quite literally better. The more lead that could be thrown, the bigger the bag, provided the target was up to it. And, if a professional who depended on his kids eating from his efforts was looking along the top of the barrel, you can be sure that a cannon was never more carefully laid. The cartridges were likely worth a week's pay each to an ordinary laborer.

The cost of the outfit was at least that of forty months' labor for one of Mottisfont's gamekeepers. Nine years later, a Best Grade double .577 engraved rifle, birthed and midwifed and spanked on the bum by John Rigby & Co., Gunmakers, a Rigby, along with Holland & Holland and Purdeys with a leather case as only the British could make them, then cost considerably less than a punt gun: You would have gotten about 136 pounds change from your 200 sterling, which convinces me that I was born not even close to the correct era. I would have liked punt gunning. Very much, in fact.

You may be sure that the blast of that minicannon rattled the inlays of anybody aboard the punt who handled it. In referring to one function of "The London" punt gun, H&H itself observed that it was "simple and certainly effective."

This was in reference to the extraction of an empty shell, but it was certainly definitive of the entire system, you can count on that.

Dan wrote to Dick from school that the best way to try things would be to treat the whole proposal as a joke. Well, it *did* come off, with the mild suggestion that Uncle Ernie and Aunt Gwavas be the recipients of the occasional duck dinner. As Dick observed, they sure as hell got them. They had a punt boat, a superb Holland & Holland swivel gun, and a bit more than 200 shells to go with it. Considering that it would be a rare day that more than two or three shells would be fired, they were set, from their viewpoint, for life. Youth.

Settling the boat by Christmas at a place called Totton, just where the Test River enters Southampton water and forms a flowage rafted over with ducks, the boys were smart enough to realize their inexperience and hired a tough professional gunner named Godwin to show them the drill. After he had accustomed them to the work at hand, Dick and Dan went out their first day before dawn, waterfowl moving most 'tween dawn and hangover. They didn't get a shot, through their clumsiness the first day, but fired their first broadside the second, at a raft of teal. The first round produced seven of the small ducks with the whistling wings, but things got better as the Meinertzhagens developed their skills. They nearly sank themselves several times with recoil and inadvisable shifting of weight in the shallow-draft punt (a deadly matter considering the water temperature in the Test flowage in January), but when the week ended, Uncle Ernie's larder was the richer.

That was the start of 1894. By January of the following year, Dick and Dan seemed to have a much better grasp of the technique involved and, despite a horrendous winter, managed to collect sixteen brent, two white-fronted, and three mergansers, but they also took sixty-seven wigeon (of which, presumably, Uncle Ernie and Aunt Gwavas got their share) and twenty-seven mallard. Eighteen ninety-five was so cold that often they could not even open the action of the punt gun; it was frozen shut. If they had tipped, they would have ruined this book, for sure. But 1896 was the year of their greatest success.

This was also the year of naval battles between the Meinertz-hagens and the local punt gunners, although Dick had the good manners to suggest that he and his brother may have well been in the wrong, not knowing the rules of the road—or maybe the flow of the flowage.

Dick calls the major antagonist, one Mr. Leigh, "a rough little rat of a man, truculent and resentful at our shooting on what he considered to be his own preserves, but of course our main crime was that the amateur should sell his bag and therefore become a professional. We did not then know the etiquette of puntgunning."[6] Leigh, like the cornered man he was, knew that attack is the best form of defense. He bared his Roquefort fangs.

The matter came to a swollen head when Leigh and the Meinertzhagen brothers were stalking the same raft of wigeon at a place called Cracknore Hard (this written with a straight face). Leigh was about a quarter mile farther away than were Dick and Dan from the target, but in the direct line of fire. The brothers would likely have been using number-four shot, as it has good sectional density and the punt gun in larger calibers was certainly sure death to waterfowl well over 100 yards, better than twice the distance that an ordinary shotgun could be relied upon even with heavy shot. The really heavy punt gun, such as Dan and Dick had, was likely a mighty painful instrument to humans up to 250 or so yards, maybe farther, depending upon shot size. Certainly a pellet would tear an eye from the skull.

Dick and Dan slewed their course a bit, but Leigh insisted on maneuvering his punt so that he was always in the line of fire, which took a touch of nerve. Unfortunately, Dick and Dan came under their first fire from somewhere between 160 and 180 yards, which made them not especially pleased. Leigh was close enough to have killed four birds, and ducks take a taint of killing. They're tough. Instantly, both brothers saw that Leigh was actually going to fire at them through the screen of ducks, using the birds as an excuse. The shot swarm swirled across the Meinertzhagen punt, marking it mightily with lead pellets, but it didn't blind either of the brothers or, as Dick fails to write, hit either of them. However, Dick's temper flared, and he decided to sink Leigh, an idea he was talked out of by his older brother. (Actually, it wasn't *that* bad an idea.)

Dick wanted to board Leigh's punt—as he playfully puts it, "ducking him"—but such exposure to the Freon-cold water would have very possibly killed the man, such performance being generally frowned upon by society and its assembled jurisprudence. In any case, Leigh might likely have had, as was the custom, a "cripple-stopper" twelve-gauge aboard, which may have well expanded Dick's guts as well as his outlook. Market hunters were not the type to fool with—armed men in general are not.

As Dick and Dan approached Leigh's boat, Dick declared that he had never heard such an innovative and prolonged use of skillful invective. It was so inventive that neither brother could resist roaring with laughter at him. Leigh, naturally, thought this most unhumorous until Dan tossed him a much larger punt gun shell than Leigh himself was using and advised him in quiet tones that there was plenty of room for all here, and if he didn't come to that conclusion he could happily pay the consequences, the consequences being at the bottom of the bay. Leigh's sense of humor prevailed in the end. Just as well; it might have been that Dan was not kidding.

That night, the Meinertzhagen brothers and Leigh made an uneasy peace at a local tavern over a couple of tots, which would be appropriate in Britain in January.

Dick writes that Dan was unavailable in the 1897 period but that he killed eleven curlews and that his high point included stalking a huge raft of wigeon, out of which he was successful in taking sufficient to give twenty-four to a cousin on his father's side. He borrowed a gown and spent the night at Eaglehurst as it was so filthy out and, the following day, took the punt back to its berthing by road to Totton. A few days later he transferred the punt by train. In 1898 he and Dan made their last shoot, decided to make a second try, and figured on Langstone Harbor. There Dan made his best and final shot—forty-eight birds. It was a great way to end. Sort of a literal swan song, or a duck song. It was his last with the punt gun.

One may be as whimsical as one wishes concerning ghosts, goblins, spooks, or spirits in general. The legend of the Mottisfont ghost is rather eerie.

Mottisfont was an ancient, Druid-festooned, strange spring, at least according to those who lived there. I have spent time with Scottish lairds of note who firmly believe in "some presence"; they have even stepped aside for them on narrow, ancient hallways in dank castles as cold as grouse drives. However, there are aspects of the world of ghosts that are less than humorous.

Like most elegant and elderly architectural appendages, Mottisfont looked like it should have a ghost. Dick was convinced it did. He'd even located its nest, that being in a gilt Buddha, which he later took to his apartment or flat, Dick being afraid of extremely little, but he surely gave that Buddha some thought in later life.

This ethereal creature was supposed—or presumed—to have been somehow created by the last prior of Mottisfont when the Catholic Church went down the proverbial tubes in England under Henry VIII.

The Mottisfont ghost certainly was the subject of a conversation among the youngish Daniel, Dick, and a gardener who happened to be there at the time. Sure enough, things got onto ghosts and the former owner, Sir John Barker Mill.

"Sure an' it appears just afore death," intoned the gardener to Sir John, who happened to be loitering about, as lords are wont, asking of such matters as ghosts, as if he had nothing better to do. Sir John asked the gardener what form the spook took and was informed that it took whatever form it wished. But the story then becomes unfunny, as a man died.

In fact, make that two men.

"Sure, and ye know, it might be th't man over there cuttin' weeds," the gardener said to Sir John.

But, when Sir John looked, there was no man cutting weeds. And Sir John was dead within a short time; as Dick puts it, "within the year."

Coincidence. Chance. You're probably right. One doesn't tend to remember what goes right. But a lot went wrong—especially with Dan.

As Dick clearly says, neither he nor Dan believed in ghosts. After all, how can belt buckles and the ever-popular chains become ectoplasmic, let alone percale cotton transcend the elemental laws of nature? Ghosts and spirits in general must have a mighty tough row to hoe.

Yet . . .

It was December 27, 1897, and Dick and Dan were out in the evening, goggling, as ornithologists are wont to do, at a flock of white-fronted geese. Dan suddenly started as he saw a form loping across the lawn. Dick asked him, "Where?"

"There he goes!" yelled Dan, pointing across the moon-tinged darkness.

Dan chased him as far as the ditch at the end of the lawn but came up empty. Nobody. Not a trace. Further, there were, strangely, no footprints. Dick, after years of experience, knew that he had better night vision than did Dan, but he saw nothing.

Later, in their common bedroom, Dan confided that he felt it was the Ghost, but Dick was not to tell his mother on any account. "Jesus," likely said Dan, "I'm the eldest son. Christ, whatever you do, don't tell mother." The curse always meant the death of the eldest son.

As Dick said afterwards, Dan was absolutely positive that he saw somebody (or something) cross the lawn, and he was uncharacteristically upset about the matter. However, as Dick said, he just couldn't believe that Dan had seen something he couldn't.

He also observed that Dan was dead six weeks later.

And Meinertzhagen's own son, also named Daniel, died at the age of nineteen in World War II. I'll always wonder if the gilt statue of Buddha remained in Dick's apartment after that.

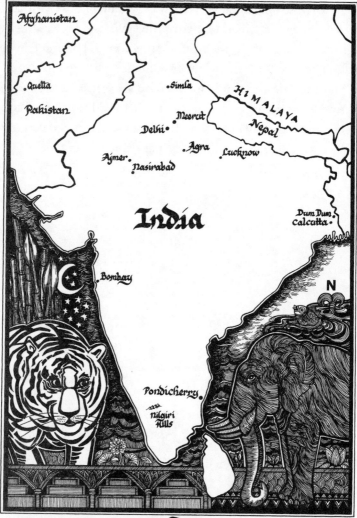

INDIA

Chapter 2

The death of Dan absolutely unraveled the fabric of the Meinertzhagen family, especially the life of Dick. Dan had been staying at Bremen, Germany, and learning the Huth family banking business in February 1898; he developed appendicitis and it was severe enough that he expressed a wish for his father to come over. Daniel Sr. immediately got in touch with a well-known surgeon, who went with him. Alas, when they arrived, it was too late: Dan had died a few hours before. Dick's father wrote the details on February 13; Richard received them on the fifteenth. His father simply said that Dan had died of peritonitis, with little pain, and that was pretty well that. Dick noted that neither his father nor his mother ever fully recovered from Dan's death. Surely he never did.

He sold the punt gun, unable to stand shooting alone. He sent Uncle Ernie 130 pounds sterling, and he notes in his diary that he and Dan had made over seventy pounds on the sale of game alone. Presumably he was not out of ammunition. I know his desolation of spirit because when my own best friend and hunting companion, my brother Tom, died in early 1981, I too felt life had changed irrevocably for me.

With Daniel dead, Richard felt emotionally depleted. His

brother had meant everything to him, but he quickly realized that he had to carry on for his own sake. His father insisted that he take Dan's proposed place at Huth's, the commercial bank, as the second eldest son, and he did, at least for a while. He studied in Germany and gritted his teeth as he bided his time.

Dick's spirit was in a state of growing rebellion. He was an accomplished ornithologist and outdoorsman, and the last thing he wanted to do with his life was to sit in some counting house, family owned or not. As he said, "I want to see the world and not moulder away in a London fog."[1] He'd enjoyed hunting roe and wild pig in the Hanoverian forests of Germany, which just fueled his longing to get out to the wild places of the world, and in the 1890s they were in abundance.

Dick had met Abel Chapman, the noted Edwardian ornithologist, big-game hunter, and author, who knew Selous. He intervened on Dick's behalf when he wrote to his father and urged him to let his son study zoology—no dice. Not even the renowned Bowdler Sharpe

Richard Meinertzhagen in the uniform of the Hampshire Yeomanry, 1897.
(Courtesy of Ran Meinertzhagen and Rhodes House Library, Oxford)

of the British Museum, promising the youngster a job in the museum if he took a degree in zoology, could prevail on pater Meinertzhagen to cut his son loose. Meeting the Norwegian Arctic explorer Fridtjof Nansen, who was invited to dinner at the Meinertzhagens', did nothing to settle Dick's restlessness. He was placed with a London firm of stockbrokers, a slow death sentence. Dick eventually wrote, "I do not think I can stand this life much longer. I am wasting my life and my youth. A stuffy office, no exercise, complete slavery and a future ruined by an atmosphere in which gold is the sole aim. I shall take the first opportunity to get out of it and if nothing turns up within six months I shall go to South Africa and join Rhodes."[2]

As an ex-stockbroker myself, I know how Dick felt. I also understand why he threw it all up, as I did.

It would seem that all came to a head when Dick made eighty pounds sterling as a brokerage fee for doing what he considered nothing in a stock transaction. Yet he made a deal with his father that, after a limited amount of time, if he still hated it as he thought he would, he would be free to do as he wished. At the end of the stipulated period, he loathed the London financial markets even more than he thought he would, and he exercised his option. The extraordinary thing was that he first did so in a secret, part-time capacity because he knew his father would object.

His first exposure to military life was on March 24, 1897, when he was commissioned as a second lieutenant in the Hampshire Yeomanry, a first step in becoming part of the Victorian British army who had held the Zulus (rather badly at Isandhlwana), who had put heavy fire into the ragged Mahdi ranks at Omdurman (and were severely criticized for the amount of ammo they used cashing in the wounded Fuzzy-Wuzzis in the same engagement), and who also made at best an uncertain showing against the Afrikaner forces in South Africa during what was termed the First War of Independence in 1881.

A brief word about the yeomanry, as it has no exact American equivalent, not even the National Guard: The British yeomanry was originally organized in 1794 as a Home Guard volunteer cavalry force and later incorporated into the Territorial Force of Britain in 1908, eventually to become the Territorial Army in 1922. The point is that a second lieutenancy in this outfit, essentially composed of small landholders, cut no ice in the British regular army. Dick rode his favorite foxhunting horse, Melksham, but first wet his hand at mock combat in the Meon Valley, sort of home ground. But, of course, combat was combat to Dick Meinertzhagen, and he made his point.

Being a cavalry auxiliary wasn't especially rough duty in 1897 in Britain. In fact, it could definitely be great fun. Sure, he had taken the sword training and horsemanship befitting a budding horse soldier and even trained in the ranks as an enlisted man in Hyde Park with major buildings looming over him even before the days of Otis Elevator. But it was on his first outing in the Meon Valley that he started to forge what was to become the legend of Richard Meinertzhagen, C.B.E., D.S.O. Of course he stayed at the George Hotel, which must not have been terribly rough duty. Even his hunter, Melksham, lived to the ripe old age of twenty-seven.

It was actually May of 1897 when Dick had his first exposure to mock battle: three days against the Aldershot Cavalry, a pretty spiffy outfit under French, better known as Earl of Ypres after his World War I record. After a day of fooling around, Dick was sent by his commander with ten men to block the local roads in Warnford. With great enthusiasm, he took his orders.

The first thing he did was to commandeer all his commanding officer's (Willie Woods, who lived locally) carts, drag them across the narrow parts of the roads, and remove the wheels. It held up the Aldershot Cavalry Brigade for over half an hour, which enabled the young second lieutenant with two fellow junior officers to smack them soundly in the flank, which was not all that unlike catching West Point with its pants at half-mast for the time. Woods, who had to have the wheels put back on, was not overly charmed, but

French gave hearty congratulations to the young scoundrel, which pleased Dick substantially. He was starting to get the drift: The object was to win, and how one accomplished this didn't necessarily matter, a principle that would mark his career forever. French was so pleased that he asked Dick to "gallop"—ride personal dispatcher—for him. As a finale, before war got to the developments of Hiram Maxim and his machine gun a few years later, Dick had a time to remember, spending twelve hours in the saddle, and was given two spare nags from a genuine lancer regiment. Heaven came down and kissed him a mighty smacker. Frig zoology: You couldn't stick anybody legitimately, anyway, besides a butterfly.

He apparently impressed French to the extent that he asked Dick to ride for him for a further three days on more maneuvers between the Test and Itchen Valleys. They were, of course, war games, in this case Dick and a slice of Horse Artillery being designated as the "enemy." Dick was sent out after dark, knowing the ground, near Winchester, in fact, his objective was the "friendly" troops near a place called Farley Down. He found the opposition after leaving his own camp an hour before witching. Their prey had no rear guard. Richard likely salivated in anticipation, the ultimate predator.

His sword slithered, steel against steel, from its scabbard in the thin moonlight. Bellowing a deep roar, he charged on Melksham, stampeding the whole of the opposing horse herd into the blackness near the old Roman road. Horses were everywhere in the murk, as were men and officers in pale nightclothes, astonished, angry, and vengeful.

Dick was not to be put off by his success. He didn't pause a second, keeping up what had now become a full gallop. He crashed clear through the encampment, chasing the confused and frightened "enemy" horses.

Dick thought he might have overdone it this time. The young lieutenant managing the show talked him out of a recharge, although at the time Dick declared he cared naught for "such niceties." Dick awakened French and told him what had been the circumstances. The future lord was delighted and commanded an immediate attack. Only there was nobody to attack, as most of the "enemy" command was spread across the plain trying to catch their horses, which Richard had scattered.

The really interesting aspect of the adventure was that Dick had personally jumped over the prostrate forms of some of the most important figures of the British effort in World War I, among them Field Marshal Douglas Haig, victorious commander of 2 million troops in World War I, as well as his future commanding general in the Near East, Field Marshal Edmund Henry Hynman Allenby, First Viscount Allenby. It was Allenby, in fact, who pronounced Dick "the only officer who has jumped over me brandishing a sword."[3] He also had other comments, not quite so flattering, when he later introduced the young man. Haig, it would seem, had more momentous things on his mind than subalterns such as Lieutenant Dick Meinertzhagen and Melksham.

Dick eventually confronted his father about his future, and Daniel, having digested the shock of his son's decision to opt out of the family calling, decided to help him. The way into the army proper for Dick at his age was through the militia. He resigned from the Hampshire Yeomanry and was commissioned as a second lieutenant in the Third Battalion of the West Yorkshire Regiment in February 1898, and starting a training process that resulted in his passing the army entrance examination in October 1898, coming third in the order of merit. Dick was in his element: "I don't think a soldier's life can be beat anywhere, it's ripping."[4]

Always the hunter, Dick was given a true-blue British army dressing down when he arrived late at parade at Aldershot. The colonel, after venting his ire, was left speechless when young Dick asked for leave to go on a duck shoot back at Mottisfont the next day. "Well, I'm damned if I've ever heard anything like that. Yes, go and shoot your bloody duck and don't forget, my boy, that I am particularly partial to duck."[5]

The colonel got his duck.

Then followed a two-month vacation at Mottisfont, where Dick shot birds, fished, and otherwise enriched his professional envelope. During that period, an old family friend, one Colonel Lethall, joined Dick for a shoot. He was as pure an individualist as is likely to wash up and one who took full advantage of the thin red line of empire that kept the Queen's petticoats unsoiled except for sundry Zulus and such folk who came along not easily. Happily for the Queen, she did not live to see the Great War and the eventual dissolution of her empire. Old Colonel Lethall positively ignited young Dick's imagination with his tales of a free life of hunting, shooting, and fishing at government expense, counting at least equally the odds of an African spear through his solar plexus with the superbness of "Army spirit and the immense advantages of a soldier's life . . . and a healthy life in the open air."[6] At the time the colonel throve, it was undoubtedly a reasonably pleasant life, managed by servants and punctuated by light duty. The Victorian army reflected a particular mind-set of superiority that went with empire. Richard was hooked. But the colonel had a friendly warning for his young friend: He told Dick never to become a staff officer or to lose touch with his troops, as they were the ones who won victories. There was no way Dick could have known that he would indeed not lose touch with his men, that he would be obliged in some instances, to "take care" of men at the point of a bayonet.

Dick received his commission and joined the City of London Regiment, the Royal Fusiliers. He was ordered to go abroad immediately and was gazetted before he could get his breath. He was to leave on January 18, 1899, the telegram arriving just when he was in his bath. Bad form, indeed; knowing Dick, it was probably a cold bath.

Dick's delight was complete, as he felt he would now be free and have a chance on active service "fighting dervishes . . . and Germans and Frenchmen."[7] He even had a little prayer going to increase his chances: "Thou seest, Dear Heavenly Father, the sad plight of thy servant Dick; grant him a nice little war, that he may better his condition and continue to praise Thy Name."[8]

Appropriately, it was the *London Gazette* that announced his appointment as the British equivalent of an officer and a gentleman of the Queen's forces. His first posting was to India, where his regiment had served for decades. "I feel like walking on air at the prospect of India and freedom,"[9] he wrote.

In the meantime, Dick's father, who had been thinking of actually buying Mottisfont, decided against it after Dan's death, and the family left the ancient abbey and magical estate in 1900.

Dick sailed for India in March 1899, having said good-bye to Mottisfont. But it would remain in his soul for the rest of his life, something I again understood when I think back on the sprawling woodland estate and lake in northern New Jersey my family once owned, where I spent my childhood and youth, and to which I have so often returned in spirit. I would have enjoyed Dick's company.

A rriving in Port Said on April 4, 1899, Dick was taken aback at the filth of the streets, the stench of open latrines, the side-weeping urinals, and the debauched citizenry. But this did not slow him down when he passed by one of the numerous brothels and saw a young girl of about twelve who looked English and who called out to Dick in his own language. Thick-set Arabs and an old crone appeared from nowhere and threatened the young officer to move along.

He did at that—to the home of the British consul, where he demanded action and got it, striding back to the brothel with Egyptian police officers in tow and rescuing the little girl in the face of a foul-mouthed and hostile crowd. Dick promptly demanded a receipt from the British consul as proof that he and his wife had taken the little waif into their safekeeping until other suitable arrangements could be made. He wrote an official report on the incident to the British ambassador in Cairo and set sail again. Dick was getting the hang of things in a hurry. He would always react decisively, whatever the consequences, when he believed in his mission, and this would earn him the admiration of some and the envy, and perhaps even hatred, of others. By the time he had reached the First Battalion, Royal Fusiliers, in Nasirabad, Rajputana, in northwest India, he discovered that he had been nicknamed "Montezuma" after the legendary sixteenth-century Aztec emperor, a name that would be glued to him to the end of his army career as surely as would his African war club.

Exotic, sultry India with her jungles and deserts, her heat, her riotous colors and aromatic cuisine, her sacred cows and holy men, the princely opulence and the unspeakable poverty, the profusion of languages and impenetrable cultures, her tigers and elephants, had long been the jewel in the British imperial crown. Dick fell into his Indian hunting stride almost upon arrival when his ever-generous and eccentric Uncle Ernie of punt-gun fame bought him his own elephant.

Richard Meinertzhagen tried out his hunting elephant and her mahout, or handler, for the first time on April 29, 1899, near Na-sirabad. Although named Archibald, she was what Dick would pos-sibly have called a "capital" cow elephant. The first game he shot from her most sturdy back howdah platform was a chinkara, the four-horned Asian antelope classic to India, which she gently passed back to her handler with her trunk. Further, as Dick ob-served, she feared neither tiger nor wild boar, the classic fare that kept British officers mighty busy for centuries of occupation. He was immensely impressed with the pachyderm, noting that, in fact, she held her breath when a shot was imminent to keep down any vibrations or interruptions! I cannot stifle a laugh when he ends his observations of the day, which suggest he will do very well against sand grouse with her as the species does not fear elephants. I've tried African sand grouse on many instances, and I wish I had had Archie along—I've always needed an ele-phant but nobody ever paid any attention.

It would appear that Dick actually bought Archibald before he had the go-ahead from Uncle Ernie, as he records in the same entry, with reference to his avuncular relative's cable, "By all means buy an elephant."[10] He'd already tried her out.

Dick had the courtesy—of which he was never short, except when he was sticking somebody—to record that Ernie was a "splendid godfather" and that God should bless him unless he was otherwise occupied. Dick told a pal of his, Bobby Roberts, a fellow officer, that he was about to buy an elephant. Robert's answer was, "You bloody young fool."[11] Judging from what transpired, Rob-erts was not wrong.

Came the dawn and Richard recorded in his diary about a month later, on May 23, that disaster had overtaken him. It was Archibald, and she was a major regimental problem. As Dick wrote, he knew that for some reason Archie was something less than pop-ular in an environment in which the largest mammal a senior officer might pretend to have was a polo pony, and she wasn't the precise pet advised for a new second lieutenant. It came to a head on the morning parade of that date.

Dick was a mite late for the dawn formation, which was a definite no-no for a budding if not blooming young British officer of the Royal Fusiliers. He was three-quarters of a mile away from the assembly grounds and, Archie being able to manage about seven miles per hour without goading by the ankh of the driver, he took the obvious solution.

Archibald went crazy.

The nearer the parade ground they drew, the faster went Archie. Dick was nearly thrown with his sword and various issued accoutrements, and the louder he shouted at the mahout, the faster went Archie until, by elephant standards, she was reasonably flying, Dumbo-style.

Archie almost caused a regimental disaster, as the troops were mostly formed and the hard-bitten veterans would not be disrupted for anything as minor as an elephant. At least not at first. After all, the British Square had stood for many decades, and the Royal Fusiliers, the City of London Regiment, were not about to break it, aboriginal animals be damned. However, Archibald managed it; she broke the British ranks—And positively!

As Dick wrote, to his horror, he could see the battalion falling in, hardly expecting a recalcitrant elephant rapidly impending on their ranks. Captain Johnson, his superior, obviously saw with some astonishment the approach of Archie and her violently swaying owner. Johnson's horse, possibly having more sense than its master, promptly threw him in a clanking mess more or less into Archie's path, which would have been a painful fate at best. Or maybe not. It would have at least been quick.

In any case, Johnson was bloody near elephantized.

To compound the problem, there was a sergeant major screaming at the troops to stand fast, as if Archie's were a Zulu impi's regimental charge, which would have been the worst advice available—and there was plenty of bad advice being bellowed.

Happily, Miss Archie was prevailed upon (probably by her mahout) to desist after she had at least emotionally and, more, physically set the British ranks adrift, but the flotsam of the incident rested squarely upon her owner, Meinertzhagen. He was ordered to take the wrath of his fellow officers, who were likely bored to death and delighted at such an opportunity. One Herbert rode up to him and instructed him to appear—without Archie—in the orderly room at 0900.

Dick was not treated kindly, at least from his own testimony. The colonel was most upset and made the same obvious. Dick was asked the standard "What is the army coming to?" and he observed in his diary that he "didn't have the answer to that one." After noting that he had put in forty-eight years of service—obviously no spring lamb—the colonel expanded his question: "What is the army coming to if subalterns can charge a battalion on parade with a bloody elephant? Answer me that, young man."[12] Dick strangled, but he struggled to keep from laughing aloud. "An elephant is most unsuitable for a young subaltern," pronounced the colonel. "You must dispose of it at once."[13] Dick was of two minds, perhaps three: He was distressed about the loss of his jumbo, and he was almost hysterical at the thought of Archibald charging the regiment, but, although he observed that he was not astonishingly popular at that given moment, he apparently made some sort of deal with the colonel that he never ride poor Archibald while in Empire uniform, which seemed a reasonable agreement to both.

India also introduced Dick to her equivalent of foxhunting: hog-hunting or pigsticking, as the sport was also called. He was a natural. The British observed a finely tuned ritual in this sport, which was organized by tent clubs such as the Nasirabad Tent Club.

Pigsticking meets would often take place over two or three days, with tentage and all the paraphernalia needed to sustain the hunters and their servants being brought in. The local villagers would be engaged as beaters, giving the local economy a boost in the process and ridding some communities of crop-raiding boars.

The idea was for one or more parties of three horsemen each to ride out, armed with their bamboo-shafted spears, which were between six and eight feet in length and which weighed between two and four pounds. The groups would take up positions at intervals, and local inhabitants would then be employed to beat the jungle or open grasslands under the supervision of their shikaris until a sounder was driven into the open. Sows and piglets didn't count, and the fun started when a mature boar with killer tushes was spotted, the horses sensing the chase and taking off after the boar when it broke cover.

Depending on the countryside, this could be tough, dangerous riding, and the environs of Nasirabad were rocky and barren. The whole idea was to be "first spear," to be the first rider, usually at full gallop, to draw blood. This brought with it the prized tushes, no matter who eventually killed the beast.

It was not uncommon for wild boar to turn and charge, their ability to inflict serious injury with their dental appendages having long become part of Raj folklore. Pigsticking was a rough and dangerous sport requiring courage, superior horsemanship, physical endurance, a keen eye, and good nerves. Dick had all this in abundance, and left Rajputana with three impressive *Sus cristatus* to his credit, one weighing in at over 300 pounds.

Meinertzhagen, by his diary comments, was a long drift from stupid, especially when it came to such matters as general field tactics. When taught how to assault an enemy position, one might have given some thought that the Royal Fusiliers were not using spears and clubs or that they were tutored by advanced and thoroughly accomplished imbeciles. The latter may have been the case, as the first words out of Bobby Robert's mouth when he woke up were "Thank God I'm a Fusilier."[14] As Dick observes, the second-in-command had surely learned nothing since Agincourt (1415), when the British got lucky against the French with the cloth-yard arrow shaft in a small French town.

Yet Dick, as a marksman, had his objections when he was taught to move his men forward in tense bunches of twenty or so, "marvellous targets for modern riflemen or machineguns,"[15] yet he noted that the "drill was splendid, shoulder to shoulder and perfect line,"[16] rather like a badly directed war movie. To cap things, Dick was caught reading a book on tactics and was almost thrown out of the mess hall. Such a thing was just not done, old boy. As Dick continued, "the battalion formed up in line, dressed by the right within 200 yards of the enemy and then walked forward cheering. . . . We should all have been wiped out."[17] A few years later they were, more than a million at a clip. This was very bad for the breeding demographics of the British Empire, which was, unfortunately, observed later. There was, of course, an unheeded historical lesson from the Napoleonic differences of opinion in which some four to five inches—depending upon one's source—was taken off the height of the average French male in succeeding generations. They were the big ones, the first assault waves, easy targets, and were in the front ranks. They fared fatally.

Meinertzhagen was certainly good at retrospect. He lambasted the Crimean screwup as well as the Boer War, best known in South Africa as the Second War of Independence. It was called the Boer War because the British bloodily lost the first one at a hill called Majuba—which ironically translates from the Zulu language as the

Place of Doves—where the Boers or Afrikaners chopped the thin red line into fish food. It wasn't even close.

Dick was getting more and more irritated at petty rules such as where he could smoke his pipe (gentlemen were allowed to do so in the billiard room but under no circumstances in the anteroom, for completely unknown reasons). He also railed at the rule that no officer might leave the mess hall while a visitor was present. As Dick was quick to notice, this was often after midnight, as one guest might well be playing whist or some other equally—Dick thought—inane game.

It was actually when he had graduated or slip-sided—depending upon your attitude—to Kenya that Dick introduced shorts into the British army. When he went shooting in India, he hated long pants and wore shorts. He was promptly smacked on the official wrist by his superiors and told to dress "properly." By 1907, however, and after Dick's battalion became the first in East Africa to take to shorts, every British regiment followed suit and was in shorts and shirts.

Dick was to have a few more adventures before he ended up as a chunk of history in East Africa. The first started with a rather strange officer by the name of Hare, unfortunately also known as March Hare or Mad Dick, neither of which titles was much appreciated by the bearer. As Meinertzhagen says, Hare was an unbalanced genius.

On the afternoon of July 20, 1899, in Nasirabad, Meinertzhagen heard some rather substantial screams coming from his compound and, on investigating, saw a fellow officer being attacked by Dick Hare, closely followed by Lyon Campbell, who was screaming that Hare drop the Samurai-sharp boar spear he was hauling with a definite will. Neville, the officer being attacked, wasn't a big man, according to Dick, yet had had the gall to call Hare "Mad Dick" as well as "March Hare" to his face. To shave a long story bare, Lyon Campbell saved Hare's life, at least by all appearances. Just as well, or the British army would have been short at least one officer. He snatched the spear away, which took some nerve. Pigs-ticking was one thing; officer-impaling quite another.

Dick quickly found that Indian foxhunting was not quite what the British variety was. One afternoon, he heard a devil of a din being raised by terriers near his bungalow. A fox had dashed into a culvert, and the terriers were not about to walk away from this snacklet.

Grabbing his hog spear and jumping onto his pony, Dick set off to pursue the fox if it tried to break cover. The neighborhood erupted as the fox eventually bolted, flying over mud walls with every four-legged critter available in pursuit.

This baying circus landed up in Colonel Abbott's compound, where the fox was speared bang slap in front of the old chap's veranda—with him on it. That he was the officer commanding the station didn't help. He was apoplectic as he confronted young Dick, spluttering that he would not have "half-naked young subalterns spearing foxes in my garden"[18] and that Dick was to kindly clear out with his curs. Exit Dick. Exit dogs. Exit one dead fox.

What next? Plenty.

Before he left Nasirabad, Dick was to have a near-fatal clash with a fellow officer, one Bobby Roberts, mentioned earlier. One did not fornicate with Richard Meinertzhagen on any basis. Since his brutal treatment as a young boy at school, Dick had developed a killer instinct to deal with bullies and assorted enemies alike. He had also developed an iron resolve to follow through, if need be. He was scared of naught, and it showed.

Dick had stayed with Roberts about a week when things became nasty. The matter came to a head late one night, when Dick left the mess hall shortly after dinner. Bobby Roberts was in a bloody mood, a dangerous thing when dealing with Richard Meinertzhagen. Dick went to bed early, immediately after dinner, and Bobby came to bed quite late, his first act being to pull off all of Dick's bedclothes with the comment that he had best learn manners and not go to bed before his superiors. When Bobby began to undress, Dick's temper snapped, and he pulled his issue revolver, a .455 Webley.

It came to a potentially deadly conclusion. Bobby had likely been toasting the Queen vigorously.

"Get out, you bloody young cub,"[19] said Roberts.

Dick made it clear that he meant business and had no intention of putting up with any more crud that Roberts wished to spread. Dick cocked the revolver with the fatal clicks that you only know if somebody has cocked one against you, and told Roberts that he would not tolerate any more bullying. Roberts had the inspired good sense that fine whiskey brings, to believe him. He and Bobby remade the bed together, but Dick was mightily disturbed at his own threat to shoot a superior officer. Roberts said nothing the next day or ever after that. Likely he didn't recall.

Dick wasn't able to sidestep disease and came down with enteric fever, which saw him being shipped back to England on six months' sick leave. He eventually rejoined his battalion in Mandalay in what is today's repressive state of Myanmar, Burma, in the good old days when it was a province of British India.

Queen Victoria had recently died—in January 1901—and something indefinable had changed. Dick could sense that an era like no other had ended with the Queen's death and that a threat to empire now hung in the air. He and his fellow officers spoke of the possibility of war with Germany. What they all knew beyond doubt was that life simply could not be the same after the demise of Victoria's "cementing influence."

Fully recovered from illness, Dick was ordered to southeast India in April 1901, to a hill station resort called Wellington, situated in the Nilgiri Hills of Tamil Nadu State. He was in command of a sick and convalescent group of British soldiers.

Wellington and surrounds offered every imaginable creature comfort to the pukkah sahib, including a local version of fox-hunting, only the quarry was the lowly jackal and the rules were a touch more informal that good old Blighty's hunting protocol. Dick's hunting records reveal that he bagged two tigers, two leopards, and three Indian bison while in the region. It was here that he would have had his first experience of the shikar or Indian big-game safari, with its elephants and their howdah platforms from which hunters would shoot their prey. Dick had already taken smaller game such as the chinkara and the blackbuck. The following incident explains to me why Dick all but dismisses his Indian experiences, hunting or otherwise, in the excerpts from his diaries he chose to publish. It was an extraordinary event that would alter Dick's life for good. It would be humorous if it were not so pathetic.

Posted back from the Nilgiri Hills to Burma, Dick was near Mandalay, the poet's delight, when he was pressured, either socially or rank-wise, into taking his commanding officer on a snipe shoot. Snipe shooting was a relatively important reason for otherwise sane young officers to come out to "Injia," as it was excellent sport. I have not shot snipe in India but have done so in Ireland, Scotland, Morocco, Mexico, and southern Africa and assure you it is all it is whacked up to be—grand.

In any case, Dick's commanding officer, a Major Bird (appropriately), asked Dick to take him out the following day, which happened to be a Sunday. Hosting the battalion commander to a shoot, Dick hardly thought it necessary to ask permission to skip church parade, as familiar a stupidity with the British army as it was with my preparatory school, which still used the "form" system of the British junior schools. "Chapel" was, among other items of curricula, somehow supposed to instill through overexposure some sort of fuzzy holiness in the troops or students. I certainly learned my hymns by rote; it ranked with the idea of algebra being some sort of mental gymnastics that would make the brain, as a presumed muscle, "stronger" and would endow the unfortunate with "mental discipline." Failing that, he or she would undoubtedly harvest the twin joys of perspective and relativity as well as something frequently referred to as "mental agility," although nobody knew precisely what that was. Further, it would impart "logic," although no member of the faculty had the faintest idea how to test this objectively. Today dinosaurs are all the rage; methinks their logic was also prevalent when I was in school. It certainly was so in Dick Meinertzhagen's time, as witness the famous snipe shoot that sent Dick to Kenya.

Meinertzhagen has written two descriptions of the incident of which I am aware, one in *Army Diary 1899–1926* and also in the preface of his *Kenya Diary (1902–1906)*. His notations are from Mandalay on the Monday following the events, January 17, 1902. He was still in the astonished stage, not having been given enough time for the famous Meinertzhagen temper to rise.

Dick, as noble a military politician as ever was commissioned, agreed to his commanding officer's request to take him out snipe shooting, but things turned nasty in the junior's mind not long after Major Bird made the request. Bird asked not only for shot shells, lunch, and the payment of the coolies who would beat the wet cover, but had a nap after lunch that had Dick from fidgeting to furious as he had lost two hours' shooting. Actually, the shoot was rather good in numbers of birds killed—mostly by Dick—and he opined that the major had never even seen a snipe before, let alone shot one.

The next morning, Monday the seventeenth of January, all hell popped out from the major. Bird sent a messenger demanding Dick's appearance at the orderly room instantly. Dick complied and was greeted by a tirade, which included some quite original language from Bird. Of all incredible questions, Bird asked what the bloody hell he was doing off snipe shooting rather than attending chapel? Dick was understandably astonished. He was, after all, with the major himself and said so. Major Bird, according to Dick Meinertzhagen, used the most incredibly imaginative foul language against him, and then Bird threatened to place him under arrest!

Well, only half the story is recorded, but it's a beauty. Dick was so angry he informed the major in writing that very evening that he would no longer tolerate serving in his battalion because of the man's attitude and that if he could not be posted to some other unit, preferably in Africa, he would resign his commission and make sure the relevant general knew the reason why. This was not an idle threat, and Dick had been around long enough for the word to have circulated that he was tough and, if pushed, dangerous.

Dick happily and enthusiastically chose the British East African protectorate of Kenya. On March 21, 1902, about two months after the sickening Bird incident, Dick announced to his diary that he had been appointed an officer in what was then called the East African Rifles (later the King's African Rifles) and that he should embark for Mombasa ASAP. He did. And it is doubtful whether there was another British officer in the Raj more delighted to get out and get on with things. India had never ensnared Dick's soul as it had so many British soldiers' before him, and he was glad to be shot of the fumbling old officer fossils, their rigid ideas, and their inferior soldiering. Three-odd years in India had been more than enough for Dick Meinertzhagen. In April 1902 the Easter Bunny gave Dick his best present yet: a one-way ticket to East Africa.

He was an action man. The blade that was to become the mature Richard Meinertzhagen had been forged in England and whetted in India, a keen, bright saber of initiative, unorthodoxy, bravery, and guile.

It was to be blooded in Africa.

Turkey

Mediterranean Sea

Mesopotamia

Egypt

Arabia

AFRICA

Nile

British
East
Africa

Lake Victoria

German
East
Africa

Madagascar

Pretoria

South
Africa

Cape
Town

Durban

N

AFRICA AND THE MIDDLE EAST

Chapter 3

With historic curiosity, Dick Meinertzhagen went from India to East Africa on the German East African ship *Safari* (the word really signifies a journey rather than a hunt in KiSwahili). He had come from Rangoon via Bombay and notes that these great events took place for the twenty-four-year-old just after he became a full lieutenant. He first crossed the equator and shortly thereafter began to develop his abhorrence of the Germans, a people he would fight in two world wars in one way or another. His opinion was based on the German treatment of a monkey belonging to the *Safari*'s captain. He never forgot it.

It would seem that the Teutonic passengers—or more likely the crew—hoisted the unfortunate primate to dangle from a mast, where it shrieked piteously until it was let down. Dick made some rather nasty comments to his diary as to the general rejoicing of the German officers aboard, who also burned the poor ape badly in the arse with glowing cigarette ends, which reach a most considerable heat. Dick was disgusted at the performance of making the monkey drunk and the German officers then laughing their socks off as he pitched around the deck. On the monkey's last afternoon before eternal primate grace, he was stoned by those who would become Dick's enemies and tied to a cord and thrown overboard. Of course, the result would obviously be a still-drunken, half-drowned, and likely shark-bitten monkey. Dick objected to the German officers but was politely advised to mind his own business. As the monkey gave a terrified yell in midair, Dick pulled his pocket knife and slashed the cord. As he later wrote, he was pretty sure the animal would quickly drown. The German officers were somewhat less than pleased with Meinertzhagen and threatened to send him after the monkey, but one look at the tall, obviously powerful Brit seemed to change their minds. Dick ended the episode with the comment, "In consequence I am by no means popular on board."[1]

Dick finally arrived at Mombasa, the tiny island off the East African coast, the old Arab slaving center along with Zanzibar. He wrote, "I shall never forget my first introduction to East Africa."[2] He was ensconced in the Mombasa Club, and "coolies" took charge of his luggage, which could not have been inconsiderable, and Lieutenants (of course pronounced "leftenants" in the Empire) Barlow and Wardle saw that their fellow officer was as comfortable as could be under the tropical circumstances. That was May 12, 1902, and Dick finished up his comments by saying, "I am full of hopes for the future in this new country and shall dream of the adventures of Harris and Gordon Cumming in South Africa. I am already in touch with the romance of Africa, and the Dark Continent has me firmly in her grip."[3] Little was he to know.

The British East Africa protectorate was barely seven years old when Dick arrived to join his new outfit, the King's African Rifles, one of the most formidable and disciplined of Britain's colonial forces, manned by blacks and officered by whites. The blacks included Swahili-speakers, Sudanese, various Kenyan tribesmen armed with rifles, and Masai levies who might number 500 or more spearmen per section, quite a lot on anybody's terms.

On May 18, Dick left Mombasa on the "Lunatic Line" railroad

where Lieutenant Colonel Patterson (*The Man-eaters of Tsavo*) had had such differences of opinion with a series of man-eating lions not long before. He woke the next morning at a station appropriately called Simba to see the sun-splashed snows of soaring Mount Kilimanjaro. Seven cock ostriches were seen eating not a few yards from the train. The joint was a seething mass of gnu, zebras, and common plains game apart from black rhino. In the overnight run on the train, he had seen roughly 6,000 assorted head. Besides counting the game, Dick noticed that falcons of various types followed the train and killed lesser birds flushed from the rush of the locomotive.

As if the Brit needed any further reminders that he was in Africa, no sooner had he arrived in the village of Nairobi and been escorted to his quarters than he was told that most of the six companies were out "protecting the railway coolies from a tribe called the Nandi."[4]

Dick was to become dangerously well acquainted with the Nandi.

The first animal he heard on his bedding down in the stillness of primitive Nairobi, Masai for "the Place of Cold Water" (bright, those Masai), was fisi, the hyena, the essence of the African night and proof wherever it serenades that some wilderness areas are still intact and that man with his plows, cattle, goats, and greed hasn't managed to ruin quite everything yet.

Dick was given command of Number Eight Company, and came to the first of his disillusionments.

He notes that they were living in tents while barracks were being built for his company and other battalion elements, no doubt. Yet his first indoctrination was that of spraying blood and whistling leather, which left an odd, salty smell and taste on the light wind. The two accused—and therefore convicted, as enlisted men did not argue with British officers—were adjudged guilty of respectively "severely frightening a British officer" (didn't know it could be done!) and, in the second case, being caught in bed with the sergeant major's wife. That definitely could be done. The first offender got ten lashes with the same hippo-hide kiboko or sjambok of which Robert Ruark spoke. Bob said directly that he would as soon hit a man with a sword as a kiboko. The second sexually indiscreet gentleman got twenty-five lashes with the same instrument. Hard place, the British colonial forces in the first few years of the 1900s—surely as bad as the British navy.

Dick was especially disturbed that his Number Eight Company was in a "shocking state." The men wore the red tarbooshes common at the time, and as Dick pried one off an enlisted man's head with his riding crop he found the scalp a seething mass of lice. Further, they were poorly disciplined, by his lights, and he was probably right.

Later that day, Dick tried to solve all the mortal problems of a Thomson's gazelle, without success, but this didn't matter at all as it was his first time out in Africa with a rifle, and that fact alone would have been enough compensation. He did perforate a Thomson's the next day with a 200-yard shot, providing dinner. Always the macabre naturalist, when he found a good many human skulls that same day, Masai victims of a year-old famine, he collected several for the Royal College of Surgeons back in England.

British East Africa in 1902 was wild and dangerous, the preserve of killer lions, as Dick learned on the twenty-seventh of May, when he recorded the rather painful saga of a gentleman named Roberts, who had had a definite falling out with a lion, ending up on the losing side except that the lion was killed.

Roberts was a civilian, one of the early big-game hunters, who came up to a lion in that clear grass country typical of the Athi Plain, near Nairobi, the same country that cost a lot of potential heroes their lives, limbs, or limps. Dick says that Roberts shot the simba in the guts at 150 yards (so it was pretty open country if Roberts could see the lion so far away). The cat was showing signs of definite exception to such treatment, which prompted Bwana Roberts to swat him again with one barrel of a double .450 cordite rifle. Roberts must not have been very swift, because before he could get the second round off, the lion had covered a football field and a half and had the gunbearer in his jaws. Curiously, Roberts seems to have had time to reload the double rifle rather than taking the second shot, which is what doubles are about, anyway. Mr. Roberts, however, hit the lion in the lower jaw and the shoulder, which brings up a point that has always fascinated me.

Presumably a lion charges head-on. So how could one hit a charger in the shoulder, which in all big-game parlance is in the side of the body? Well, to be perfectly honest, I have shot genuine charging lions in the butt, but it was only when they received a frontal shot causing them to spin around and giving me the chance to attempt to break the pelvis before somebody got very dead.

The lion, however, was by no means finished yet, leaving the torn-up gunbearer and choosing Roberts as his next opportunity. Roberts stuck him twice more, but he didn't swerve from his charge one step, despite another .450 in the chops and one more in the chest. Lions are a lot tougher than they are reputed to be: I have known a big male to take eleven shots from major calibers all in the right places and not change his mind until he was dead, one man also dead and two more in the hospital for enough time to earn a doctorate.

Roberts, however, even in the days of potassium permanganate (which probably did more harm than good to open wounds such as created by enthusiastic felines), was smashed down and actually sat upon by the shot-up lion. As Dick gives him credit, he got out another cartridge (he must have carried more than the average battalion), loaded it, and redecorated much of the Kenya plains with the lion's brains. Incidentally, the lion was chewing on Roberts's (presumably left) arm all the while, which is unpleasant. How he loaded the double rifle one-handed when his attention was otherwise engaged by a lion trying to tear off his arm remains a mystery. Roberts survived, although the incident lowered Dick's opinion of the new cordite rifles (cordite was a new propellant at the time, used until the 1950s) that were all the rage. He felt that if Roberts had had a twelve-gauge Paradox (or other brand name of rifle that fired a solid or capped conical slug as heavy as a surf-sinker), the incident need not have happened.

It's curious in retrospect that Dick seems not to have been much of a gun writer, not even giving the bore of the famous punt gun. By deduction, he himself favored a .256 Mannlicher, a bolt-action magazine rifle with a full-length forestock, which his son now has. The bullet had great sectional density—the relationship between bullet length and weight to velocity—and end results were obviously successful for Meinertzhagen. One of his pals, "Deaf" Banks of Uganda, once killed three bull elephants with one shot from a .256: He shot the topmost bull on a hillside, causing an animal avalanche that took the other two elephants with it. Of course, they looked the same on the score sheet. His reference to Roberts's .450 double is unusual. He did, however, quote one of his heroes, Sir Frederick Jackson, a major figure in the assorted ramifications of East African government, a gentleman of considerable experience with dangerous game whom he had first met at the British Museum about eight years previously. Jackson, author of contemporary erudition and eventually governor of Uganda as well as holding other major diplomatic posts, was only deputy commissioner at the time Dick started with the KAR. However, he espoused one of the classic arguments of big-game hunting, a theory concerning calibers and bullet construction. Jackson was convinced that if a man were hit in the chest with a fist as opposed to a skewer, the blow would penetrate but would "not knock down." If he is hit by a fist, that is, a major caliber, the blow will be sufficient to floor whatever is unlucky enough to be struck.

Dick, with his limited experience, however, took the opposite view, maintaining that penetration was the major factor, and since Jackson had never tried the alternative viewpoint, he could hardly judge. Dick implied this but did not say it. The ideal is a *big* bullet that penetrates; but ammunition and bullets generally have come so far along the path of excellence since 1902 that the current conclusions are hardly comparable.

If you've been recently to Nairobi, Kenya, the descriptions Dick gives from 1902 compared to those of the balloon safaris, the American fast-food restaurants, and the air-conditioned safari clubs of today make one wonder if Jules Verne wasn't on the right track. Mind you, nobody opposes comfort, which is the elemental product of successful labor. There's just something irretrievably lost— and not just in Kenya—that went with the wilderness. Forever.

When Dick was there, the only proper store was a duka, run by enterprising Indian brothers who lived behind a curtain in the small rear and were saving to bring their wives and brothers over. As Dick said, it sold every item from cartridges at the exorbitant price of eight cents (sterling) each, to hot beer at an astonishing five shillings a throw, sardines, jam, bully beef, and what was called paraffin and still is throughout much of Africa, which in America is called kerosene. Dick notes that they might have to close down, as nobody would honor the tenuous credit offered.

There was only one street when Dick arrived, a morass of mud during the short and long rains, and scorched plains of red, rutted dirt during the dry season. It was Victoria Street, the same name as my own address, surely being as popular as the Falls or a thousand other byways throughout the British Empire. But it did have a hotel, also run by Indians, who doubled it with a soda water factory, which should give some idea of the inhabitants' pleasures. There was little to do but get drunk, shoot lions, or fool around with the Masai women.

Dick shot lions and felt light-headed with happiness at the game-packed Athi Plain, which, he said, "exceeds my wildest dreams of Africa's big game."[5]

Meinertzhagen, largely the professional Victorian, rather liked the noncommissioned officers, especially the "mustangs" who won their commissions under fire, such as one Mackay, who captured his at Omdurman, when the British and Egyptian forces under General Kitchener thumped the military daylights out of the Sudanese in 1898. But he essentially disliked his fellows, commenting that his company commanders were either heavily in debt, gay, or alcoholic, and in some cases all three. He was scandalized when local women were brought into the officers' mess and wrote out a formal objection, threatening to send it in at once if they did not reform. Of course, today this seems a touch foolish and priggish, but, after all, it was 1902, and many people around the world still don't understand the concept of "class" as it is interpreted in Britain. It's the way things work. Dick ended his complaint with the quatrain:

> They say I'm a quarrelsome fellow,
> God rot it, how can that be?
> For I never quarrel with any,
> The whole world quarrels with me.[6]

Around the sixth of June, Dick had a formal chance to examine his company. He was both elated and disappointed, depending on the personalities. He had a hundred and a quarter Swahilis, an Arabic-extracted tribe, generally, from the coast, but not known as great fighters; a couple of Sudanese, who almost lived to fight; and four Masai, whom Dick pronounced "worthless." This probably didn't help the "noble savage" concept overly, for it would seem that all explorers loved and admired the Masai. Dick started to learn KiSwahili that day, noticing that the native officers maintained but little control and the sergeants even less. His object was immaculate discipline, and his intention was to make his men into "an efficient fighting machine."

Despite removing one of his men's tarbooshes and discovering the small sea of lice, Dick really got the drift of the early KAR in several more practical ways. First, it was their weapons, thirty-plus-year-old Martini-Henry .577/.450 single-loaders that thumped as badly at one end as the other. They were getting old when the British bearded the Zulu lion in 1879. They happily came along with bayonets and every soldier was given a machete, which, as Dick observed, was an excellent choice for bush-clearing and arbitrary decapitations of the enemy.

Unfortunately, his company would have done better to have thrown stones than to have tried to use the rifles, as they were so frigged up. All were rusted and one was completely blocked by cleaning material, and another's breech was frozen by rust. Dick asked for twenty-four new rifles but was told that he would shortly be equipped with the .303 rather than the old-style single-shot. Of course he inquired about extra ammo for target practice and was told he could have ten cartridges per man and practice on game. His comments on this did not endear him to his superior.

Another incident happened along the path that further disendeared him. One of his soldiers was dragged to the orderly room for insubordination, having informed his sergeant in a moment of pique that his superior's mother was a hyena and his father a crocodile. This was not done in the British colonial army and the man regretted his comments the moment he had said them.

He got twenty-five lashes with the kiboko or sjambok anyway. Dick had to oversee the operation, which turned his stomach. It was horrifying, but it was also colonial Africa. The man was tied to a wooden triangle, his pants removed, and he was thoroughly beaten with the kiboko until his legs were streaming with blood. Dick was holding down his gorge, but barely. Shortly after the punishment, he went to the orderly room and expressed his astonishment at the brutality of such a lashing. His fellow officers were taken aback! They accused him of being squeamish (that's certainly one thing Dick wasn't guilty of) and told him it was impertinent to question a punishment authorized by the orderly room.

Dick's answer was that he would never again have a man flogged unless he were discharged; certainly he could not revert to his regiment. He wasn't off to a very good start with his new regiment—nor were they with him.

Dick's sighting of his first lion coincided with his first actual foot safari when he and thirty-five men set out on the four-day march to Fort Hall, northeast of Nairobi, where he was to take command of the detachment based there in the shadow of Mount Kenya.

At dusk, as the African night was about to set in with its unique orchestra of sound, Dick was outside his tent when one of the escorts yelled "Simba!" The lion was only a streak of tawn at 500 yards, which Dick just glimpsed, but his heart surely pounded in his throat with sheer exhilaration, giving him a hint of how he would feel at his next encounter with the beasts. Twelve days later, he'd been following the blood spoor of a wounded impala when he saw eight lions entering a reed bed in the Tana River. That he and a fellow officer, Hemsted, proceeded to walk up the lions in the dense reeds, hearing them crashing on ahead, was "foolhardy," as Meinertzhagen quaintly puts it. In retrospect, it was enough to make Dick take up croquet as a lifestyle!

Dick, now at Fort Hall, was in Kikuyu country, whose people were noted for their belligerence. In fact, Dick had thorn barricades, or zaribas, built around his encampment when out on hunting trips, just in case the locals got ideas of surprise attacks. His basic impressions of the Kikuyu were further enhanced by an old Kikuyu chief who came to meet him when he was out hunting and had set up camp for the night. When the chief offered Dick a fowl as a most welcome addition for dinner, Dick noted that the old boy's right hand was missing its fingers. Not quite: The chief fished out a tobacco tin, which he proudly opened, to show Dick his fingers, which had been severed in a fight. "This did not improve my appetite for my dinner off his chicken,"[7] Dick wrote.

With Fort Hall as base, Dick was honing his hunting skills on a great variety of game, which included rations for the locals, culminating in the Coronation Day celebrations in June 1902. He was astounded at the huge quantities of meat the Kikuyu could consume, and this reminded me of an amazing, documented story I read soon after I came back to South Africa to settle. A gigantic Zulu used to give public demonstrations, for a fee of course, of his eating an entire goat at one sitting. When I tried to find out several years later what had happened to him, the trail had gone cold. He had probably died from his gastronomic antics.

One of the more interesting entries that Dick made in his journal was on July 25, 1902, in which he mentioned his pay. When in India, he made 108 pounds sterling per year, in British East Africa he found himself with 400 pounds per year "under cheaper conditions,"[8] which included ammo and booze. He said that eggs were three pennies a throw, a chicken a half rupee, and a sheep three rupees. Dick reckoned that his own expenses were about two shillings per day. The case of W. Robert Foran, an early Kenya pioneer and author of several grand hunting books, gives an idea of the value. He literally suffered a mental breakdown over the value of the rupee to the pound or shilling. It also illustrates the world Dick had entered in early East Africa and the colonial stupidity of the British civil service.

Foran, a major in the British forces despite having gotten a fine reputation as an ivory hunter, quit the game when his gunbearer was killed by an elephant. Foran felt that he had been somehow at fault. In any case, he ne'er again looked at his rifles through the express sights at Bwana Jumbo. He did, however, go temporarily crazy through his extended exposure to the British army in East Africa.

The problem was twofold, both parts related to the army, in which he was, after all, a field grade officer with the Queen's commission. Foran was attached to the BEAP, the British East African Police, and, when he obviously started to crack up, in the opinion of superiors, he was granted leave for twenty-one days to hunt elephant in the area of Mount Elgon to the north. Foran had walked for 200 miles when a runner came with a note in a cleft stick advising him to get back to the fort immediately. He returned and covered the distance in record time. Two hundred return miles was a hell of a trip through *that* country in 1909. It still is, on foot. The emergency? A junior officer had gotten it into his head that the inspector general was going to pop by for an inspection. Of course he did not, and Foran's twenty-one-day leave was ruined, sure, but it was more than that.

Foran wasn't home for very long before classic British jots and titles began to descend on him. It was the beginning of the end of W. Robert Foran, soon to become ex-major.

The major had never been able to make it even remotely intelligible to those droves of British civil servants thousands of miles away that, since the tribesmen had no money in the European sense, they could hardly be expected to pay hut taxes and such in the coin of the realm. Thus, they paid in cattle, hardly an unreasonable approach to such classic matters of international finance. The problem was that, unlike shillings, pounds, and guineas, which hardly ever got gravid no matter how hard they were rubbed, a herd starting off at one bush post never arrived with the same number of head as that with which it departed. Lions and leopards and hyenas ate the slow, older ones, and new calves were born.

Nope. Foran was feathering the British Empire in favor of his own nest, or so they saw it; at least by thrupence—three cents'—worth. An important aspect to add to this concept, stirring the whole lot well, was that British East Africa had two currencies, the British shilling and the Indian rupee, which were irritatingly officially disparate in such urgent matters of exchange rates as the British and most other armies of the day used to pay their troops—simple mathematics. It is truly curious but typical of any military organization that they would drive an officer that cost tens of thousands of pounds sterling to train into another profession over a lousy three cents. Why we're not slinging clubs and eating sea urchins on Saturday mornings certainly is no fault of the British or anybody else's army. It's the way armies work; or are at least *supposed* to work.

Foran was led kicking, screaming, and likely crying from his counting table for a long rest back in Britain. Later, he was to become a prime correspondent on Teddy Roosevelt's safari in Kenya, the editor of the *Straits Times* newspaper in Singapore, as well as a well-known author of several books. God help him.

He lived out the remainder of his life until 1968 when, feeling death stalking him on quiet pads, he ordered a bottle of champagne and toasted his eighty-eight years of life, including the accumulation of some terrible facial injuries in World War I that kept him mostly solitary. Apparently he was something less than hand-some. He drank his bubbly at the Sportsman's Arms Hotel in Nan-yuki, Kenya, and died. He was a grand gentleman by all accounts who stoutly defended Meinertzhagen in a major incident that was to have a pretty devastating effect on Dick's later life.

But back to the bush.

Dick, the young British officer and big-game hunter, was soon to start hunting the most dangerous game of all—man.

In early July 1902, a youngster came running into the boma at Fort Hall with the news that four members of the official mail party had been wiped out by the WaKikuyu along the Thika River as they were making their way to Nairobi and that several horren-dously wounded people were still alive. Dick was so stunned that he at first thought this was the work of a man-eating lion but when confirmation arrived from fellow officer Hemsted, Dick went into overdrive.

Now, it must be understood that there were few things as sacrosanct as the Royal Mail, which held the empire together by a whispery wisp of gossamer done in India ink. To fool around with it was definitely a gaffe that would bring in the military and any-body else they could round up. Dick immediately set out with twenty men, most of whom couldn't keep up with him. He had something of a shortfall of personnel when five of his eight porters disappeared into the bush, but it bothered him little and he "en-listed" another five road workers, likely at rifle point. He reached the Thika in the early hours and dovetailed with Hemsted, who was himself left with two suspect policemen. He was mighty glad to see Dick, who mentioned that there had been an additional threat to that of a Kikuyu ambush: the ominous presence of a no-torious man-eating lion.

The night was as dark as your sombrero at midnight with no

moon and a wet match, and the lion was performing not far away, keeping parallel with Dick's few troops and porters. Dick ordered his men to fix bayonets and "proceed with great caution."[9] I doubt if the lion he heard was the man-eater, as the last thing a hunting lion wishes to do is to advertise his presence vocally. It was nonetheless a chill and scary early morning.

Hemsted got to the scene first and was confronted by a horrific scene. The blood had already clotted over the three dead porters, who smelled like a bag of liver forgotten in the closet since last November. They, of course, had not been buried, but there were eleven wounded in the most pathetic state, two women and nine men, who were a seething mass, a swimming swarm of maggots and other opportunistic African larvae. As is typical of Africa, Dick mentions that there were several untouched survivors of the attack who had not done the remotest to bring water or otherwise help the injured, despite it having been quite a while since the attack.

The mail party had built the usual thorn barricade to protect them for the night against not only lion but also attack by the area's particular branch of the Kikuyu, the Kihimbuini, who were known for their blood lust. The attack came, the indigenous throwing spears and shooting arrows everywhere but correctly. One shot from a local askari solved the problem, and the Kikuyu all vanished to apparent banana leaf–shaded homes and hearths, none wishing to come back with any blue-edged holes. The mail bag was intact, as well as some of Dick's trophies, which he was sending to Nairobi.

In any case, Dick was left with eleven wounded whose best hopes were painless progression on the road to immortality. He suggested to Hemsted that he go back to Fort Hall for some medical supplies, the white man's tomfoolery, and he even sent to Nairobi for a legitimate doctor, but his task was for the most part hopeless. There were two women seriously wounded, one with a long spear under her right armpit, Dick being astonished that she was alive at all, as it came out under her left arm. The other lady had received a severe spear wound in the stomach, which was a crawling morass of most enthusiastic maggots.

The first lady was the victim of Richard's attempt, eventually successful, to remove the spear, with a "severe tug,"[10] which likely meant that he had to use one of his feet to get some leverage. He packed the wound with permanganate of potash but, of course, she eventually died in presumable agony. The whole item was so gruesome that Hemsted, a professional British army officer on frontier duty, couldn't face it. Dick did.

The other black woman had a great deal of her intestines hanging thither and yon, courtesy of another long spear thrust or thrown, the gaping wound a mass of maggots. Dick was obliged to cut off some several feet of her guts with a pair of scissors, also giving her the permanganate treatment. Among other comments, Dick noted that "the flies are a great nuisance."[11]

Dick would soon get revenge. But not before dealing with man-eating lion.

Dick had just seen his first lion on June 11, 1902. It was a male, but 500 yards away, which put the Englishman off, as it apparently did the lion, which obviously had some sense. The second pride he ran across was on the twenty-third, eight in number and, as most lions are, not disposed toward junior officers. Dick suggested in later years that eight lion all in a bunch made his mouth water mightily at the time.

Dick repented his sporting misdeeds—if they could remotely be considered such—years later, when he had already collected or otherwise accumulated his 20,000 bird skins alone. He did it when he was ecologically safe. Obviously, retrospective philosophy is most selective.

Before he met his next lions and had a tiff with them, among other items that bite were a pair of rhinos (in 1902 there was certainly no shortage of them in Kenya), whose hunting he completely screwed up, killing the female. But it was 1902, when black rhino were as thick as flies in never mind.

Dick finally admitted in print that his "stop-gun" was an eight-bore, or an eight-gauge Paradox-type gun, which would handle everything from snipe with number-nine shot to a solid slug in the other barrel heavier than your-mother-in-law. The last several inches of the barrels were rifled. Good idea! He learned, through field experience, as I did over the years, that a solid, nonexpanding bullet was more efficient, provided the shot was properly placed, on heavy game such as rhino or buffalo. Cartridges and alcohol were cheap, in line with the cost of living mentioned earlier. Which brings up an interesting point that became obvious in World War I, still some years in limbo but well anticipated by Meinertzhagen: White British officers were much more economically kept in the field than were their troops, especially the Indians, who had religious dietary laws that incurred massive imports of such things as were acceptable to their diets. The British officer of noncom, could, on the other hand, live off the land on game and fish, which did not have to be hallaled—the throat cut before the animal was dead (curiously, the hippo was and still is considered to be a fish, as it lives in water)—as appointed by Islam and other religions and was obviously not at all practical under field conditions. The British should have gotten their clue in 1857 at the outbreak of the Sepoy uprising in India, which enlivened the British press to expound such concepts as the Black Hole of Calcutta. Well, they changed their caliber of service rifle, as so many had been captured or otherwise absconded with. It was a huge blow to the empire and to Queen Victoria, who thought the whole exercise most un-Britanic. She was, of course, correct. It was a knock in the knuts.

Dick was not fortunate enough to evade the other half of the equation, the man-eating lion. A party of fifteen police had arrived from Fort Hall in the meantime, bringing medical supplies, which included morphia. Dick gave the two severely injured women a good dose each and was about to turn in when a human shriek ripped through the night air. Grabbing his sidearm, as he thought the Kikuyu had somehow managed to get into the enclosure, Dick was just able to make out the dull silhouette of a lion jumping over the thorn barrier or zariba "with a man in his mouth."[12]

Actually, I think this was largely imagined or literarily magnified by Meinertzhagen, based on my personally having held several professional hunter's licenses in Africa since 1968. I've got stacks of late-1800s illustrations showing lions, with their mouths full of contraband such as calves, jumping ten-foot thorn barriers. However, I have long disputed the accepted observance of so-called naturalists that lions almost always break the necks of their prey, especially buffalo, by causing them to fall on the forward spinal structure. In my opinion, not so. I've never seen one that did not differ from what I consider the standard of tackling a buffalo by the throat, or, rarely, by the back of the neck. The same goes for most game, although I suppose a lion would grab an impala wherever he could. It's hard to tell later—not much left.

Certainly, it stands to reason. An average African weighs perhaps 140 pounds; a lion perhaps 400 pounds for a reasonable specimen. *Nobody* clears ten-foot thorn fences with that kind of weight in tow.

What had actually happened was that Dick had been deluged by more than one man-eater. At the supposed jumping of the lion over the zariba of thorn, Dick says that a porter was grabbed by his arse, but at his screech the lion let him go and nabbed the next man in line by the throat.

He was, presumably, killed instantly, which a bite in the neck by an adult lion will do every time.

The dawn brought as much as you would expect: a broken

necklace, slices of cloth, quite a bit of human blood, and God's own amount of lion tracks. There were also some fragments of bone and human skin, as well as some chunks of the lion's mane. His last victim fought to the end. Dick, however, had his revenge: On November 26, he killed both of what were presumed to be the man-eaters. The survivor, bitten by the lion in the butt, considered himself lucky. Dick observed that the carbolic he poured into the wounds may have been more painful than the acquisition of the injuries themselves.

The wounded from the ambush of the postal raid were in very bad shape, the woman with the maggot-ridden stomach wound "exuding a sort of green fluid,"[13] and Dick noted that she was in terrible pain and gave her more morphia, using his shirt and pajamas as bandages.

As soon as they could, the party returned to Nairobi, restocked, obviously planned on how to deal with the Kikuyu outrage on the mail party, and was back in Fort Hall a few days later. In fact, in Dick's absence, the Kikuyu openly threatened to attack the outpost, and when Dick heard of this he warned his fellow officer, one Tate, that if such a thing ever happened, he'd not only defend Fort Hall but would burn down every village within a five-mile radius in one day flat. This was not idle bombast. Meinertzhagen was a killer waiting for his first blooding, African-style.

Perhaps one of the most colorful summations made by a British officer on duty in East Africa at the turn of the century is contained in Dick's own words, which really caught the flavor:

Here are we, three white men in the heart of Africa, with 20 nigger [sic] soldiers and 50 nigger [sic] police, 68 miles from doctors or reinforcements, administering and policing a district inhabited by half a million well-armed savages who have only quite recently come into touch with the white man, and we are responsible for the security in an area the size of Yorkshire. The position is most humorous to my mind, but we seem to be handling it quite well. A small chief gets drunk, threatens to stamp out our authority, and is fined 5 goats. The humour of that alone is sufficient to allow us to drown our fears.[14]

Richard left his mark elsewhere, at least on a questionable moral basis. Being at least a historical Victorian, he was both amused and furious with the English-reflecting conduct of one Smith, who advised concerned native girls that they could not possibly become true Christians until they had slept with one of the fold's anointed. Precisely how they got anointed was not disclosed, but one can pretty well imagine. This incident followed what Dick called "an infliction" of three Italians, and his sentiments were all with Karurie, a former subject of "king" John Boyes, the traditional king of the WaKikuyu. This did not especially help British-Kikuyu relations. They were members of the Order of White Fathers, and, as Dick observed, "They are certainly not 'white' but doubtless will soon be fathers."[15]

Dick gave Smith his marching orders after checking with Karurie and seven of the no longer vestal (or vestigial) virgins. Last heard from, Smith was outraged but packing his bags like a good boy.

It was starting to chill off into the bone-binding cold, the air permeated with the smell of dead, burned grass that was typical of Fort Hall in Kenya. Hyenas chuckled a dirty joke, jackals chortled, and bush babies crooned their insane wails through the grass-sooty blackness.

Meinertzhagen and his men, back a mere four weeks at Fort Hall since the mail party massacre, had not yet finalized plans to deal with the perpetrators when they were sent reeling with the news of the murder of a policeman not one mile from the boma of Fort Hall. A clear message was being sent to the Brits, a crude challenge: Come and get us!

Meinertzhagen and his peers, McClean and Hemsted, held their council of war in soft tones under the brittle, smoke-smudged stars. Dick strongly advised immediate action against the Wa-Kikuyu for the death of the policeman, in addition, obviously, to the mail party massacre. McClean didn't think it such a grand idea. McClean was the replacement of Tate, who had seen greener pastures elsewhere. Tate, clearly, also saw what was coming.

Dick blamed McClean directly for the entire incident, at least in retrospect, and he was likely right. The dead man, the policeman killed by the natives, had been sent out to a WaKikuyu stronghold to arrest the chief for some heavy-handedness for which he was believed responsible. Unfortunately, the native policeman didn't have the gift of the gab, speaking—call it shouting—in the unknown language of KiSwahili at the headman. He made the fatal mistake of arousing two medicine men by loading his rifle in a threatening manner, grabbing the headman in the middle of an orgy, and suggesting rather forcefully that he come along nicely. The medicine men disagreed and encouraged the villagers to slaughter the policeman. That the medicine men were publicly hanged at Fort Hall the following October for a further offense did little except stop the trouble temporarily.

What Meinertzhagen then wrote in his diaries at this point has always put him in a certain form of jeopardy, as he erased many of the thoughts in his diary around World War II, and we really don't know if they were replaced with more modern conclusions or not. In any case, he says in his presumably edited notes from his diary that "the Kikuyu are ripe for trouble, *and when they get educated and medicine men are replaced by political agitators there will be a general rising*" (italics mine).[16] That certainly proved to be correct in the 1950s with Mau-Mau.

This comment was theoretically written in Dick's diary of October of 1902. Personally, I don't believe that anybody could see Mau-Mau looming its dusky Kikuyu hulk roughly a half century before it bloomed. I don't in any way call Meinertzhagen a liar, but his comments in 1902 are awfully convenient. Make your own choice. If nothing else, he was certainly a soothsayer in print in that year, which is mighty early for the subject.

Whatever the case, the policeman was most definitely dead, probably speared and bludgeoned until he stopped twitching. McClean reckoned it was a bad idea to raid the village, but Hemsted agreed with Dick that if such a crime were left untended it would breed more frolics, any inaction being immediately interpreted as weakness. Dick sent a most reliable black man from his command to find out what was happening with the WaKikuyu, and he found the worst: The man returned at three in the morning saying that the adjoining villages had joined forces with the bad guys and there was a lovely orgy going on. The policeman had been mutilated beyond recognition.

Dick discovered through the intelligence for which he would become famous that the WaKikuyu were slated to do rude things to Fort Hall at dawn. He adjusted his schedule as only he could do; Dick himself puts the engagement rather thinly, however. He and his force of twenty-two men had marched, surely not in step, from Fort Hall in the middle of the morning, which is godawful black in equatorial East Africa, to the village and found the WaKikuyu dancing around the mutilated body of the policeman.

Dick and his force attacked the village with what was classic colonial vengeance. One tribesman tried to break the slender cordon of British and askari troops and, failing to respond to a challenge (in language unknown), was instantly killed by rifle fire. Of course, the remainder of the population of the village didn't stop their precipitous rush, and when the rifle smoke finally cleared, there were at least seventeen dead WaKikuyu. Dick lost two of McClean's policemen and one of his own men. He mentions that he damned near took a spear through the skull as explorer Richard Burton did through his cheeks somewhat earlier when he was looking for the source of the Nile.

Dick's mentioning that he almost got on the casualty lists the hard way when a Kikuyu spear whispered by his head with that odd, thrumming vibration that large spears generate, is genuine, I can assure you. He and his force torched the village into cinders, "killed a few more"[17] and lost three of his own men to poisoned arrows and spears in the process.

Dick reckoned that it was a pretty good deal, at least based upon the reaction of the villages near his strike. He stayed on the battleground for about twelve hours—that he had lost four of his own men by that time, plus McClean's policemen, shows that the WaKikuyu were hardly helpless—and he departed with his troops at about three the next afternoon.

The logical question is, Where did this tiff end up? Was it worth it? Well, given the time and place, the confrontation was not only bound to come to conclusions, but they were in the British favor. When he got back to Fort Hall, Dick found a bunch of WaKikuyu chiefs more or less suing for peace. They agreed to bring in the local chief, the British lion having by no means been remotely satiated. McClean decided to fine them only fifty head of cattle and suggested that twenty-five would be returned if the murderers of the cop were turned in. Ah, politics.

The chiefs swore to deliver the killers of the policeman the following day upon Meinertzhagen's assuring them that he and his men "are quite prepared to continue tomorrow what we began today."[18] Meinertzhagen observed that such ideas as attacking British installations were "completely driven from their stupid heads."[19]

He also observed that order once more reigned in Kenya District.

Things started to heat up with the WaKikuyu by September 1902, when the Kihimbuini clan, responsible for the mail party incident, continued to defy His Majesty's Government. Richard felt rather "embarrassed" at his force's lack of cooperation with other units of the British as they went about a scorched-earth policy against the WaKikuyu under a force headed by one Maycock.

Richard and his force were totally unaware of the offensive and were only tipped off by the fires of burning villages. There he and his men pitched in. Although short of ammo, in three hours Dick and his force had captured 170 cattle, over 1,000 goats and sheep, and had taken prisoner seventeen men and thirty-four women and children with a loss of two of his own force killed and three wounded, most likely by poisoned arrows. His men killed seventeen Kikuyu warriors.

The whole matter came to a most grisly head over the fate of a captured white settler. His last thoughts were surely of the English spring.

The enemy was clearly identified as the Kihimbuini clan, Dick finally making heliographic (reflected mirror) touch with Maycock, whom he met just as the sun went down over the badly tonsured nape of Kikuyuland's woolly neck. The news was not good.

Maycock told Dick that the day before, the Kikuyu clan had captured a white settler and condemned him to a particularly savage death. The poor bastard was just trying to buy some sheep from those charming, enlighted, and certainly inventive people. They decided to drown him to death in human waste, after which he was mutilated and disemboweled. Great place, Africa. Lots of innovation in 1902, and even today, where several "witches" are burned alive every year in an area of South Africa, located in the Northern Province, a mere few hours by road from my home.

But back to the settler.

First, the Kikuyu pegged him down with long skewers and rawhide, banging a wedge into his mouth, most likely against his molars. Then the people were assembled at the village, where he was dragged from his indiscretion of trying to buy some sheep in the forest. Essentially, he was drowned, his esophagus completely blocked with urine and feces by every woman, child, and man in the village.

Richard commented to his diary that Maycock had given him a free hand to deal with these somewhat unenlightened chaps, and he decided to do so as the sun broke the cockatoo crest of cloud at first light the next morning. He and his troops would enlighten them. And they did. During the night, although historically he wasn't *that* much of gentleman, Dick had raised a tent for the women and kids and gave them a bucket of milk as well as meat, vegetables, and wood to keep their fires going. Considering what had happened to the settler, this was pretty good care on Meinertz-hagen's part.

It must have been an eerie sight, watching the villages burn, dull orange exclamation points about the area. That the silence of the darkness was thumbed in the eye by the war cries of the WaKikuyu fighters shaved very little ice with Meinertzhagen. He thought of his fellow Englishman with rage; committed to his diary that he did not feel overly merciful toward the Kihimbuini and that "I shall teach the offending village such a lesson at dawn tomorrow as will be long remembered among the WaKikuyu."[20]

Dick waxes both militarily and politically to his diary, men-tioning his ire at the central command not advising that he and his fellow officer should have closed the country to settler/traders as they should have done to avoid such instances as the death of the sheep buyer by incredible means. He wrote, "Our little camp is by no means safe tonight, as we only have 40 rounds per rifle left, no machine gun, and a large perimeter. We can but hope for the best and trust that the Kihimbuini are as apprehensive as we are to-night."[21]

Dick, on August 9, a month after his earlier entry in his diary, observed that "I have performed a most unpleasant duty today."[22] Oh well, it had to be done to keep a semblance of military balance. Dick and his men made a night march and surrounded the village before dawn, the village where the settler had been killed. The drums were thumping all night long, but Dick and his men were able to encircle the village and actually see the black warriors cavorting about the corpse of the Englishman.

This did not especially augment Dick's sense of fair play. He was brutalized and gave a brutalizing order: "Every living thing except children should be killed without mercy. I hated the work and was anxious to get through with it. So soon as we could see to shoot we closed in. Several of the men tried to break out but were immediately shot. I then assaulted the place before any defence could be prepared. Every soul was either shot or bayoneted, and I am happy to say that no children were in the village. They, with the younger women, had already been removed by the villagers to the forest. We burned all the huts and razed the banana plantations to the ground."[23]

Meinertzhagen found the body of the Englishman without trouble and assisted in washing it in a nearby stream. Before returning to his home camp, Dick had the body buried just as the sun came up outside the village.

He commented decades later that he regretted his actions and was not certain that he was correct in his decisions to kill all men and women. As he said, "I am not sure whether I was right. My reason for killing all adults, including women, was that the latter had been the main instigators of not only the murder but the method of death, and it was the women who had befouled the corpse after death. McClean, who was with me as Political Officer, was naturally consulted; though he refused to give his consent to my action, he told me he would not interfere if I thought it was a just punishment, so the responsibility is entirely mine.''[24]

The blade had been blooded.

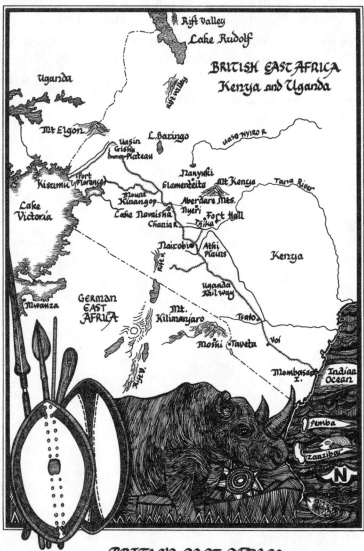

Rift Valley
Lake Rudolf

BRITISH EAST AFRICA
Kenya and Uganda

Uganda

Mt Elgon

Uasin
Gishu
Plateau

L. Baringo

MASO NYIRO R.

Kisumu
(Port Florence)

Nanyuki
Elamenteita
Mount
Kinangop
Lake Navaisha
Chania R.
Nyeri
Aberdare Mts.
Mt Kenya

Tana River

Fort Hall
Thika

Lake
Victoria

Nairobi
Athi
Plains

Kenya

Mwanza

GERMAN
EAST
AFRICA

Mt.
Kilimanjaro

Uganda
Railway

Moshi
Taveta

Tsavo

Voi

Mombasa
I.

Indian
Ocean

Pemba

Zanzibar

N

BRITISH EAST AFRICA

Chapter 4

ast Africa at the turn of this century meant wild animals, tribal clashes, primitive conditions, and disease. It was inevitable that Dick would succumb to malaria or "fever" as it was called in his day, a most accurate term, being a combination of sweltering sweats and incredible chills that had the sufferer alternately steaming and freezing. Curiously, I have never managed to catch malaria despite likely locations from Brazil to East Nevermind and more African locations than I can spell, although I do have relapsing (recurrent) tick fever, which does its damndest to equal the best that malaria can offer. I suppose the difference is that the first malarial prophylaxis—chloroquine phosphate, as best I remember—came out about the time I started hunting professionally and generally gallivanting around the boondocks, and, most important, it was effective. Anyway, I never got "fever."

I have always been interested in the logic that dictates that professional hunters don't take an antimalarial pill, even given the degree of sophistication they have achieved—the pills, not the professional hunters. Pros insist that the malaria pills tend to "mask" or otherwise obscure the symptoms of malaria, although I really can't agree. I suspect the decision depends upon whether or not one has the disease to start with. I am certainly not a doctor and claim no medical expertise, but if you are a safari client and don't take preemptive medication or a malaria prophylaxis, perhaps you had best rethink your game plan. See your doctor, although be warned that most Western physicians have never even seen a case of malaria, let alone treated one. A good case would be that of Dean Witter Jr., to whom I dedicated my first book, *Death in the Long Grass* (New York: St. Martin's Press, 1977). Dean, who died of heart problems, picked up a walloping case of malaria in East Africa in the 1960s and spent several years before he found a doctor in the States who knew what he was confronting on Dean's behalf.

The next few days drifted by casually, Dick taking his quinine, which gave him respite from the malaria. He shotgunned four black-and-white colobus monkeys swinging on the tall, feathery exclamation points edging the Tana River, Kenya's largest, the home of grand ivory, and noted that hut tax had been instituted among the Wa-

Richard Meinertzhagen in Nairobi, 1903. (Courtesy of Ran Meinertzhagen and Rhodes House Library, Oxford)

Kikuyu, the formula being based upon goats, sheep, and cattle. It didn't, of course, work, for the biological reasons mentioned earlier. Dick, incidentally, skinned the monkeys in bed that evening. He makes no comment as to the state of his sheets. After a while, the sheep held for hut taxes by the British became virtually worthless, as all were suffering from hoof rot.

In between military duties and hunting, Dick chalked up several firsts in British East Africa. During an expedition into the Aberdare Mountains west of Fort Hall, for example, Dick became the first white man to ascend Mount Kinangop, from where he had a spectacular view of all the Kikuyu country to the east, Mount Kenya soaring into the sky, and the Rift Valley with Lake Naivasha to the west. As he turned to face south, he saw forest and the Athi Plain sweeping toward Mount Kilimanjaro, the Aberdares continuing northward. I've always wondered if anyone since 1902 has dug up the six-foot stone cairn Dick assembled on the summit of Kinangop, in which he buried a bottle of beer with a note that the finder drink to his health and drop him a line at his London address. Nice touch, that.

That same trek into the Aberdares saw Dick locate the headwaters of the Thika and Chania Rivers and make a discovery of infinitely greater importance. On September 5, 1902, Meinertzhagen was thrashing along a high, heavily bambooed game path too dense to survey. After six and a half hours he had managed a sweaty but chilled nine miles, the ambient temperature being 46 degrees Fahrenheit. The occasional salt lick was stamped flat with elephant and buffalo prints, and both species seemed much in residence by their spoor, which was practically smoking in its freshness. It was then that it happened.

It was nearly dusk, which lasts for only a few moments in East Africa, a time between heaven and hell, darkness and light. The equatorial sun guts itself all over the western sky for only a few moments like a samurai warrior committing seppuku. Then it dies, and the hungry hyenas, lions, and jackals take over the murk, and quite competently, too. It was in these few moments that Dick was most likely to have been the first white to have seen the bongo antelope, the will-o'-the-wisp of African hunting, the prize extraordinaire, the toughest trophy to acquire in the ragged-toothed

Aberdare Mountains, although there is a western species that requires not quite so much effort.

Of his first encounter with the bongo Dick wrote, "Unfortunately I caught only a fleeting glimpse of them. The larger was a huge red antelope of sorts with white stripes. I could not see the head, only the rump. It seemed even larger than a haartebeeste [sic]."[1]

Bongo are members—the largest—of the bushbuck family, with semicurled but not centrally axised horns such as have the lesser and greater kudus. Their tribe includes more bushbucks than you are likely to come across no matter what your bank balance. If you were to insert a more or less common denominator into the family, it would be that they are fatally aggressive, from the smallest buck up to the bongo. They have very little fear, except for perhaps leopards, which haunt their joint riverine coverts. They're ectoplasmic but they are most capable and inclined to kill you if cornered.

I recall being with a most well-known professional hunter when we visited "Jack" Block's home on beautiful Lake Naivasha in Kenya about 1971. Meinertzhagen met him in 1903, "recently arrived from South Africa and exploring possibilities of making his fortune in this country."[2] He asked Dick's advice, and the young officer told Block to buy land. Block replied that he only had a little cash, a pony, and a sack of seed potatoes! The man I met was old, wildly wealthy, and a Kenya legend. He also kept us waiting for three hours because the imported largemouth bass were biting and we were hired help anyway. He wasn't a terribly polite person. In any case, while we were waiting for his imperial appearance, we noted that he had several Aberdares bongos enclosed behind a chain-link fence. I made the unfounded assumption that they were likely captured as fawns, or whatever one calls baby bongos, and were suitably tame in their incarceration. Nope. I found out nearly the hard way as two of the bulls hit the chain-mesh with astonishing savagery, trying to place me en brochette. I have never seen animals so vindictive or savage. They hit that wire like a Cape buffalo given an unexpected enema. A bull bongo weighs about 500 pounds, sometimes well over, and after that performance I would have guesstimated 5,000!

It was to be a day of firsts for Dick. The curious thing was that Dick saw not only the bongo (of whose hide the drum in its aboriginal form is named by the very primitive WaNdrobo for its resonance, and this was before ovens that tightened the skin), but at the same time he caught a glimmering, dark glimpse of "an enormous black pig."[3] Little did he know that the largest and rarest African pig, the giant forest hog, would bear his name as *Hylochoerus meinertzhageni* upon his sending some samples of skin to the British Museum. The giant forest hog is sort of a nightmare composite of your ex-wife and a tax collector, although it is both rarer and has larger teeth than either.

Dick had to wait for almost two more years before he was able to shoot a fine specimen, a sow. He sent the complete skull and skin to the British Museum, making eventual zoological history in the process.

Famous and very well-heeled hunters such as Mr. James Mellon have spent as long as seventy days in the Kenya mountains without a glimpse of a bongo through what is literally a bamboo curtain. I am told that the Aberdares bongo is forever preserved in Linnaean Latin as *Tregaluphus eurycerus isacci*, which probably serves it right, and I further note with interest that the best head was taken by my then next-door neighbor in the 1970s, Baron George de Dozsa, as we both lived on a private island, of which I was president, in Naples, Florida.

The Western bongo, which has the same Latin name less the *isacci* frill, lives in a more hunter-friendly part of the bush. Personally, I would make them two separate classifications based upon horn structure and conformation, the spiral-horned and the twisted-horned, such as the bongo, sitatunga, and various bush-bucks compared to the greater and lesser kudu.

Dick picked out a gunbearer from his ranks of WaNyamwezi from German East Africa and from among the Manyema tribesmen of the then Belgian Congo. He chose Simba "lion" from the latter tribe, a huge, close-mouthed and powerful hulk of a man whose tribe was known to practice cannibalism. He stuck close to Dick, who was obviously pleased with him. It would have made me a trifle jumpy under the circumstances.

But faithful gunbearers in the bush can sometimes make the difference between living to tell the tale and not living to tell it. Dick had had to pass up a splendid lion because the magazine of his Mannlicher jammed. When on safari in Botswana where I was gathering material—literally—in 1986 for a book (see *Peter Capstick's Africa*, New York: St. Martin's Press, 1987), my pro hunter colleague Gordon Cundill, a superb shot, had a couple of hangfires and a dud in the middle of a de facto lion charge. Our gunbearer, a splendid old man of the Subiya people, Karonda, stuck close to us, firing too, and there is no doubt he would have tackled that lion alone had one of my slugs not finally done the trick. Gunbearers don't have to be pretty. They have to be brave. And, in Dick's case, a Manyema cannibal in the early Kenyan bush was an asset.

Dick's Nairobi was still so raw that he was awoken by a devil of a din when a lion tried to force entry into the cattle kraal just 100 yards from his digs. Dick grabbed a kerosene lamp and his revolver, fellow officer Barrett snatched the sentry's rifle, and Maycock burst out of his tent brandishing a spear! The cattle stampeded, snorting in panic as they smashed through the kraal, and the lion was mobbed by hyenas, which were lurking in the murk, lighting up the night with their contrapuntal whoops, chortles, and shrieks to the lion's double bass grunts and growls as it disappeared into the African night.

Dick remarked that "one does not expect such incursions in places like Nairobi."[4] Oh? What about the elephant that promptly crotonized the subcommissioner's croton bushes in his garden not four weeks before the above incident? And the most recent horse race that was interrupted for over one hour because of a black rhino in a blacker mood bang slap in the middle of the Nairobi racetrack? And the zebra that dropped its foal on Dick's parade ground? And the lion that nailed a zebra just 100 yards from the officers' mess? With buffalo in swamps not two miles outside Nairobi and leopards frequent visitors to the soldiers' cantonments, Dick's Nairobi was indeed still the place for "such incursions." The dangers in the real Kenyan bush of that time, compounded by restless, warring locals of whom more will be heard in a moment, can but be imagined.

Meinertzhagen, in the meantime, was out hunting most Sundays from Nairobi and had already collected a variety of plains game and gamebirds, including creatures such as caracal, warthog, and ostrich. Dick's *Kenya Diary* lists thirty-eight species taken in Kenya. His first big-game animal was a pregnant female rhino—a no-no that exhibits the bad judgment of a novice—but remember, the Kenya of 1902 was awash with black rhinos, and Dick and his times cannot be judged with the hindsight of the 1990s. As Dick remarked in December 1902, "The number of rhino here is incredible. We and our men have in the last few days been compelled to kill 17, and yet the country is teeming with them."[5] Dick took sixteen of his own black rhinos while in Kenya and witnessed a number of incidents with rhinos that must have made him wonder how he'd managed to dodge death as he had. Take the case of one Mr. Eastwood, who was mauled by a black rhino to the extent that he lost an arm.

Eastwood, a Uganda Railway official, was near Baringo, on Lake Victoria, where he had shot a rhino, when another started toward him. He wounded it with a .577 cordite rifle and then twice again in the chest, but he couldn't stop the beast. He ran instead of climbing, had he been able to, and the rhino caught up with him, crunching his left arm in two places and sticking his horns into the man's chest, crushing ribs and injuring a hip. Eastwood lay in the sun until rescued by his men, who were not expected by their bwana. His people finally found him when the vultures became so thick as to be obvious.

It took two days for a Dr. Falkner to arrive from Nakuru, which was some eighty-five miles distant, and when he did, he had to amputate Eastwood's arm there and then, in the bush. No jet-propelled medical evacuation or 911 niceties. There appears to be no record of whether Eastwood actually survived and for how long after that ordeal.

There were to be several more close ones with rhinos. Dick had sent one of his officers, Collyer, to purloin a pachyderm for the porters when he ran into a rhino. Dick and his men watched helplessly as Collyer trudged the half-mile to perforate the damned thing, but were frustrated that they had no way of conveying to Collyer that there was another rhino between him and his intended. The Englishman and the rhino met at the top of the distant rise, and each did what he did best: the rhino charged and Collyer fired.

Now, Collyer weighed at the time perhaps a dark shade over 224 pounds (15 stone) and had accumulated something of an impressive reputation in rugby football as being stronger than old underwear plus last year's trout-fishing gear thrown in. He was apparently just what the British Empire needed at the time.

Impasse.

Collyer missed, or at least thought so. So did the rhino, at least partially, smashing the man with his shoulder but not his horn. Crikey! Collyer later reported to Dick that his first sentiment on being charged was anger. Happily—for Collyer if not the rhino—the animal ran out of steam about 200 yards away and did his finishing act.

Of course, there will be those who are completely horrified at the concept of killing—yes, killing, not "disposing of" or otherwise euphemistically ending the existence of a black rhino, but, as already stated, this was 1902 and retrospect is the rudest, least constructive form of conservation. Everybody is a Green Expert, from Girl Scout up. Or perhaps down. Why weren't we there when the Kenya birth rate was rampant? Why weren't we there when they were eating one other en masse in the Congo or under Idi Amin Dada in Uganda? Why didn't we intervene when "Emperor" Bokassa in the Central African Empire had a walk-in freezer full of corpses? Where was the Western expertise in Somalia, Sudan, Ethiopia, and Rwanda? Green People? The point is we have far, far, far too many people already, despite the most reasonable liberal attitude toward population, and it's not getting better but hugely worse. Destruction of habitat and out-of-control human population growth rates are the main threats to the survival of wildlife in Africa today, followed by chronic levels of greed and corruption in high places that are linked to poaching operations. The problem is positively not the presence of licensed trophy hunters paying huge amounts of money to keep the wilderness wild and the cattle and goats out.

Now that I have vented my bilges, living full time in Africa as I do and seeing daily what actually goes on, let's head on back to that poor bastard Collyer, who had essential bad luck with rhinos. He must have had a bruise that looked like a commercial-sized chunk of mastodon liver. Rhinos don't fool around.

The interesting thing is that Dick, not three days later, bumped into a rhino to which the hapless Collyer would lay legitimate claim. It's worth quoting:

I took a stroll around camp this evening after work and coming around a corner met a rhinoceros face to face walking in my direction. There was no cover, so I fired at point blank at his chest at but 20 yards. He staggered and nearly fell, but recovering himself made off. I gave him another shot as he ran but failed to stop him. He bolted towards the camp, when all my men and about 100 Masai spearmen gave chase. I yelled to them to let him be, but it had no effect and the hunt continued. The rhino could neither go fast nor far with his wounds, and was soon brought to bay and charged the whole crowd of us. We scattered and he stood. I fired again and the Masai encircled him and tried to spear him, which prevented me firing again for fear of hitting a man. He soon charged again, and singling out a Masai hunted him as a terrier does a rat. Nobody could fire for fear of hitting a man, so we yelled and tried to divert his attention. But he stuck to his victim, caught him up and tossed him some 10 feet into the air. The man fell clear of the rhino, who did not turn but went a short distance and stood. I quickly got the men out of the way and dropped the rhino dead with a shot in the neck. The Masai who had been tossed suffered a bad rip up the right thigh, but no artery or bone has been damaged. Dr. Mann has him in hand and thinks he should be about again in a month or so.

On cutting up the rhino we found 15 Martini [Henry] bullets in him which had been fired by my men, three Mannlicher bullets of mine and two .303 bullets. These latter rather puzzled me, as none of us had been using such a rifle. There were also 37 Masai spears sticking in his hide when he fell dead. He looked like a Christmas tree.

When we were finishing the cutting up, Collyer, puffing and blowing, arrived on the scene and claimed the rhino. The .303 bullets had been fired by him some little time before I had met the rhino face to face. So, as he could prove first blood, he took the horns, which were quite good.[6]

Meinertzhagen seems at times without humor, but there is a story he tells, gleaned from a fellow officer named Dr. Mann, that shows that this is not so. Jenner, one of the prime accomplices, was serving in Jubaland in what is part of today's southwestern Somalia. He had a full set of false teeth; his colleague, one St. John Wake, had a wooden leg; and Dr. Mann a glimmering glass eye.

In any case, they were at a rather prestigious meeting at Kismayu and the weather was sultry to say the least. Jenner was first, feeling uncomfortable with his false teeth, so he slid them out, placing them on the conference table with the sound one might expect. The Somalis were bug-eyed but said not a word in their Nilotic language. Wake, also suffering from the heat, unscrewed his imitation leg and put it beside Jenner's porcelain or hippo ivory teeth. Mann, possibly seeing the value of all this, quietly removed his substitute eye, and "tossed it in the air and put it in his pocket."[7]

Of course the Somalis freaked out, running at top speed from the meeting, convinced no doubt of the madness of the "mzungus."

Meinertzhagen, in between punitive expeditions against the locals, was to meet many of the people who would become part of the legendary fabric of early Kenya. One such character was

John Boyes, known as the King of the WaKikuyu (see *The African Adventurers*, New York: St. Martin's Press, 1992), whom Dick met in November 1902. He states that Boyes stole ivory from Karurie, one of the main Kikuyu chiefs, and that Boyes had not paid for a rifle Dick had sold him. Dick had long since met the old Kikuyu chief, who had thirty-nine wives and in excess of sixty kids, not to mention his wealth in cattle, sheep, and goats.

I have always believed that Boyes would not have soiled his own nest. He was very possibly the object of a certain envy, as he had single-handedly subdued the most savage tribe of the day in British East Africa. The rifle? There is no mention. But when Boyes died in Nairobi in July 1951, just shy of eighty years of age, the who's who of Kenya Colony turned out for the funeral.

It was soon after this that Dick bagged his first leopard and hippo down on the Tana River. He was soaking in the sight of snow-capped Mount Kenya when he saw the leopard grooming its flanks. Dick's first shot sent the leopard bounding toward him in a blind rush, before it was stopped at twenty yards.

Dick's local entourage were salivating at the prospect of the huge bull hippo he'd shot. They were all Muslims and got around the religious dictate of having to slit the throat of the hippo by declaring it a fish, as it lived in water. This points out the difference between one region and another in Africa and local prejudices. In the Luangwa Valley of Zambia, where I met my first hippo, the local people, the Awiza and Senga, firmly believed that hippo meat caused boils, and they would not touch it.

I note that shortly after, Dick killed a waterbuck but found that the locals wouldn't touch the meat, nor would he. Frankly, I have never eaten waterbuck, as I could never get anyone on my staff to skin it farther than the headskin. The waterbuck has a natural insect repellent in its hair, which usually taints the meat.

But more urgent matters descended on Dick when news came through in December 1902 of a party of Indian traders who had been butchered by the Tetu branch of the WaKikuyu. Dick was back to man-hunting with a vengeance as he geared up for a series of punitive expeditions against that tribe.

Dick and his men passed through Tetu country early in the morning, the sun coming up like a bloodshot agate eye. Of course, the Tetu WaKikuyu were active as usual, and had dug as many as fourteen pits within 100 yards—man traps—studded with sharpened stakes and reminiscent of the punji sticks we faced in Vietnam. Progress was deadly slow as Dick's men probed in front. These pits scared the Masai speechless, which very few things will do.

Dick divided his force into what he called raiding parties of twenty-five Masai spearmen and fifteen riflemen—not the sort you'd want to bump into on a moonless night. As Dick put it, "We were not altogether unsuccessful in surprising the enemy, and burst on the cultivated area, with little organised resistance. I remained with a central reserve and rapidly built a camp and zariba, clearing the ground for 100 yards round camp."[8]

Almost as an afterthought, Meinertzhagen mentions that he went to the assistance of some of his men who had been met by resistance in a neighboring village. He survived the arrows and spears, killing "some 20 of them and returned to camp. It was a busy day."[9]

Dick lost only two men, five being wounded. His forces captured 665 head of cattle and "many" sheep. The racket kicked up by the cattle, sheep, and goats that night kept him awake and no doubt left him frayed around the edges and in no mood for what awaited him. He and his men came across the party of slaughtered

Indian traders who had been stripped and mutilated. When a primitive tribe took the trouble to mutilate you, you stayed mutilated. The putrifying Indian corpses were stacked and set alight.

Pliny was quite incorrect: There's nothing new out of Africa; flame, blood, revenge, and hopelessness are still her innate fiber. It's Africa by definition.

Dick spent the night by leaving his camp standing, despite his worst nightmares, yet he lost "one of my best men,"[10] Laiboro Matumbato. He did, however, capture an additional 1,600 head of cattle, although I am horribly shy of round numbers. Obviously, the WaKikuyu placed considerable value on their stock, as they attacked twice on the night of December 12, 1902, pouring poisoned arrows into Dick's camp in sheets. Two bearers were hit through the rain, which was stiff enough to give considerable thought to refitting the Ark. They seemed to have higher opinions of the KAR force than they did of themselves, but at about 1:30 in the wees they again attacked from two sides, hitting seven of Dick's men in a sleet of poisoned arrows and rather nasty-looking spears. The furore of Dick's men, hardened as they were, coupled with the clatter of the two machine guns, caused some cattle to head for the Carpathian Mountains which, of course, delighted the enemy, who recovered them.

Dick was now in his element, which was essentially lead and steel alloy composed of bayonet and bullet. He rallied his personal Masai shock troops of elite warriors, who were Nilotic. They loathed the WaKikuyu, who were Bantu. Dick, of course, led the charge. He personally killed the first two WaKikuyu, likely with rifle fire as they were outlined against the flirting flames of combat. The Masai carried the early hours until the WaKikuyu slid away like boiled butter into the shadows of the thick bush with their few

cattle. They'd paid enough for them. Dick's losses were nine dead
of his combined force, and eleven KAR and fourteen Masai vari-
ously skewered by local indigenous innovation. When, however,
the Kenya sun cracked like a stale, pale crust, he and his men found
thirty-eight WaKikuyu in various stages of advanced death within
a few yards of his zariba. Nice guns, the .303 and the Maxim.

It certainly was a singular pean of praise from Meinertzhagen
as he reflected on the bloated, fly-swollen WaKikuyu corpses, "I
must own I never expected the WaKikuyu to fight like this."[11]
One didn't get better from the imagined Viking berserker.

Before leaving Dick to the mossy dentures of December 1902,
just about his most astounding adventure against an armed enemy
recalls T. E. Lawrence's comment mentioned earlier in the first
edition of Seven Pillars of Wisdom, of Dick's being "a silent laughing
masterful man," although the Tetu Kikuyu clan likely saw very
little in his humor.

On the eighteenth of December, Dick's troops, under command of a mere Masai corporal, had a hell of a hullabaloo with the
WaKikuyu in bamboo as thick as your forearms before your face.
After a four-hour running fight, the KAR totaled their dead at three
and the wounded at eleven, so it must have been a noteworthy
encounter, although nobody seems to have been taking notes. Dick
Meinertzhagen appears to have been losing his patience. It is not
known how many the Kyukes lost, but there must have been plenty
of local gentlemen with extra belly buttons.

As he put the tactical situation, "Before dawn this morning it
was evident that a considerable body of savages were in the vicinity
of my camp. Now the WaKikuyu have the habit of entering our
old camps as soon as we leave, digging up the dead, and mutilating
them. So I decided to teach them a lesson. I arranged that we should
break up camp, and that I and 15 Masai spearmen should remain

in ambush within the zariba and pounce on the savages as soon as they entered the place. We were successful beyond our wildest dreams."[12]

Dick obviously had in mind precisely how many spear- and arrow-armed enemy he would choose to engage, at what range, and that he would use Sheffield steel rather than Eley bullets. He also, of immense importance to the engagement, permitted himself to be outnumbered by more than three to one; sixteen against fifty.

A single shot was fired. All the rest of the hot, steaming human blood on that frosty, mountainous Kenyan dawn, in the carefully cleared zariba area, was vented by blades, something WaKikuyu never forgot.

Dick and his fifteen Masai spearmen hid behind piles of firewood, small stuff mainly of panga-slashed brushwood. He had advised Dr. Mann to stop within two miles of the camp and to return with the force the second he heard a rifle shot. (Who precisely Mann was and his background remain a secret although you will notice farther on that he was not an especially gifted individual. Likely he was the regimental surgeon.) As the dawn broke like a newly sliced watermelon over the high Kikuyu giant bamboo and the scalpel-sharp whistling and wait-a-bit thorns of the zariba, the WaKikuyu started to appear as dark shadows, their bright winged spears and arrowheads glinting evilly in the first, early light. The slithering sound of soft iron simis, short swords, being drawn from their red leather sheaths mingled with the almost dead campfire smoke that wafted over Dick and his fifteen picked spearmen, men who were only admitted to manhood by killing a lion by themselves.

Dick let fifty fully armed KiKuyu enter the boma before he neatly shot the last man and jammed the entrance with the corpse. With blood-frosting war cries, the lone white and his few men set to slaughter the astonished Kikuyu with spear, Masai short sword, and bayonet, despite being outnumbered three to one. Richard straddled the body and blocked the door with his own, shielded by a picked Masai on either side to deflect spears and arrows. Slowly but with stark, ruthless efficiency, Meinertzhagen held the portal with his bayonet and killed every man who tried to escape, afraid to fire with his rifle into the swirling melee of sweating black dusty skins and gleaming iron in front of him as his Masai went into individual combat. As Dick said:

> The Masai were out like lightning and began to kill at once. The whole affair was quick and quiet, and as it all occurred in the open and within a few yards of me I had an excellent view when I was not myself kept busy. I held the entrance with my bayonet, being shielded on either side by two Masai with their massive shields of buffalo hide. A good number of the enemy bolted for the door, but none got past me. I was surprised at the ease in which a bayonet goes into a man's body. One scarcely feels it unless it goes in to the hilt. But one frequently has to make a desperate tug to get it out. *In the end not a single one of the enemy escaped, all being killed* [my italics]. I had my shirt ripped up by a spear, 3 Masai were killed, and most of them had been cut about. One could hardly avoid it in a pure hand-to-hand encounter.[13]

Dick makes a rather lengthy comment about the Masai and their way of fighting:

> The Masai fought with their shields in front of them and used their spears as stabbing weapons throughout [which the Amazulu under Shaka in the 1820s did, calling the spear the isiqwe for the sucking noise it made when withdrawn

from your kidneys in a hurry] rather than throwing implements. I never saw one use the knobkerrie or short sword (seme). Once their man is down they use their short sword, inserting it on the shoulder near the collar bone and thrusting it down, parallel to the longer axis of the body, through the heart and down to the bladder. The length of the sword is such that it does not protrude.[14]

Dick surfaces by saying: "I doubt if the people of Tetu will worry us again for some time."[15] He was correct, too.

It was around this time that Meinertzhagen met the notorious slaver Tippoo Tib and learned something about Arab hospitality. Dick had had a bad fall from his pony and was given time off to recuperate from three broken ribs, so he headed for the island of Zanzibar, arriving there on January 30, 1903.

Zanzibar was the main center of the slave trade in the nineteenth century, from where merchants would go inland to capture "black gold" and elephants for their "white gold"—ivory. One such trader was a Zanzibari-born Afro-Arab, Tipu Tib or "Tippoo Tib," as Dick called him. When the British proclaimed a protectorate over Zanzibar in 1890, they set about putting an end to the remains of the slave trade, officially declaring it dead in 1897, a mere six years before Dick's memorable meeting with one of the most notorious and ruthless traders of them all.

The old slaver was confined to Zanzibar, and rumor had it that his servants were in fact still slaves. Dick tried to get the old boy to open up and talk of the "good old days" of slave raiding but this apparently seemed to embarrass him. On drinking the fragrant coffee, Dick remarked on the beautiful silver pot used. The next thing, he was its owner, not knowing that if you admire something in an

Arab household, the owner is obliged to give it to you. Dick kept the silver coffeepot, which his son, Ran, has to this day.

In mid-1905 Dick was to think back on that rather strange meeting with Tipu Tib when he was near the Ugandan border at a place called Kitale. An old Sudanese by the name of Mubarak fell in with Dick, who discovered the old boy had served with Arab slave raiders and had spent a lot of time at Kitale, which was a major slave market. When Dick and his Sudanese chum arrived there, the remains of the slave stockade could still be seen, surrounding the market area of some four acres.

Mubarak still had vivid memories of his slaving days under Tipu Tib and proceeded to tell Dick of what went on at the Kitale "holding pen." Young captured boys were castrated to serve later as eunuchs while young girls became the literal sex slaves of the merchants. The adults captured were mercilessly driven to the coast shackled together in iron chains, those too weak or ill to continue being shot out of hand. The images of such cruelty shook Dick, but old Mubarak could only speak of "plenty food, plenty women; very lovely."[16]

When Dick revisited Kitale over fifty years later, the remnants of the slave market could no longer be seen. Instead, the colonial club stood in its place. This was to be one of several experiences Dick would have where past memories would return to oddly haunt him.

Talking of ivory, Dick met Arthur Neumann, possibly the best-known elephant hunter besides "Karamojo" Bell, at Elementeita soon after the Tipu Tib encounter. Neumann had discovered the hartebeest named after him, a large, reddish antelope. Dick described Neumann as "a professional ivory hunter, conducting his work somewhere around Lake Rudolph [now Lake Turkana]. He is a quiet, unassuming little man, with a faraway and rather sad outlook on life. We had a long chat together about game and the glories of the simple wild life in Africa. Neumann's native name is Bwana Nyama, or the Lord of Meat. This was given to him on account of his fussiness in always insisting on his meat having a fly-proof cloth tied around it, a precaution the natives could not understand. Neumann is just off back to Rudolph."[17]

Arthur Neumann was later to blow his brains out in a London hotel room upon finding that a lady he treasured would not be his. Too bad; his book, *Elephant Hunting in East Equatorial Africa,* in its first edition, is one of the great acquisitions in African hunting literature, and my copy occupies a special place in my library.

It was in June of 1903 that Dick mentioned that he and other officers had started pigsticking on a regular basis. At this date this sounds ludicrous, but it was a most formal affair of gentlemen, especially officers, at that time. It would not be unreasonable to suggest that it was a test of cojones. Certainly it was a leftover from "Injia," where it was an essential of camp life, especially if you read a book such as *Wild Sports of the East.* By heaven forgive me, but I collect pigsticking (or hog-hunting) books. As Dick said, "Last January we started pig-sticking seriously. Our previous efforts were rather hampered by the lack of proper spears (our improvised weapons were bayonets lashed to bamboo poles) [Crikey!], but we imported some proper hog spears from India and then began serious business."[18] Dick hunted with a fellow officer named De Crespigny, the scion of an ancient and wealthy family of Norman origin.

Of course, Dick and his pals had to improvise, as *Sus scrofa,* the European and Indian wild boar, was not on hand, so he and his fellows had to manage with the African warthog, which is surely a formidable foe, I assure you. I've seen females take on lionesses. An average boar warthog weighs about 250 pounds or considerably more. As Dick said in his diaries:

The African warthog is a very different beast from the wild pig of India. His home is underground, and if chased he makes straight for his hole, from which nothing will turn him. If one gets between him and his hole he charges at once. Neither does he jink like the Indian pig but makes a straight run, which makes spearing easier; but on the other hand, if one is anywhere but directly behind him he has a nasty habit of suddenly turning into one's pony's forelegs, which entails a crash if not worse. Since we started in January, we have killed 27 pig.[19]

Dick makes the comment in his books that he and De Crespigny once chased a cheetah like mad for two miles, then they ran him down. The cheetah was exhausted, which was my experience in Ethiopia. The animal doesn't have much staying power as opposed to speed. I have personally run them down on foot (when I was a great deal more lethal), and I kept a cub for a few months in Sidamo Province before I released it. It was as tame as a kitten.

There's an interesting photo in Dick's diaries of his Masai orderly and Natalie, his pony, with a dead hartebeest, which he speared on what would likely be the Athi Plain outside Nairobi, a definite feat as the hartebeest is reputed to be the fastest of African antelopes.

Dick seemingly stuck a lot of stuff, including wild dogs (*Lycaeon pictus*), and, once, at least, got into a tumble with an old baboon. They killed no animals that day, but Dick had a rather close thing when the old "dog" male baboon turned and came for Natalie. Bull baboons are definitely something you don't want to fool with, especially if you've inspected their fangs, which are astonishingly lengthy and adept at dismembering other baboons, leopards, and anything that crosses them, including humans.

African warthog sticking was one thing; lion sticking with jobbing lances quite another.

It was on the swarthy, oatlike grass of Nairobi's Athi Plain in August of 1903 that Dick and his pal Claude de Crespigny, both still toting a bayonet lashed to a bamboo pole as a spear, first saw the tawny form about 800 yards away. It was, of course, a lion, the kind that bites with essential efficiency. Neither Dick nor Claude knew what might happen if the lion were "ridden" with an eye to doing something rude to a critter nearly as big as their ponies, but it was Claude who semishouted, "I'm off—come on!"[20] Certainly, he was well off, given that he was attacking a full-grown African lion with a lashed-on bayonet spear.

It would seem that De Crespigny had the better horse, and he pulled ahead of Richard, thundering down on the lion, ersatz lance-head flashing. As the British officers approached, the lion rose and stood in what must have been pure amazement. At twenty yards the big male crouched, but De Crespigny's horse wasn't up to the challenge and swerved at the last moment, depositing Claude on the Athi Plain within ten feet of the lion, who was spending his off moments watching both Claude and Dick as he approached on a lathered and moon-eyed Natalie. Dick felt like a fool coming up with a lowered "spear," the lion watching him with considerable interest and quite clearly ready to charge him and any other fools present. Yet the smoothness of the plain was punctuated by a sharp report as Claude's pistol fired and the lion, possibly more astounded than either of the officers, fell dead with a .455 Webley service pistol bullet in his brain!

At the instant of the firing by Claude, Dick's spear entered the lion's chest, so he had stuck a dead lion, yet he didn't know that until an instant later. Major gonads, Mr. Meinertzhagen. There was not a word spoken while they unzipped the lion and Dick confided that he was scared stupid. Of course, he knew De Crespigny well and suspected that he was faking it when Claude commented, on being asked if he had any sense of fear, that he had enjoyed the episode thoroughly. He in fact said, "Of course I did! . . . I was afraid of myself, not the lion."[21] There was no more conversation during the skinning. Dick finishes up the matter with his personal comment: "No more lion-sticking for me. The risk is not justified."[22]

Dick puts this performance down to family tradition, a triumph in fact for the De Crespigny family, who must have been a bunch of screwballs in the first place to beard lions in their lairs.

When word got around of De Crespigny's triumph, Colonel Harrison, Dick and Claude's superior, threw a champagne supper for them. Harrison forbade them ever again to "ride" a lion and incur such stupid risks, but he did say, "My God, I should like to have been there!"[23]

Chapter 5

Richard Meinertzhagen's experiences in the 1903 diaper-clad Kenya Colony took a new twist on October 8 when one of his men, obviously a Swahili Muslim by his name, Juma bin Suliman, announced to the bwana that he had caught an exceptionally fine snake just outside his lordship's hut. With what may be presumed to be a flourish, Juma then produced an immense puff adder, probably the most dangerous reptile in Africa due to its prevalence, from under his hat! Unlike most Africans, Juma had no fear of snakes; obviously neither had Dick as he took it in hand, a rather risky item. He took a photograph and then placed the deadly creature in alcohol.

Just over two weeks later, Dick was again nearly struck by a puff adder, which would have been mighty bad news. This snake's venom causes immense tissue damage, although it may not always kill. The skin suppurates, sloughing off. Puff adders tend to lie in warm paths such as the indigenous use and they bite whenever trodden on, especially by bare feet. My wife, Fiona, came within a snake's scale of stepping on a puff adder in Zambia, where we were on safari. She was about to get down from the safari vehicle when the tracker's incredible eyes spotted the curled, camouflaged snake just beneath her. He grabbed her and hauled her back up just in time. We were all silent with shock. The snake snoozed on, watching, no doubt, and waiting for the next unwary human. Its photograph is captured for all eternity in *Peter Capstick's Africa*.

Puff adders are the most common poisonous snake and, given their massive dose of venom, victims are difficult to medicate. Once, Dick was wandering through fairly thick stuff and very nearly stepped on one. He jumped clear, but barely, as the snake actually struck but missed him. One can only appreciate the speed of an African reptile through experience. Their reaction-strike time is nanoseconds.

Dick leaped at the same instant that his dog, a terrier called Baby, joined in. He gave the pooch a horrendous kick in the ribs, effectively punting it some yards, which probably saved its life. He then decapitated the snake with his trusty shotgun but had a hard time trying to explain to Baby why he had kicked her so rudely.

A day later Dick witnessed a migration of elephants traveling from Mount Kenya to the Abedares that he estimated at being 700 strong, backlit against Mount Kenya as the sun rose. The local rhinos didn't like it a whit, eleven of them showing through their erect tails that they resented this intrusion. But this awesome sight, which included tiny calves, and the sweet dung-filled morning air, punctuated by the strange rumbling communication signals elephants make, touched Dick, who was all the more aware of what a great spectacle was flowing a mere eighty-odd yards away from him when he was told by some Kikuyu that such migrations took place only every three or four years.

Funny thing about Dick and elephants: In all his long life, he never shot an elephant. This may have had something to do with his pet elephant in India, and in fact he becomes sanctimonious and inaccurate in condemning the hunting of elephant. Strange that he should bag everything else in sight, including dainty dik-diks, ground hornbills, and hyenas caught in traps, but preach about wicked, unintelligent humans and their propensity for playing billiards with balls made of ivory. This didn't slow him up from making inkstands out of rhino feet, however. Did Dick figure sporting morality by weight?

Dick would be aghast at today's Kenya and much of Africa from the elephant point of view. And I shall state to all comers until I die that the legitimate sport hunter is not the culprit in the decimation of African game but rather the heavily armed, internationally backed poaching syndicates, often with the collusion of people at the top. Period. If game does not have a value on the ground that also benefits the local inhabitants, it will disappear. I have said this, written this, and argued this until I am hoarse, and the facts now speak for themselves. Zimbabwe is a grand example of hunting as *the* conservation tool, and South Africa, with its flourishing game ranches, is equally so. If you want game to survive, let the ethical hunter and his bank balance take charge. If you want cattle, goats, and poaching, suppress hunting and let the foreign revenue dry up along with the game scouts, their vehicles, weapons, salaries, and morale. The bush will evaporate, man in his breeding millions will move in, closely tracked and controlled by the poachers and their expatriate masters, and you can whistle Dixie about ever reestablishing the natural environment. Kenya banned the hunting of rhinoceros in 1977 as well as all other hunting. Poaching took off like a rocket. The rest is history. Meinertzhagen, of course, was penning some of his thoughts decades after the event, and I understand the "green" pressure in his English environment. That doesn't make him right. I live in Africa. Full time. I make my living by knowing the facts about sport hunting. Ecotourism is a vital part of the equation, no doubt. But it is the hunter who generates the most money to conserve the wilderness and the animals living there. Money buys the whiskey, not sentiment.

Dick's run-in with snakes was not over. Just a few days after the migrating elephants filled the horizon, Dick heard an anguished squeal. He came out of his tent to find a tremendous python constricting a jackal. Dick was not known for being unarmed, but he had to run back to his quarters for his shotgun, with which he blew off the head of the python, which was only making a living at the best of times. Personally, I think I would have taken off the head of the jackal, there being enough in this world for us all. An emotional decision. Curiously, some ten minutes after Meinertzhagen had laid the prostrate body of the jackal in some grass, it recovered and went off into the star-spangled blackness, obviously much relieved of its former drapery.

Dick then set off with his cat, "the China Ornament," and his dog, Baby, to the Mboni River north of Nyeri, where he had to do some surveying. The next day he walked eleven miles and crowned it off by shooting a duck that had a fresh egg in it. There was clearly nothing wrong with Dick's appetite as he dined that evening on duck, five boiled eggs, and a fruit tart, the essence of which his men had gathered. Obviously, the availability of labor was no problem in early Kenya, especially if one happened to be a British army officer. In any case he had a Goanese chef, which doesn't hurt too much in the bush. He, however, was almost sans chef when the poor man caught sight of his first rhino and, for some very odd reason, it sent him a little crazy and he started going walkabout in the bush. Had he flipped at the thought of Dick's possibly bagging the critter and then expecting rhino mince on toast the next morning for breakfast? Hard to tell with hired help.

In perusing Dick's books, one finds a lot of technicalia as to animal counts and weights. Well, he was an ornithologist and something of a perfectionist, as much of his writing indicates. For example, his game census for October 23, 1903, tells of "18 elephant, 34 giraffe, 17 rhinoceros, 198 zebra, 436 oryx, 66 waterbuck, 186 Grant's gazelle, 109 Thomson's gazelle, 5 bushbuck, 3 duiker, 88 impala, 46 eland, 18 warthog and 44 ostrich." As an afterthought he adds "also 88 haartebeeste [sic]."[1] Meinertzhagen was a pioneer in methods for measuring and weighing sport-hunted animals.

Curiously, on the same day, Dick had the chance to see two separate leopards, one at about 500 yards, which was long gone before he could bring a shot to bear—such are leopards—and another stalking a herd of Thomson's gazelle in broad daylight. He watched it for some twenty minutes. Personally, I am fascinated by this because, as a professional hunter for over two decades, I have very rarely seen a leopard hunting during the day. I once saw one flowing down a tree (they bail out of their roosts headfirst) in 1969 in Zambia when my client and I surprised it, probably sleeping, as it was midday. So I guess we can presume that there must have been God's own amount of leopards in business in Kenya in 1903 for them to be hunting in broad daylight when they are essentially a nocturnal animal.

On returning to Nyeri from this latest expedition, Dick noted that he hadn't seen "a single native."[2] He would doubtless recall this very shortly when he was once more to be in the thick of punitive campaigns against locals who were starting to step out of line. But an odd piece of news came to him when back in Nyeri, which was to echo decades later in his life.

The British were anxious to colonize British East Africa as fast as possible, some say to help pay for the Uganda Railway. There was a harebrained scheme to bring out Finnish settlers. Then someone hit on the idea of resettling the persecuted Russian Jews on the Uasin Gishu Plateau in the Naivasha region. Meinertzhagen noted, quite astutely, that this wouldn't even remotely work. Jewish elders actually came out to the Uasin Gishu but "what with elephants by day and lions by night, together with an encounter with Masai warriors in full war regalia,"[3] they left, convinced this was no place for Russian Jewry.

Dick notes:

> I hope they refuse it, for it is just asking for trouble. In the first place, the Jews' home is in Palestine, not in Africa. The scheme would only add to political confusion, and God knows there will be enough trouble here in 50 years when the natives get educated. Also, the Jews are not good mixers— never have been; they have their own religion, customs and habits and would constitute a most indigestible element in East Africa if they came in any numbers. Why not persuade the Turks to give them Palestine? The Arabs are doing nothing with it, and the Jews with their brains and dynamic force would be a tremendous asset to Turkey.[4]

Dick's passionate backing of the Jews-in-Palestine cause would see him going into actual combat with the Haganah, the forerunner of the Israeli Armed Forces, but more on this later.

Dick could never be accused of racist favoritism when taking action against people who rattled the British Empire's cage. Take the Gibbons affair, in which Dick rather roughly handled a rogue white man who had installed himself in the Embu country southeast of Mount Kenya. This character was reportedly filching taxes from the local blacks, keeping a harem of fourteen young girls, having reputedly murdered a tribesman and extorted ivory from the natives.

Dick got word of Gibbons, who was traveling with thirty armed Swahilis. Dick and his twenty-five askaris set off to bring him in. His company did about twenty miles in the dark, ending up about fifteen miles from Gibbons's stronghold. He walked at night so as not to alert the locals to his force. Finally, on November 14, 1903, he and his men reached the camp about two hours before dawn, surrounding it. There appeared to be no sentries except for one at the door of the thorn enclosure, and Dick, like a gray cat in the half-light, got past him and into Gibbons's tent, where he covered him with the Mannlicher rifle, throwing back the flap and shouting that if he didn't raise his hands, he was food for hyenas. Gibbons had the ill sense to appear to go for a revolver and Dick was a whisker away from sending him into permanent meditation when the man thought better of his options. Gibbons further had the idiocy to be flying the Union Jack, which Meinertzhagen hauled down, probably primly. Apparently, some especially vile language was spoken by Gibbons, who should have known better than to speak such to an armed man. Dick had the tents ransacked and took the man's revolver and rifles as well as those of all his men, which he had burned. More's the shame.

The local natives, curiously, were most irate at these proceedings, as they thought of Gibbons as a "government official"; in any case they were paying taxes to a white man. Dick haggled with the locals and suggested that they come to Fort Hall with him under armed arrest. They quieted down considerably. Dick took the fourteen concubines with him and told them that he would release them on the Tana River. The native chiefs agreed to go with him to look after such a volley of presumed virgins so there were no more immediate problems. Within about five hours of his arrival, Dick started his column of assorted enemy and his own people. The bunch totaled sixty-seven souls, but then his men each had 150 rounds of ammo on them.

Meinertzhagen was his usual hard-assed self, especially with Gibbons, who had corrupted the King's English with assorted unspeakables. Tired of this performance, he threatened to tie Gibbons's hands and he confined him to his tent surrounded by four sentries with direct orders from a British field officer to kill him if he so much as twitched. Dick, who had a unique talent for this sort of thing, was convinced that Gibbons would try to escape or kill him that night. He wasn't wrong, either.

Meinertzhagen stayed awake until after midnight, and about an hour after that, he heard whispers in KiSwahili. Easing his tent flap aside, he saw Gibbons standing in the moonlight talking with a sentry. Dick attacked with his rifle, Gibbons immediately trying to tear the sentry's rifle away. Dick hit him full in the face with the butt of his Mannlicher, likely doing extensive damage: Dick was a big, strong man, and a butt stroke to the bridge of the nose isn't pleasant. Gibbons fell like a dead bird. He, of course, had tried to bribe one of his guards, almost succeeding. I wonder what eventually happened to the sentry, given our knowledge of Meinertzhagen's wrath.

Dick did untie Gibbons at dawn so that he could eat and drink, but he or his men would not have hesitated to kill him. He let the fourteen concubines go as promised on the Tana and surrendered Gibbons to the army authorities at Fort Hall. Gibbons was to be remanded for trial in Nairobi the next day.

Dick's superior officer was so pleased at the mission that he gave every soldier a sheep and five rupees. Dick and his men had managed eighty-two miles in seventy-eight continuous hours carrying ammo to the tune of 150 rounds per man, their own food, and their arms. Meinertzhagen was correct when he pronounced it "not a bad performance."[5]

Previously, and the instances are well worth telling, Dick had had a small adventure with a pride of lions and killed a female. He notes, however, that man-eaters had been "worrying" the neighborhood and he was shown where a lion pulled a most unfortunate gentleman from a tree branch roughly ten feet up the trunk, which is not unusual, as a lion can reach up approximately twelve feet, although Richard reports that this particular lion had some trouble with the local chap and left quite a few scars on the lower bark. He got him, though, exercising the most elementary of demographics, sort of a form of retroactive birth control.

Speaking of Dick's lions, there was a humorous circumstance among his fellow officers in which an officer named Lawson killed a lion and, not wanting to go to the trouble of having the skin tanned, gave it to another officer named Hinde. Dick had never liked Hinde, the same man who brought his wife on campaign. Hinde promptly—according to Dick—hired two tribesmen to spend all their time stretching the skin until Meinertzhagen wrote that it now looked like a crocodile and Hinde was still having it stretched. In fact, Hinde came crashing into a room where Dick and Mrs. Hinde were and, not seeing Dick, excitedly pronounced, "It's now over ten feet, darling."[6] And one wonders what started the green movement. Hinde, curiously, was a qualified medical doctor turned army officer in the thither parts of the world. What do you suppose was behind that story? Damned if I know.

Early in December 1903, Dick killed two lions, the last one severely wounded when he came across it with a definite fright in very thick cover at two paces. Nice gun, that little Mannlicher 6.5mm or 256—excellent sectional density of bullet and ballistic coefficient. A few days later, Dick killed a bull giraffe using a ruse imitating an ostrich, carrying his rifle in his right hand and a stick with a false head in his left. He shot it at forty yards with—what else?—a neck shot, and giraffes are bloody difficult to stalk. About three or four days later, he bagged a hippo on the Tana River while surveying, also picking up a considerable amount of pot meat for his 400 men, which is quite a few people no matter how you count them.

He amply demonstrated his idiocy by breaststroking across the Tana River, with its crocs and hippos. The hippo wasn't all that big but the Mannlicher killed him as dead as courtesy through the brain. More's the wonder, he got seven of his men to follow him into potential perdition. This naturally drew barbels (African cat-fish) of an impressive size, one of which took a chunk out of one of his men's feet with its teeth. Dick caught several, the largest of which went nineteen pounds, which is not precisely a sardine. This episode reminded me of the day I swam across a section of the croc-infested Luangwa River in Zambia to set up a row of beer cans on the opposite bank for some off-duty target practice. It obviously wasn't my time to clock in at the Pearly Gates!

The day after Christmas, Dick managed to kill the man-eaters that had given him such crap earlier on the Thika River, whose source he had discovered. Freezing wet at those altitudes, he first walked to the Athi and spotted a lion about 200 yards off, slithering with high-shouldered grace through the yellow, feline-colored grass. As Dick was about to shoot, he was somewhat aroused by a snarl at his shoulder. It was an angry lioness, which got his definite attention: "Turning at once, I found a lioness charging towards me through the grass. She was already almost on me when I fired from my hip and jumped out of the way. By a great bit of luck my bullet had hit her in the head, and she rolled over dead on to the spot where I had been standing."[7] Dick shot her again through the heart to make certain that she was dead, a mighty fine policy indeed. He was damned lucky to have scored a killing shot the first try, as lions are notoriously difficult to kill when in that position: mouth-on. The brain is small and tapered to the rear, and I have tried as many as five cartridges to pull this one off, and that's with a much heavier rifle than a .256.

Dick fired at and hit the other lion but was unable to find the carcass and left it. Not done. However, he was quite sure that these were the two that constituted the well-known Man-Eaters of Thika, which had caused the deaths of over fifty tribesmen. He was, in fact, right, as he and a fellow officer found the body of the lion some two miles from the shooting, stiff and hyena-wearied by watching for vultures, which are the essence of Africa but for the hyena at night.

Meinertzhagen is possibly the only British army officer to have almost been raped by an ostrich. It will be recalled that he had an "ostrich costume" for stalking and found, to his dismay, that male ostriches found such an arrangement convenient. The only animal he had had problems with were rhinos, which had a collectively waning sense of humor. Warthogs didn't like him much, either. As may be appreciated, wearing a used but not abused ostrich was something of a chore, but it showed that Dick Meinertzhagen must have had considerable spare time on his hands. He had to plunk himself on his butt and manage to shoot from that position, but, on the other hand, he was able to get within twenty yards of warthogs and at one circumstance got within three steps of a ground hornbill, one of the more nervous birds of Africa.

He got quite close to such species as roan and oryx antelope and was dying to try out his technique on wild dogs and various birds such as oxpeckers, but his adventures with that bull ostrich gave him a clue. He tried to experiment with a flock of wild ostriches, but the cock came within ten yards and began to stomp his foot on the earth, a very bad sign of an attack, which Dick, being an ornithologist, recognized. He was obviously upset, as this is also a sexual threat as well as a mating ritual. He immediately divested himself of looking like an ostrich at ten yards from the male. If you think ostriches are cream puffs or marshmallows, you should have been with me recently in Namibia when a huge male apparently wanted to mate with the Toyota hunting vehicle. That bloody thing chased us for at least 800 yards and with considerable gusto, I might add—most intimidating behavior. I've seen Cape buffalo with less chutzpah.

Dr. Adams, of whom you shall hear quite a bit more, was apparently the regimental surgeon, and, as mentioned, he doesn't seem to have been cut out for frontier duty. He wandered about the Kenya bush gaily with but one cartridge hunting lion, and he was obviously not exceptionally adept at the sport. Happily he missed a lioness with his single round for his .450 cordite, but was able to (presumably) hide in the long grass from her ire.

Speaking of ammo, Dick experienced the same thing that "Karamojo" Bell, one of the best-known elephant hunters, did with the early .256-caliber cartridges, which gave him any amount of grief, although they were of German and Austrian manufacture, same as the rifle, as far as I recall. Dick mentions that about 20 percent of his cartridges hit the ground twenty to thirty yards in front of his highly polished boots. He got this ammunition from some of my good pals in London, who are hardly known for purveying such products, being one of the world's best gunmakers. Well, the century had hardly severed its umbilical cord and the .256 was still a relatively new cartridge, which is minor relief if one has a rampaging lion on one's chest, but that hardly brings respite from dangerous game. What does one do when there's a fault such as the bullet almost hitting one's bootlaces? Call 911? The gunmaker?

February 1904. Back in Fort Hall, Dick was briefed on a growing crisis involving the Irryeni branch of the Kikuyu, who were interfering with caravans passing through their neck of the woods and who had slaughtered several policemen sent out as messengers to try to reason with them on behalf of the British. A series of punitive expeditions was about to be launched, and all the tricks Dick had learned to date would come in handy.

What tuned his nervous system was an odd experience late one bright, moonlit night as he lay sleeping in his grass hut. His cat, the China Ornament, became very agitated and started jumping about on his bed, obviously in an effort to wake Dick. He got one hell of a shock on seeing the huge face and jaws of a hyena completely filling the opening that served as a window, its forepaws resting on the ledge, possibly the first step to entering this human's abode to snack on him before dawn. Dick managed to get hold of his shotgun, which he always had close to him, and was about to pull the trigger when the hyena had a change of plan and made off into the moonlit bush. I could immediately identify with that chilled shock Dick must have known. Experiences in Botswana and Namibia have brought me eyeball-to-eyeball with hungry hyenas, and let me tell you straight off, hyenas are not mere lowly scavengers; given just a tiny chance, they'll hunt you down and cash in your chips quicker than you can blink. They're fearless predators, and humans are just another source of protein. Dick was lucky that night. His cat is probably the reason he survived and, ultimately, that this story is being shared with you over ninety years later!

Five days after this brush with eternity, Dick set out at the head of a column of sixty rifle-armed troops and 250 spear-toting and likely drooling Masai against the Irryeni Kikuyu clan. In a rough pincer movement, the other column was headed by an officer named Brancker, with Tate as his political officer, who had 100 rifles and 200 Masai. As usual, Dick kept to his normal game plan and marched all night to surprise the enemy at dawn. They reached their position at four in the morning after about a seven-hour march, which is not hugely pleasurable through the African blackness.

Now on the edge of enemy territory, Dick split his men into four raiding parties who then descended like black lightning onto every village in the area with orders to confiscate livestock wholesale. The result was 325 cattle and 550 goats and sheep, which were herded back to Fort Hall while the Irryeni Kikuyu, totally taken by surprise, scattered into the adjacent forest without being able to offer any resistance. The extraordinary thing was that there were no casualties on either side that first day, but the psychological impact of that dawn raid was immense. Cattle, especially, signify wealth to rural African communities to this day, and their instant loss, especially to another tribe, meant loss of wealth and a sense of security as well as a profound sense of humiliation.

If you're a shooter, you will be aware of the term *mixed double*, in which a gunner takes two different species in succession with the same lift of the gun or rifle. Well, Dick possibly had the most unusual mixed double of all time the day after the capture of the livestock.

Dick and his men marched on to an Irreyni Kikuyu chief's village deep inside the adversary's territory. As they were edging through the bush, they came across a reed bed in a stream about two acres in size. With no warning at all, arrows suddenly wooshed through the air at Dick and his askaris. It looked at if they had been loosed on them from the reed bed, which prompted Dick to fire a couple of shots into the reeds.

Human hell erupted. Twelve armed Irryeni Kikuyus charged out of the water-logged cover, the air electric with their whooping and yelling as they punched the skies with their weapons and rushed Dick's party. But they weren't alone: A massive lion boiled out of the reeds on the other side, clearly intent on finishing any human that was dumb enough to come within clawing distance.

One of Dick's men, Adams the doctor, shot at the lion and wounded it. Dick must have instantly recalled the ancient Chinese curse "May you live in interesting times!" Twelve armed and hostile tribesmen and a wounded lion make for interesting times!

The lion slunk back into the reeds with a sickly gait while Dick let fly at the first four tribesmen, killing the last one just as he was about to shove his spear into Adams. The rest of the askaris followed Dick and joined him in slaughtering the remaining Kikuyu. He lost one man but the day was not over, as Adams insisted in going into the reeds after a wounded lion.

Dick and Adams had hardly gone a few yards when another armed Kikuyu leaped out of nowhere. Dick shot him as he was poised to spear Adams and at that same instant a black-throated roar announced the return of the wounded lion, which was now just a few yards off Adams. Dick fired again and killed it with a shot to the neck.

All this happened in a few terrifying seconds. Adams hadn't even managed to get off a shot. Dick had long since lost any confidence he may have had in the man being able to take care of his own hide, so he kicked him out of the reeds and got his men to set fire to the stuff. After this highly unusual "mixed double," Adams had the gall to be irate that his lion had been burned. Never mind that his inept skin had been saved from certain death. No good deed ever goes unpunished.

Dick injects that Adams later gave him a silver tobacco holder but that he eventually died of morphia addiction.

Nonetheless, the day's festivities weren't anywhere near a halt:

Dick's men moved in under menacingly thick tree cover when one was suddenly wounded by a Kikuyu arrow. The foliage was so jungle-dense that it was impossible to make out any enemy. The only way to clear the way ahead was to set up two machine guns, which Dick did, pouring ammo into the cover. This got things going. Kikuyu warriors started moving about in the branches, and, as they came into sight, they were picked off by rifle fire, five thudding to their death as they were hit. A final warrior was hit and landed close to Dick, his head split open by a bullet to the brain fired by the hitherto pretty useless Adams. It was the end of another busy day. The expedition against the Irryeni Kikuyu was now at full blast.

Cattle raiding continued as the Irryeni had it hammered home that to interfere with law and order in the British Empire would bode ill for them. Dick's men were now on the outskirts of the bamboo forest on the southern side of Mount Kenya, preparing for a lightning attack on a village where some of the Kikuyu enemy were holed up. Before the actual expedition set out, Dick had warned his entire force that if anyone killed a woman or child he'd be shot out of hand. Clearly he was not believed by a couple of idiots.

In rushing the village from where the Kikuyu were firing their arrows, Dick's ears rang with the terror-filled shrieks of a woman who was being dragged from her hut even as one of the Masai was tugging his spear out of the body of a small boy. As if this weren't literally the bloody limit, Dick caught sight of one of his Masai levies with his knobkerrie raised, on the point of crashing it down on the head of a little girl.

Dick yelled but the levy simply didn't or wouldn't hear the boss and killed the girl anyway. As for the woman being dragged along in the dirt, she was bayoneted to death just spitting distance from the outraged Dick. He raised his rifle and, unblinking, shot dead his man and the man's companion, who seemed about to shoot Dick. Three of his levies tried to escape as they saw Dick carry out his warning, but he downed the lot of them before they could get to the perimeter of the Kikuyu village.

The air laden with that peculiar smell of fresh human blood and the powerful stench of human sweat in fear-filled combat, Dick ordered his men to fall in right in front of the corpses of the woman and what were apparently her two children. Not a single one of the men so much as twitched when they were challenged to step forward if they were in any way unhappy with their commander's actions. They knew he'd shoot them dead right there if they dared to challenge him.

Dick hadn't finished. His men were ordered, no doubt with a rifle pointed at their guts, to bury the woman and her children. Significantly, the five men Dick shot dead were left to the ultimate insult when their corpses were simply abandoned to hyenas and vultures. This was another pointed lesson for anyone still stupid enough to doubt the resolve of the young pommie captain just days away from his twenty-sixth birthday.

With a few more Kikuyu scalps to his belt and thousands of head of livestock captured, Dick and his men headed back to Fort Hall, the Irryeni expedition over and the word well and truly out: Stay clear of the captain! In under two weeks of the start of the campaign all the Irryeni chiefs descended on Fort Hall to renew allegiance and, not only that, to offer the Brits help in a forthcoming blitz against the WaEmbo people, an offshoot of the WaKikuyu but who spoke a different language and who had different customs.

When the weeklong WaEmbo campaign got under way, Dick passed through Irryeni country to cheers, smiling faces, and such cordiality that he recruited about 150 spearmen to help with the rounding up of the livestock Dick and his men would be confiscating from the WaEmbo. Some 250 WaEmbo died in the expedition, and going on 2,000 head of livestock were confiscated. Even more awesome statistics were attained in the Irryeni campaign.

Of course, there has been armchair psychoanalysis and nose-wrinkling claptrap about Meinertzhagen's killing days both as a soldier and, for some, as a hunter. Let those who have never been in mortally dangerous combat, who have never had to deal with murderous insubordination of troops, and who have never had to stand their ground against animals intent on eating them kindly hold their collective peace, not flaunt their ignorance or their sanctimonious hindsight, and let someone who *has* been there tell it like it was, warts and all:

> I have no intention of making a laboured defence of my action in this matter. In my own mind I did the only thing possible under the circumstances, and am satisfied that I acted rightly. What I did was contrary to military law and therefore illegal. . . .
>
> The lesson to be taught was discipline, and my object was to stop once and for all such barbarous habits as the killing of women and children in cold blood and to enforce the carrying out of my orders.
>
> Some may think I was too harsh, others may concur with what I did. I acted with a cool head, fully weighing the consequences, and would do it again under similar circumstances. War is necessarily brutal, but it need not be made too brutal. If black troops and undisciplined levies are allowed to get out of hand, as they most surely will if not ruled by iron discipline, disaster is the result.[8]

Dick's tour of duty at Fort Hall in Kikuyu country, which had lasted almost two years, had come to an end. He was sad to take his leave of the WaKikuyu, a people against whom he had waged bloody campaigns and whom he had come to like and admire in a way perhaps only soldiers can understand.

In Nairobi once more, Dick got to know one of the greats of the old Kenya and one of the first game rangers to head the fledgling game department, Blaney Percival. He found Percival not only to be a keen orthinologist but, obviously, a man with an encyclopedic knowledge of big game. Dick, although only a young man, had already developed an insight into the need to set aside reserves for game, which, he believed, couldn't coexist with cattle and farms in general. His idea was scoffed at by the commissioner, Sir Charles Eliot, who bluntly told the young soldier that sentiment concerning the future of British East Africa's game couldn't be allowed to stand in the way of progress, that is, vigorous white settlement in Kikuyu country, which Dick thought wrong. What neither man could ever have foreseen was the true danger to African game: rampant human population growth.

Dick had no sooner had time to catch his combat breath than word came through of the Nandi tribe far to the west of the country, on the shores of Lake Victoria, who were threatening an American mission station north of Kisumu, where one of the missionaries had gone missing.

As the train pulled in to the terminus of the Uganda Railway on the shores of the Victoria Nyanza Lake, Dick felt a thrill of delight at this expanse of water stretched before him with its gorgeous birdlife and total change of pace after the Irryeni and WaEmbo campaigns. Expecting to be plunged into a bloody confrontation with the Nandi, Dick was to discover that the missionary had pretty well asked to be speared through and through by that tribe, as was eventually discovered. The supposed American Quaker missionary had pitched up at the mission in Kaimosi, sponged off it wholesale, and then set in motion a weird chain of events that would get him killed.

There had been some trouble with the Nandi in the region of the mission, and an expedition had been sent out to force them to give up firearms said to be in their possession. The administrative officer of the immediate region, one Mayes, apparently then decided to have a shoot-up against the Nandi and confiscate some of their cattle, a dumb, illegal thing to have done.

The Quaker, hearing the gunfire, decided against all warnings to leave the mission and have a closer look. The Nandi spotted him and his policeman escort and killed them both, viewing them and all whites as legitimate targets under the circumstances. And another missionary, seeing the cattle nearby, thought he'd be doing the government a favor by helping round them up. The Nandi had had confidence in the mission's neutrality, but when they saw their cattle being herded together by a member of the mission, this was as good as an open declaration of war against a people whose status, security, and wealth were vested in their cattle. The only thing that staggers me on reading Dick's account is why on earth the Nandi didn't make a proper job of it and exterminate the entire mission. I too, do not blame the Nandi for bumping off the Quaker. My library shelves positively groan with the indiscretions and down-right arrogant illegalities perpetrated in many parts of Africa by the white man in the name of his god, and often to the ultimate det-riment of the locals. Let me not pump my bilges a second time!

The Nandi episode quietly sorted out with no reprisals, Dick then heard that he was to be granted home leave in England. Before leaving for England from Zanzibar on a French mail steamer with a bunch of "moth-eaten" French people from Madagascar, Dick was to have a few more experiences that are worth sharing. One gives a quite chilling insight into his character.

Out walking near the Athi River on July 18, 1904, with his pet dog, Baby, Dick saw a huge troop of baboons in the under-growth, and he decided to stalk them and scare them off. Either he had not had a chance to understand what dangerous animals baboons can be or he had fallen into that easiest of traps after months of successful hunting experiences—complacency—because he was unarmed. One simply did not saunter off to the Athi River unarmed in 1904 British East Africa. Dick did. He regretted it.

He and Baby had chased the baboons into the Athi River when the animals suddenly spun round on their pursuers and nabbed Baby, tearing her into bite-size morsels before Dick's speechless, horror-filled sight. The shrieking, raucous mob then scampered up a rocky cliff face overlooking the river, some of them with bits of Baby in their gleeful mits. Dick, as he admits, had murder in his heart as night fell and he was forced to return to camp.

Dick requested and was given "30 men at 3 a.m. tomorrow with rifles, bayonets, and 100 rounds each. No questions were asked."[9] Dick was out to avenge the death of his pet dog by leading an armed assault on the baboons' cliffside fortress. The order? The baboons were to be mown down without mercy.

Dick and his men arrived well before dawn, and he positioned his men for the baboon blitzkrieg so that they were surrounded. The first soft rose flush of dawn tinged the bush and river as a scops owl mournfully greeted the new day and a jackal howled in the distance. The blurred flurry of bustard wings broke from the grass near Dick, and, gradually, nature stirred in unison. The baboons on the cliff face? Not a twitch.

So Dick fired a shot to get things moving. The cliff erupted as an old female led the troop in an apparent escape attempt, her barks bouncing off the riverbanks. The men opened up, bullets and baboons exploding in utter pandemonium as the creatures frantically sought a way out, bolting in all directions and being scythed down from all angles. Two old males tried to hole up on the cliff, but Dick dislodged huge rocks, which forced the old males out into the open and certain death. The baboon bag for the day equaled twenty-five and fifteen escaped. As Dick and his men prepared to return to camp, he remarked, "We killed every full-grown male, and I was pleased."[10]

He'd avenged the death of his pet dog, which used to sleep in his bed and accompany him wherever he went, posing on top of dead rhinos and generally keeping the boss happy. The ferocity of his reaction to the death of his pet points up the extremes of Dick's nature. He could understand and exonerate the Nandi for killing a fellow human, the Quaker missionary, but the sight of his pet being ripped to pieces by baboons turned him into what some would call a psychopathic killer. Once his emotions were roused, his sense of fair play offended, Dick's killer instincts took over. And this was to happen many times over before he sheathed his claws and died in 1967.

The very day after the baboon debacle, Meinertzhagen was with the renowned ornithologist and author who would go on to write of his African hunting adventures, Abel Chapman, who had come out on safari, being one of the very first to do so in the infant Kenya Colony. He found Chapman oddly distant and generally sour about life, not even willing to talk birds with the young Dick. More's the pity because the two men had a feast of game before them in the area south of Nairobi toward the Athi River. Although nothing was shot, Dick and his distinguished companion were privileged to see a pride of lion hunting down zebras and making two kills. It thrilled Dick as he watched the lionesses fly at the zebras, which were in full gallop, the zebras being grabbed in the throat and downed in an instant, the rest of the pride then moving in to feast.

Such scenes fresh in his mind, Dick was on his way back to England via the "Lunatic Line" train from Nairobi to Mombasa. Something of his empire arrogance and sheer ingrained prejudice comes to the fore when he meets an old Boer on the train who had come up from South Africa after the civil war, which had seen Boer and Brit tearing the country apart and causing generations of bitterness afterwards.

The old boy launched into his tirade against the British and their concentration camps in South Africa in which thousands, mainly women and children, did, in fact, die between 1899 and 1902. Dick was told how his people starved the Boer people and raped their women. This ignited the Meinertzhagen short fuse and he lit into the old codger, telling him that "Dutch women were so notoriously ugly that no self-respecting Englishman would touch one with the end of a barge pole."[11]

I have lived in South Africa full time for over twelve years as of this writing, and I now have insight into this incident that would not have been possible for an outsider to have had otherwise. Among my shooting companions in South Africa have been distinguished Afrikaners, people of the old Boer/Dutch stock referred to in this passage from Dick's diary. I quickly learned that the Anglo-Boer War was still being fought in some quarters and that the hatreds and prejudices on both sides still flickered like a badly tended camp fire nearly a solid century after the event! As for Dick's attitude, it was typical of his time, and we shall see this empire mind-set come to the fore again and again in his long life with all its suffocating arrogance. He looked down on those who were not true-blue Brits and was to take numerous swipes, sometimes with absolute justification, at those who were not graced with British birth. As an American, I can stand back and view this lot with some amusement, if not irritation.

But it is Dick's thoughts, decades later, as he looks back on his first tour in British East Africa that are of intense interest. He tells us quite bluntly that he has no belief in the sanctity of human life and in the dignity of the human race. Neither have I. He tries to convey the primitive conditions of the time, and the need to take action in emergencies. He does not excuse his tough military discipline and is not about to apologize for his hunting, which also often provided rations for his men. As Dick states:

When I arrived in the country I was obsessed by an unashamed blood-lust. Hunting is man's primitive instinct, and I indulged it and enjoyed it to the full. . . . The hunting of big game gave me good healthy exercise when many of my brother officers were drinking rot-gut or running about with somebody else's wife; it taught me bushcraft and how to shoot straight. After all, the hunting of men—war—is but a form of hunting wild animals, and on many occasions during World War I I thanked my God that I had learned several tricks of my trade when hunting wild and dangerous game.[12]

Chapter 6

"I have had a good leave in England, but I feel that my ties with my family and my home are even looser than before. I prefer Africa and the savage to England and the over-civilised society which lives there."[1]

Dick's almost eight months' absence on home leave in England was over. The frills and niceties of genteel Edwardian England and the alienated relationship with his large and strange family were reason enough for Dick to be glad to get going and get out. His mother was as distant as ever, his father unable to really express his kindly nature to his son, and the horde of sisters with their left-wing leanings no doubt irritated him. And Dick irritated easily—very easily.

Docking in Mombasa on St. Patrick's Day, 1905—March 17 in plainspeak—he no doubt felt that odd sensation of recognition, of relief at the sights, smells—stenches, perhaps—and exotic noises that greeted him as he once again set foot on African soil and prepared for a new tour of duty. I recall the surge of emotion that washed over me when I saw the Luangwa River in Zambia again after a long absence, the lump-in-the-throat response to familiar faces and to the sounds of the African bush no amount of big-city hype could ever displace in my soul. Life had a real feel to it that energized me. I know firsthand what jumble of emotions coursed through Dick's mind as he saw his baggage being humped onto the quayside by burly Swahili dockworkers as they cheerfully shouted their conversations to one another, as he caught sight of fellow officers smartly turned out and waiting to greet their brother officer back into the home-from-home imperial fold of "the Club," of the purpose and excitement of kitting up once more for his new assignment as company commander at Nandi Fort in the wild northwest region of the country, of the anticipation of hunting again, and of a new command and fresh challenges after tame, effete Blighty. Dick and I would have gotten along just fine in reminiscing about the hold Africa had over him and that she will have over me until I die.

Dick's previous experiences in dealing with tribal groups who stepped out of line were mere dress rehearsals to what lay ahead. The Nilotic Nandi tribe would see to that. Kenya, with its many tribal groups, was already best known for the Kikuyu and the Masai of the central highlands region, and Dick, of course, had had extensive experience with both groups during his first tour of duty. Now, his eye long trained as a hunter and soldier in the African bush, his wits sharpened like the deadly thorn zaribas he had so often helped construct when out on expeditions, and his nerves toughened by repeated encounters of a bloody kind, Dick was to become better acquainted with the Nandi.

During the construction of the railway, the "Lunatic Line," between 1895 and 1901 from Mombasa to the shores of Lake Victoria in Uganda, a 600-mile haul through desert and scrubland, over deep gorges and through treacherous swamps, the British and their motley work crews had to face not only heat, disease, and wild animals; they were repeatedly threatened by hostile tribes, and the Nandi were right in there with the worst of them.

The railway completed, it then had to be defended at several points in Nandi country because of the guerrilla strike-and-run raids and the refusal of that tribe to acquiesce to British rule. Dick's Third Battalion of the King's African Rifles, with its tiny handful of British officers, its Sudanese core of veteran fighters, its local troops, and the indomitable Masai spearmen, were up against something else when it came to the Nandi. Settlers who had started farming operations in Nandi land were often attacked and their livestock stolen in lightning raids. Non-Nandis who got in the way landed up looking like human hedgehogs with Nandi spears decorating their anatomies, like spikes of cloves in baked apples at a traditional Meinertzhagen Christmas.

The trouble was that, as Charles Miller points out in his superb book *The Lunatic Express*, "a punitive campaign against the Nandi had been called off in 1900, out of fear that large-scale hostilities might delay completion of the railway. As a consequence of that act, the Nandi regarded themselves as victors, a superior force, and saw no reason to cooperate with Government."[2]

Dick had already had a taste of Nandi intransigence just before his home leave when the American Quaker missionary decided to go walkabout and got himself thoroughly dead at the hands of the Nandi. He was no doubt briefed before boarding the train in Mombasa, and his thoughts were probably only semidistracted by the vast herds of game close to the railway as it puffed and belched its way inland, climbing higher and higher until the final destination of Kibigori, near Lake Victoria, from where Dick marched to Nandi Fort.

At about 3,000 feet above sea level, Dick had a bout of what could only be called altitude sickness, but he quickly recovered to deal with the appalling state of his military outfit: rusted rifles, soldiers in filthy clothing, and discipline a word with little meaning. To add to this was the distasteful presence of Walter Mayes, that "common seaman from Glasgow"[3] Dick had met for the first time the previous year in May and against whom he took an instant dislike. That feeling hadn't changed. In fact, it got worse when he discovered that Mayes was ripping off the local Nandi by confiscating their cattle and then pocketing the proceeds and falsifying official reports. Dick braced the little man and got his attention. When Mayes came down with a sore throat, Dick fed him "some excellent broth out of grey parrots and dried vegetables."[4] Was this a new recipe for disposing of former Glaswegian sailors? It's not the parrots; it's the dried veggies.

Whatever, the two men were out hunting for rations a couple of days later. A rumor had already started that they had been bumped off by the Kamalilo clan of the Nandis. On getting back to camp, the local Nandi chiefs pitched up and seemed a bit put out that Dick and his tame Scot were still breathing. There was more fun and games when Mayes's deserted Mauritian Creole wife suddenly appeared, a "slut of a woman"[5] who was howling and creating a devil of a din. Add to that Mayes's half-dozen Nandi concubines in the house and it's easy to understand Dick when he said, "I left them to fight it out among themselves."[6] Warfare with the Nandi would probably seem a little more orderly after that lot.

The mood now changed. In between dodging a black mamba, hunting blue buck, and trying to treat a case of sleeping sickness with arsenic, Dick got orders on May 5, 1905, that had been issued to every military outpost in East Africa, namely to beef up defenses without delay. Trouble was brewing among the Nandi against the white man's rule.

For the first time, there is a glimpse of the cunning that was to mold Dick into a formidable intelligence operative later on. In having the bush cleared around his house and around his men's quarters, he chose the distance of 150 yards, but not before flattering one of his Nandi acquaintances into showing him how far he could shoot an arrow—134 yards, maximum; or throw his war club, the rungu—68 yards, or toss a spear—42 yards. Dick was a calculating man, literally.

News was now coming in of murders and daring raids by the Nandi from every military post in the district. Dick's own lines were attacked one night by the Nandi, who made off with some cattle from the Masai levies, resulting in one dead Masai and two dead Nandis. Dick, in pajamas, was out in a flash with his rifle at the ready in the moonlight as the night air rang to the sounds of the Masai war cries. Things were hotting up. Even Dick's vegetable patch was being raided by hyenas, jackals, duikers, and forest hogs, the hyenas kicking up a "hideous din."[7] Of all the sounds in Africa, the hyena's repertoire of vocal gymnastics is the one thing I could never term a "din." It's music, the bushveld Met. The hyena's voice proves the game is still out there. When the hyena can no longer be heard, the game has gone. For good.

Dick had come to realize that if he was to have any hope of launching successful operations against the increasingly restless Nandi, he needed information. To that end he began organizing a rudimentary intelligence service by using the Masai, who lived near his house and who could move about unhindered among their fellow Nilots, the Nandi. His aim was first of all to try to discover what their chief witch doctor, by the name of Koitalel, was plotting, as he already long knew that in such societies, the witch doctor played, and still plays, a pivotal role in the tribe's affairs. How difficult it must have been for British officers, out on a tour of duty and with no intention of settling in Africa, to try to fathom such beliefs. What Dick didn't do was underestimate the deadly dominance, the total power a man such as Koitalel had over the Nandi. He was feared; he was believed; he was obeyed. And he was busy preaching to his followers that the white man had to be thrown out by force. The man was becoming politically dangerous.

Dick was all for definite action, as he knew that the Nandi interpreted lack of resolve or categoric response to their increasingly provocative attacks and ambushes—Dick surviving one—as fear. He wanted a stiff ultimatum sent to the Nandi and for Koitalel to be brought in and have the British facts of life drummed into him. Dick was now beginning to suspect that the Brits were actually afraid of Koitalel's power and of the consequences if he were ever arrested. Dick despised fearful behavior and supine, placatory gestures.

Stories had already reached Dick's ears that Koitalel had told the Nandi that the white man's bullets would simply turn to water when fired at them. What made this sort of thing very dangerous was that Koitalel's subjects unquestioningly believed him and it was this that would turn them into deadly foes on the battlefield because they would be mentally drunk on their invincibility, totally fearless and out of control once in the fighting mode. They outnumbered Dick's garrison to a ludicrous degree, even when the final Nandi Field Force was mustered for the eventual showdown, boosted by troops from Uganda and from as far away as Nyasaland, today's Malawi, not forgetting a further police detachment and something like 1,000 extra Masai spearmen.

Examples from African history simply emphasize the life-and-death power of the soothsayers and witch doctors in tribal cultures. Take the appalling tragedy that occurred in 1857 down in the Eastern Cape of South Africa. A young girl by the name of Nongqawuse, who was a spirit medium and who belonged to the Gcaleka section of the Xhosa people, had a vision that if her people were to undertake certain acts of blind faith, the white settlers would be driven out of their country and paradise would reign. These acts included the willing destruction of all tribal cattle and crops. Anyone who refused to carry out these instructions would be transmogrified into something unspeakable, be scooped up by a terrible wind, and drowned in the sea.

The people obeyed the spirit medium until they had destroyed all their food supplies. The fateful day dawned on February 18, 1857, when a bloodred sun was supposed to rise, remain static at one point, and then set in the east, signaling the death of all whites and the miraculous appearance from the skies of cattle and crops and long-departed ancestral heroes come to celebrate.

The day dawned. The people waited and watched. The sun rose in the east, went on its usual merry way, and went to bed in the west. And none of the predictions materialized. Anywhere between 25,000 and 30,000 people eventually starved to death, and as many were forced to migrate. The consequences, political and otherwise, were staggering, and the young medium fled to British soldiers for protection. One of Africa's ironies saw her actually being placed for her own safety on Robben Island, off Cape Town, where Nelson Mandela, the president of my adopted home, was incarcerated for most of his twenty-seven years in prison. The poor girl eventually died over forty years later on a farm, no doubt haunted to her last day by the vision that went wrong.

There is more of this, much more, right up to the oathing rituals of the Mau-Mau in Kenya in the fifties and what they were told to believe. And before we are tempted to denigrate such events from our supposedly sophisticated perspective, let's not forget the skeletons in our own supernatural closet: the People's Temple Sect of one Jim Jones, who ended up committing mass hara-kiri in the Guyana jungle in 1978, and, closer to home, the mind-control goings-on in various cults that sometimes result in tragedies such as the Waco, Texas, debacle that had the world's only true superpower in an uproar just a few years back, with the at times farcical events plastered all over the world's television screens. Divinely inspired suicide bombers in the Middle East and Japanese cult warriors letting fly with nerve gas attacks on subways in the nineties are another topic, but back to the Nandi.

Dick's temper was beginning to fray. He wanted nothing more than to "take on the young men of Nandi and smash them up, as they are becoming too full of themselves."[8] His ire increased when his house was bombarded one night with Nandi arrows and rungus, a hail of stones thumping the tin roof. It got so bad Dick had to board up his windows. So what to do? Lay an ambush.

The culprits were caught late one night—five young boys and a girl. The boys were each given "7 hard smacks on the bottom"[9] and the girl had to dig in Dick's garden for a whole day. The Nandi hooligans were then sent packing with a rupee each and a warning that if any more stones and arrows were directed at Chez Meinertzhagen, they'd be shot. Dick's reputation was long out. He was not an idle chatterer. He meant shot dead and everyone knew it.

Which explains the presence of his name on Koitalel's death list.

The commissioner, Sir Donald Stewart, a hard-boiled old British Colonial Office hand, issued an ultimatum to the Nandi and their witch doctor boss: Produce 300 head of cattle within three weeks to compensate for the many past misdemeanors or face a punitive expedition to sort them out forever.

The Nandi, not unexpectedly, ignored the ultimatum and were now "completely out of hand"[10] according to Dick. The foot dragging and the hesitation, coupled with the climate, resulted in Dick's succumbing to quite severe depression, but his bird and butterfly collecting, his great interest in botany, and his ability to get out into the bush and be active instead of moping back at the garrison pulled him through. What recharged him finally was the news that a full-scale expedition was now, after all, to be launched against Koitalel and his people.

Dick's first act was to get the sixty-odd porters in his company onto the shooting range with single-loading Martinis and water-filled kerosene tins as targets at 100 yards. The porters apparently had a ball each time they managed to hit a tin and see the water shoot up into the air. They were getting the hang of things pretty quickly, but Dick wasn't so sure about their cool under combat conditions. Kerosene tins were one thing, marauding Nandi in full battle cry quite another.

In the meantime, Dick's bush intelligence service came through with some hot news. He was using a group of Masai who hated the Nandi on simple tribal principles. A couple of his agents were living with the witch doctor himself and the rest were scattered about thither and yon, ears to the ground, eyes at the ready, brains recording anything of interest for Dick. Koitalel had just held a major gathering of the Nandi where he stated that the Brits were obviously scared stiff of them, that no expedition would be launched by the foreigners, and that, therefore, the Nandi were to double up on all aggressive acts and drive the white man and his trappings clean out of their land. Apparently near-riotous bedlam broke loose at this meeting, where it was also decided that Dick was to be murdered. The odds were a bit disconcerting—about 25,000 Nandi against a handful of Europeans.

The witchcraft part became a bit more worrying for Dick when his spies reported back to him that Koitalel had told his followers that the white man's bullets would certainly be rendered useless if parts of Dick's anatomy such as his brains, liver, heart, and eyes could be procured, boiled up into some brew, and then sprinkled on the warrior Nandi. My files give closely documented accounts of such ritual slayings and beliefs involving present-day Kenya, Zambia, Zimbabwe, and South Africa where, for example, a special governmental commission of inquiry was established just a couple of years back specifically to look into the whole witchcraft scene.

Dick was left in no doubt. He was on Koitalel's death list, and

something had to be done about it. Dick's agents were also reporting back of plans to have him poisoned. This plot actually
materialized in the form of a young girl sent across with a powdered
poison substance hidden in her nether regions to be administered—
the poison, that is—to Dick so he could be on his merry way to
wherever white men went when the time came. Dick's agents had
him prepared for this, and when the young girl was searched and
the stuff found on her, there was much howling and wailing for
mercy. Dick sent the poor kid right back home to Uncle Koitalel,
suggesting he take the poison himself. This whole Nandi/Brit issue
had, as Dick put it, become "a personal quarrel between me and
the Laibon [the Masai word for a witch doctor] and I will bet a
small sum he falls first. I strongly object to anyone wishing to kill
me."[11]

In the middle of the biggest buildup ever against the Nandi, as
if for comic relief, Dick's diary suddenly tells of his beetle-shooting
expedition at Nandi Fort when he noticed large beetles buzzing
about and decided to collect a few for the Natural History Museum
in England. This reminded me of a glorious late afternoon when I
went dragonfly shooting with my BB gun (real men all have BB
guns!). I didn't have a museum to appreciate my prowess, though.

Mobilization orders finally came through on October 2, 1905,
for a full-blown expedition against Koitalel and the Nandi,
numbering about 6,652 men, which included Somali levies and
two armored trains on the Uganda Railway. Dick was convinced
that the key to the whole operation was the early capture or killing
of Koitalel. He had been around long enough in Africa to know
that the witch doctor held total sway over the people. Neutralize
the witch doctor and the people will follow as surely as dawn fol-
lows Stygian darkness.

This made me think back on that grand old man of the Mozambican African bush, Wally Johnson, whose story I was privileged to write in 1988 (*The Last Ivory Hunter*, New York: St. Martin's Press, 1988). He survived a potentially fatal encounter with poachers when the witch doctor was nabbed in front of a hostile mob. On seeing their chief medicine man with a gun to his head and incapable of doing anything about it, they decided to cooperate, hand in their weapons, leave the hunting concession to the bona fide hunters, and go back to where they came from. Wally came close to dying that day. Had he not had the witch doctor completely under his control, he would have died at the hands of the mob of poachers.

Dick discussed his plan with fellow officers to capture or kill Koitalel, and they agreed. He was then supplied with a pretty accurate plan of Koitalel's village, where the witch doctor would sleep in a different hut every night, such was his fear of assassination. The tracks leading to the village were all heavily guarded, so Dick realized that a surprise attack on his village would be impossible. He even changed villages, which only spurred Dick on with his idea of inviting the old hex across for a meeting, so revealing his latest address for future executive action.

It was then reported to Dick that Koitalel had a plan to invite *him* over to meet on the eve of the actual expedition. Dick and his party would then be ambushed and killed. To compound matters, Dick's interpreter was revealed to be one of Koitalel's spies. It was clear the Brit was to be murdered. On contemplating the meeting on October 19, 1905, Dick made a strange remark in his diary when he said that he didn't care whether he or Koitalel died. I've always wondered what lay behind those words. Was the whole primitive African scene finally getting to him? Or was he so fired up at the thought of Koitalel and his threats that he relished the idea of mortal combat and really didn't care if he died in the process, as long as he went down swinging? We'll never know.

What we do know is that Koitalel invited Dick across for what was obviously going to be a terminal chat. He was told to bring only five men with him. Dick, forewarned through his own bush counterintelligence system, was as ready as you ever can be when you are about to come eyeball to eyeball with someone intent on obliterating you.

This final stage had been preceded by a series of "wires" in pretty strange French. Dick had resorted to rusty French to try to safeguard communications. He did a double take when the Goanese wire operator came in, grinning. French was his native tongue, and he then told Dick that he'd worked it all out: The wire traffic obviously referred to the chief witch doctor of the Nandi, Koitalel.

What to do? Here was a potential security leak that could sink the entire long overdue expedition against the Nandi. Dick fixed the Goanese with a cold stare, no doubt, and said, "All right, my friend, if you divulge the contents of this message to anyone I shall convene a field general court-martial, of which I shall be president and court. You will be convicted of treachery and sentenced to be shot, and I shall shoot you with my own hands."[12]

Richard Meinertzhagen in Kenya, 1906. (Courtesy of Ran Meinertzhagen and Rhodes House Library, Oxford)

Funny how you just know Dick would have followed through. The Goanese kept his mouth glued shut.

The late October nights were crisp at that altitude as Dick and his force made final preparations. He'd informed his seniors of his plans and had been given the nod if he was "sure" of his plans. This, as Dick correctly interpreted, shunted the responsibility onto his shoulders alone if the operation against Koitalel backfired. Dick wasn't to be put off. A lesser man would have withdrawn. His so-called superior's ambivalence just fired up the Meinertzhagen war machine. He was ready, his multiethnic forces were as ready as they'd ever be, the Masai no doubt baying for Nandi blood. The day broke at the meeting place, Kaidparak Hill, ten or so miles from Nandi Fort. The name would come to haunt Dick for decades afterwards.

Dick and 80 men set off at dawn, a machine gun in tow. On arriving at the summit of Kaidparak Hill, Dick's field glasses picked up large numbers of Nandi warriors hidden in the bushes on the opposite hillside. His consternation increased when he saw Koitalel approaching with twenty-two warriors, quite contrary to the agreed arrangement of five men each. It was clear to a corpse that Dick was about to walk into a lethal trap. This was confirmed when the Nandi interpreter, Koitalel's spy, came trotting across to say that the actual meeting would no longer be held in the open, in full view of Dick's men, but that it would now be held in a hollow, out of view of his men.

With the stipulated five men, Dick then advanced down an incline to the meeting place, the rest of the force hidden higher up with a fine field of fire and orders from Dick to open up if they saw that he and his four men were about to be overwhelmed by Nandi warriors and their witch doctor supremo. Rifles cocked, bayonets fixed, it's pretty certain that the party had gone silent with tension and anticipation as they negotiated the rough bush terrain, thoughts drumming in their heads, their hands clammy with the sweat of intermittent fear and anticipation of combat. No soldier worth a damn can say he does not feel fear in anticipation of combat. It's the same in critical moments of big-game hunting. Only fools shoot the breeze about not knowing that gut-fluttering adrenaline rush of fear, however brief. This is nature's way of getting the human mind into gear to survive. Those who disagree simply haven't been there. A soldier or hunter full of bravado doesn't last long.

Then followed an extraordinary scene. As Dick and his four men advanced, Koitalel came forward, flanked by about fifty warriors, one even placing a poisoned arrow in his bow. Not exactly friendly body language, however fluent your Nandi. As Dick shot a glance about the immediate bush, all he saw were shields and spears. He was staring at the prelude to his own slaughter, and he knew it.

The Nandi thought he didn't.

Just four strides short of the witch doctor, Dick asked him to step forward and shake hands. He refused. Dick, as a white man in 1905 British East Africa, wasn't about to make the first advance at the behest of a black man. It just wasn't done. So he told the tribesman, via the treacherous interpreter, that they'd just have to conduct their talk at that distance and no closer.

Now, it will never be known if the interpreter conveyed exactly what Dick said or whether he added a deadly frill to the proceedings, because no sooner had he spoken to Koitalel than a poisoned arrow whined through the early morning air, piercing his shirtsleeve but missing his body. Quicker than frozen credit, Dick's backup force opened up, and before the Nandi had time to quiver more arrows and toss more spears, Koitalel lay dead in the dust, with another twenty-two or so of his people nicely heaped up about him. Dick, apparently, also shot at Koitalel just as one of his men did. Another arrow sent Dick's helmet for a loop.

The effect was electric. As Dick and his men retreated in an early example of unaided hot extraction, moving at a cracking rate through the bush, their retreat covered by their backup force, the Nandi stood about, stunned at Koitalel's sudden death, at the obvious preparedness of the enemy.

But they suddenly got their druthers together and set off in even hotter pursuit of the enemy, all but catching them in the last few miles out of Nandi Fort. Dick's force had just about run out of ammo, and there is no doubt they were exhausted and tiring quickly now. The Nandi had not only lost their spiritual and temporal chief, they had lost a whole hierachy, as this was a hereditary position and Dick's diary tells us that most of his male successors had been gathered at Kaidparak Hill and, presumably, had been wiped out with the boss.

Back inside Nandi Fort, the marauding Nandi having been forced to withdraw by a patrol from the fort, Dick sent a short message to HQ announcing the success of the operation. The very next day, congratulatory "wires" came in from the acting commissioner and other senior officers, three of Dick's chums immediately sending a vigorous recommendation that he be awarded the Victoria Cross.

The Nandi campaign was now at full blast. Livestock for Africa was confiscated, the Nandi in disarray with no leader to call the shots and organize resistance. The Nandi abandoned their huts and fields, leaving everything behind, food included. Only old people and women had been left to look after livestock, as they couldn't keep up with the flight. Pockets of warriors were scattered about, some within poisoned-arrow distance of Nandi Fort, which was bombarded with arrows just five days after Koitalel's death. The air erupted with rifle and machine-gun fire as the fort blazed away into the blackness of the African night at the unseen killers. Dick took over at a machine-gun emplacement when the gunner was hit by a poisoned arrow and was promptly hit in the hand by the deadly Nandi weapon.

His hand went black in ten minutes flat as he quickly made a rough tourniquet out of his whistle cord to block the flow of blood from the wrist upwards. Then followed the standard treatment, an injection of strychnine. It worked for Dick, but of the seven men hit by the Nandi arrows, two died after Dick gave them strychnine shots.

My files contain evidence of poisoned arrows dated as recently as February 1994, when a Canadian tourist died in the Tanzanian bush less than one hour after having been struck in the right calf by a poisoned arrow in an attack just outside the Serengeti National Park. And hanging on my den walls are a couple of quivers with de facto poisoned arrows from my elephant hunting safari with the Bushmen in what was Southwest Africa in 1989, which featured in *Sands of Silence* (New York: St. Martin's Press, 1991). I saw the poison being prepared and applied. I saw it work in the bush. Poisoned arrows and Africa have a long and documented association, but they were particularly dangerous in Dick's time because of the primitive treatment and lack of all modern facilities to casevac people to safety.

Skirmishes abounded in the next few days, complicated by clashes with assorted tribes on the way, but it was clear the Nandi morale had been hammered. The British Army Act was then put to a fine test when Dick's corporal, a Manyema and a practicing cannibal, came back from patrol sporting five black hands stuck in his belt, telling Dick they were for his supper. Her Majesty's Empire couldn't put up with this sort of thing on expedition, and the poor chap was told to bury his supper promptly and then appear before

Dick, who ruled out any further mutilation of enemies. He did enlighten Dick on the finer points of cannibal cuisine, however, when he said that while fingers were the most succulent, the pièce de résistance was undoubtedly "the buttocks of a young girl."[13]

The first phase of the Nandi expedition was drawing to a close. They'd lost 80,000 head of livestock, and 500 warriors had been killed. They were suing for peace. Dick was talking unconditional surrender.

It was then that the first dangerous and ugly rumors about Dick started doing the rounds.

It had taken several months, huge expense, loss of life, injury, and general trauma to sort out the Nandi, who were now confined to a reserve after accepting the terms of surrender dictated by His Majesty's Imperial Government. That part of Africa was not to see another indigenous uprising of such magnitude until the Mau-Mau of the fifties. There can be no doubt that had Dick not dispatched Koitalel to Nandi kingdom come on that fateful October day, the entire expedition would have dragged on and probably ended very differently and very much later on. Many admired Dick for his role in the expedition, a couple hated and resented him for it and sought ways to sabotage his name and military career. It was only human nature.

Dick heard the rumors for the first time in early December 1905 that he'd acted treacherously, that he'd had no intention of speaking with Koitalel but was intent on luring him into a death trap from the word go. He was accused in these rumors of killing the official interpreter, presumably to make sure he didn't talk about his dishonorable conduct. He was accused of brutality.

The stories persisted. As is the way with rumors, when they persist, they grow more imaginative and more damaging. Not one to sit back and have anyone wipe their verbal feet over his honor, Dick demanded and was accorded a military court of inquiry.

In between shooting for rations, killing a puff adder in camp, and crossing spoor with leopard and forest hog, Dick attended the first of three military courts of inquiry into the Nandi affair on December 1, 1905. The court cleared Dick of any treacherous behavior and concluded that the witch doctor had been killed by a "native officer of the 3rd King's African Rifles."[14] Dick had wanted to cross-examine the vulgar Glaswegian sailor Walter Mayes, whom he suspected all along of being behind the rumors, but this didn't happen. In fact, the black levies who had taken part in the expedition were not allowed to give evidence. Was this because they were simply shunted aside as mere servants whose opinions counted for naught? Maybe. Dick had wanted the levies to testify because they were bitter and angry that any accusations should have been made against Dick in the first place, and the chances were good that they would have accurately recounted the events on that day and stood by Dick.

Thinking the affair now settled, Dick was back doing survey work and hunting along the way. Up on the Uasin Gishu Plateau in the northwest, he came across a colossal croc in the Nzoia River and got the chills when he thought that just the previous day he'd actually swum in the croc-infested murk when going after Uganda cob. Of all the animal-versus-human incidents in my files, croc attacks are the most frequently reported. And we can be sure that many more such attacks just don't make the press because the African bush is often so isolated, lives are so anonymous, communications so poor, people so inured to such events.

Dick's senses, ever tuned, received a fresh jolt when he heard the screams of francolins as they flushed in large coveys from the grasslands. They sounded just like distressed human babies, and the screaming gets worse when they're fired at. Dick, no doubt, was beginning to relax and wind down after the prolonged tension of the Nandi expedition and the court of inquiry. These forays into the bush were good for the soul. But the Koitalel affair was far from dead.

Fresh accusations against Dick had been made by two officers, egged on by Mayes who, like an inferior whiskey, simply wouldn't leave the system quietly. Dick faced a second court of inquiry, where "native evidence" was heard. Dick was cleared again of any treacherous behavior and one of his accusers ordered back to Blighty. Dick headed back to the relative peace of the bush and his surveying tasks.

For an ornithologist there could have been few treats to match the day Dick was seduced by the African honey guide with its excited chattering calls as it forced Dick to take notice as it kept flying off into the Kabwuren Forest near Nandi Fort, always sticking to exactly the same flight path and then returning to perch near Dick, chattering nonstop.

Dick couldn't resist. He got up and followed the bird, which had now been joined by two chums in chorus. The birds finally settled in the branches of a small tree and wouldn't budge. The bees' nest had to be close at hand. That's what the folklore said, so Dick searched and found the nest under some rotting bark. His men broke apart the comb and spread open the yellow-gold feast. Down swooped the honey guides, each making off with a chunk of comb, only to return for more until they were positively bursting with the stuff, all puffed out with happiness. God, the memories that tugged at my heart as I read this grand description of one of Africa's true joys.

Dick heard a superstition about honey guides of which I have heard similar versions, namely that if you find the nest and take all the honey, leaving none for the birds who got you there in the first place, then next time they'll guide you straight into the embrace of a snake or worse. The story reminded me of my elephant safari in 1989 in what is now Namibia. One day I was out with my host and superb professional hunter and outfitter, Volker Grellmann, when we came across some Bushmen taking honey from a huge hive at the base of an old termite heap close to our camp. I can remember being profoundly moved when it was explained to me that a fair piece of the hive was always left behind, as man would only court disaster for himself and his kind if he took it all for himself, depleting nature through sheer greed.

As I watched an elderly Bushman at work among the bees, I couldn't help noticing the uncanny harmony between the bees and this human. They would surely have stung one of us half to death in true "killer bee" fashion but, somehow, with the Bushmen, there was this symbiosis, this understanding. That old man knew more about conservation and respect for nature than half the world's learned fossils droning on at conventions in any of a hundred faceless cities everywhere. I've never forgotten that day in the scorching Namibian sun, the air alive with the thrumming of wild bees, punctuated by the Bushmen as they spoke among themselves in a soft stream of click-sounds about the job at hand or some other issue. A striking little Bushman boy stood close by, absorbing as if by osmosis one of the skills he would hopefully still be left in peace to perfect and enjoy. I left that scene, moved and saddened because I knew, as we all did who had been there, that these gentle people are doomed because their lifestyle is doomed.

The new year of 1906 had come, and with it came a third court of inquiry with Walter Mayes center stage and full of accusations against Dick. Dick proved the Scot a liar in court, and the court concluded that Mayes had been motivated by personal hatred in his reports about Dick on the fateful Koitalel/Nandi expedition and it was recommended that Mayes be kicked out of government service. He resigned soon after being posted to some dump on the coast, soundly demoted and dishonored. This vengeful little man turned out to be an embezzler to boot.

Three courts of inquiry, much finger-pointing, now, hopefully, peace. There were mopping-up operations among those Nandi who were slow in moving onto the reserve set aside for them. Sporadic attacks against government patrols took place as Dick and his men had to undertake a pretty distressing task. In an official effort to force Nandi compliance, villages were razed, granaries burned, stock enclosures destroyed, Nandi captured or killed, and livestock confiscated. Dick felt that burning down villages and evicting the inhabitants did not constitute soldiers' work, and there is little doubt this must have hit military morale. Poisoned honey offered Dick by two young Nandi girls hit his stomach, and he came close to "swotting finals" as they say in South Africa. Driving lines were formed to round up the straggling Nandi and confine them to their reserve. It is a bit shaking to read in the late nineties of a ring of military posts that were set up around the reserve, the soldiers under orders to shoot on sight any Nandi found outside the designated area. But then the 1990s ethnic cleansing in Bosnia by so-called enlightened, civilized folk comes to mind and one thing is obvious: Human nature is the same, often tragically so, all over the world.

The expeditions against the Nandi finally drew to a close in late February 1906, and with the end came Dick's conviction that he'd better get out of Africa after this five-year tour of duty. As he bluntly puts it in the terms of the day; "The climate is making me feel depressed, and altogether I feel I want a change. I want to be more with my own folk than with these savages."[15] These sentiments aren't quite what Dick proclaimed when he arrived back in

British East Africa as reported at the beginning of this chapter. There are examples by the bagful throughout Dick's published diaries that show this sort of contradiction or inconsistency.

Feeling as he did, a fresh assignment came from the brass, which fired up Dick's engines as if it were latter-day mental rocket fuel. An espionage mission to German East Africa! Like pronto. Dick actually wrote in his diary on the day this new task came through, March 1, 1906, "Sooner or later we are sure to have a war with the Germans."[16] But first back to Nandi Fort to pack up and be off to the Teutons.

All seemed to be conspiring to help Dick on his way. He was destined to spend a night at the third-to-last station on the Uganda Railway Line, Kipigoro, before the terminus on Lake Victoria, Kipigoro serving Nandi Fort. Ah, what a night. Marauding elephant were into the Nandi fields, indulging in elephantine culinary forays. The antidote? Let Dick tell us: "I never heard such a din as went on last night from sunset to dawn . . . drums beating, women shrieking, dogs barking; and all this accompanied by the continuous hum of myriads of mosquitoes. As though this were not sufficient, some railway coolies sleeping near me kept up an intermittent but gorgeous chorus of snoring such as would awaken the dead."[17] The fabled German sense of order probably seemed rather appealing after this lot.

Dick had been detailed to cross into German East Africa to reconnoiter the Voi-Taveta-Moshi Road and see what the Germans were up to at Moshi itself. Taveta was the last stop before German territory. Dick went by train to Voi and then proceeded to footslog across the Serengeti Plains to Taveta. Dick was tough. And focused. He was on the spoor of that most dangerous of animals—man.

Deluges of rain, mud that resembled clayey plowed fields, no mod cons, close, humid nights, and mosquitoes by the battalion greeted Dick as he sketched, noted, and filed into his zariba-sharp brain all those elements the Brits would have to know about in order to plan against the Germans in a future battle. Road conditions, water sources, strategic high ground, suitable ambush sites, the presence of settlements, and the attitude of the locals toward the Germans all fitted into the jigsaw of reconnaissance missions.

Once over the border, Dick headed for Moshi and the German fort, where he was given accommodation. He was bombarded with questions about the British army, strengths, military customs, and the Nandi expedition, about which the Germans had obviously heard. Dick bluntly told them he'd dispatched Koitalel, and his hosts cheered. It seems pretty obvious from this that Dick's military identity was made known to the Germans at that point.

Dick had understood one key element in intelligence gathering: let the others yap their heads off; just listen intently in return, observe, note, feign no particular interest in anything, feed the egos of the targets. Sooner or later, someone starts spilling useful information out of bravado. It worked for Dick. He learned all about political attitudes concerning the French, Belgians, and Russians, as well as German communications plans in their territory. He landed up even inspecting a German company on parade where he could note the weaponry and the level of marksmanship, which, according to our roving spy, was "vile."[18] Only one shell of twenty-four from a .37-mm gun hitting a twelve-by-eight-foot target at 800 yards is fairly "abominable,"[19] as Dick put it.

He was taken for a South African by many Germans, who chatted to him on that basis. Boer families were moving into German East Africa and, of course, into British East Africa after the Anglo-Boer civil war in South Africa, which had ended in 1902 and left the Boer people bitter and defeated. Rather than genuflect to the Brits, many cleared out on a fresh trek to freedom way north. The Germans were pretty scathing in their opinions of the Boer trekkers, whom they branded as thieves and people who maltreated the locals and ignored German regulations. In fact, Meinertzhagen was told that these Boer families couldn't take the Prussian way of doing things and were heading north to British East Africa, where life appeared less harsh.

As he made his way towards Taveta, pouring rain enveloped the countryside, dense mist shrouding the summit of Mount Kilimanjaro, turning everything damp and mildewed. Multicolored slugs and enormous snails decorated Dick's path through banana plantations in WaChagga country, a people who had been subdued by brute German force and who resented them as a result—another useful piece of info for Dick's intelligence report. In fact, a chief of the WaChagga who had had his cattle confiscated by the Germans—and that is equivalent to somebody cleaning out your bank account and safety deposit box under your nose and in full view—asked Dick why the Brits simply didn't come across the border and throw the Germans out, saying that his people would join in with glee. As Dick puts it, "He is credited with having great influence with his people, and should the occasion arise I shall not forget what he said."[20]

A British officer, even if on a lone espionage mission, still ate well in the African bush. Never mind the green mold on the bread because of the rain, heat, and humidity; Dick assures us the inside was still just fine, especially if you coupled it with tinned caviar and pears. One morning he shot a great bustard for his dinner and enjoyed the eggs "along with ostrich liver and the tongue of the Waller's gazelle."[21] The Explorers Club in New York, of which I am proud to be a member, is known for its exotic dinners. Dick would have felt quite at home there, with these gastronomic inclinations.

In what was to be a foretaste of clandestine wartime activities down the line, Dick's retinue intercepted a black soldier of the

Germans on the Serengeti Plains at a place called Maktau where Dick had decided to halt for a while. The askari was carrying a letter for a certain "Count Cudenhove" some distance off. He had been told to avoid Dick's camp and go straight to Cudenhove.

This was too much for our British agent. Dick told the poor chap that, in the failing light, he'd be wise to spend the night at his camp because of marauding lions; quite tidy to have wild and hungry lions handy in order to terrorize the askari and get hold of the letter. Dick instructed his men to take it once the askari was asleep. Once done, Dick artfully unsealed the letter in true John Le Carré style. Its contents were illuminating.

Cudenhove was doing a mirror-image job of what Dick was doing: reconnoitering for the Germans in the event of future British/German military disenchantment. The Germans, according to the letter, suspected the actual nature of Dick's visit to German East Africa and wanted, via this Cudenhove chap, to lay their hands on any notes or maps he may have made. The letter was resealed and replaced. And Dick started plotting, in between recording the speed of a black mamba as it chased one of his porters and before recovering his wounded lesser kudu. A man has to do what he has to do. The porter? He tripped and, with the mamba almost on him, Dick blasted it to serpentine Shangri-la—all five feet seven inches of it.

Using local whites at Bura, one with a grudge against the Germans, Dick ascertained the whereabouts of Cudenhove, who was posing as a geologist and prospective settler and arranged for the white farmers to invite Cudenhove over for some good old-fashioned English hospitality and be absent from his camp for a bit. The German's black staff would be simultaneously ordered up to the British government station in the district, close to Cudenhove's camp, to be "registered." That should keep the Cudenhove camp deserted for a bit: Stage One.

Dick, in the meantime, and as a precaution, moved his notes, maps, and himself to the safety of a French Roman Catholic mission station. The missionaries were not overly crazy about the Germans, and accepted Dick as a paying guest. The pseudogeologist was already enjoying English hospitality with Patterson the planter, and the entire askari staff had been marched up to the government station for due "registration." Stage Two complete and counting.

Chez Cudenhove now clear, Dick and the fellow Englishman who hated Germans descended on the camp, searched it, removed two dispatch cases and maps from under Cudenhove's bed, sloshed paraffin all over the place, struck a match, and left. Quickly. Very quickly. Stage Three now at full flame.

As soon as the fire was spotted from the government station, "all hands rushed down to try to rescue Cudenhove's belongings, but too late. Grass huts burn very quickly."[22] Dick's own men did the neighborly thing and also rushed down to help. When all was lost, Dick offered shelter and food to the Cudenhove crew, who were now paranoid with fear about the boss's reaction when he returned from English high tea to see the smoldering remains of his camp.

Dick strode out to meet Cudenhove, who was now due back. The poor man went pale when he heard Dick's name and must have had tachycardia when Dick respectfully informed him that his camp had burned down in his absence. To crown it all, the German was grateful for Dick's hospitality under the circumstances and spent the evening trying to pump him for information. You have to hand it to the German; his sense of duty came first. All Dick gave in response to the incessant questions was "shooting information."[23] As in duds and hang fires.

After breakfasting together at dawn on March 28, 1906, Dick headed for Voi and the German for Moshi, across the border on the German side. Mission accomplished. So much so that the accurate, highly detailed military reconnaissance maps by the German on the Voi-Taveta Road and key surrounding areas, together with Dick's careful reconnaissance documents, would prove invaluable during campaigns in World War I in East Africa, a solid decade down the line. The "silent laughing masterful man" had played a brilliant hand of espionage poker, the maps and relevant documents being passed on to the War Office in London.

Dick's German East coup revitalized him, and he makes no further mention of the irritation and depression that had affected him earlier and made him think seriously about going home. He was buoyant and on his way back to Nairobi.

Nothing could have prepared Dick for the shock awaiting him when he reported to the orderly room on May 5, 1906.

The Colonial Office, in its imperial wisdom, was ordering Dick out of British East Africa and home because of the Koitalel affair despite three military courts of inquiry clearing him of any wrong-doing. He was unctuously told that while his good faith was not being questioned, his killing of the Nandi medicine man had brought the British reputation for honesty and straight dealing into question, and Dick's presence in British East Africa, as a result, was now deemed "undesirable."[24]

He was accused of undertaking the Koitalel expedition on his own responsibility, when it was clear he had been given orders by superior officers to proceed. All efforts to obtain an explanation for this sudden turn of events proved useless. Frederick Jackson, the deputy commissioner, told Dick he thought he'd been scandalously treated. It was clear something had happened between British East and the Colonial Office about which Dick knew nothing. He had no choice but to pack up and go home. But Dick was not a man to be trifled with.

After a farewell dinner given him by the officers of the Third and Fourth KAR in Nairobi, a night to remember, especially if you had been either of the two officers who attacked Dick after dinner that night and ended up with a smashed face and a broken nose, Dick headed for Mombasa to board ship. Ever the gentleman, before leaving he called on the two officers to present his apologies. Finding them hungover and surly, he left a note with some sage advice about keeping fit.

Dick's last shoot in BEA was in Mombasa, where he obtained a Grave Island gazelle. This is somewhat prophetic—part of Dick's name had been flung into a hastily dug bureaucratic grave over the Koitalel affair. Despite family connections and vigorous effort, Dick was denied access to all the official documentation on this life-changing incident in his military career. Even when he returned to Kenya on a nostalgic visit in 1956, a solid half-century later, his name was still linked to the killing of Koitalel as an example of British treachery. He was also to discover that because of the Colonial Office's attitude, he was not considered for the VC and that the Army Council would have viewed the whole matter differently had it not been for the Colonial Office poison. The War Office said it would not let this episode count against Dick's military career, but it clearly did.

It wasn't until 1959 that Dick was finally able to see the official documents. The governor of British East Africa at the time of the Koitalel affair, Hayes Sadler, had simply forwarded all relevant documents to the Colonial Office, backing the recommendation of General Manning that Dick be recalled, stating that despite the outcome of the three courts of inquiry, Dick's behavior had brought discredit on the British. Yet the very day General Manning wrote this, he had actually congratulated Dick in person after exoneration by the third court of inquiry.

He accused Dick in the dispatch to the Colonial Office of acting unilaterally in meeting Koitalel. No mention is made of the fact that the two senior officers of the day, Colonel Harrison and

Major Pope Hennessey, sanctioned the plan beforehand. And a faceless Colonial Office clerk named Ellis was responsible for reviewing Dick's case, implying that because Dick and his party escaped unscathed from the Koitalel ambush, therefore he had acted with treachery. What an office clerk knows about combat is debatable, but this type would know all about professional jealousy and toadying to senior types such as Manning and Hayes Sadler. Dick's forthrightness and effectiveness had made him enemies in BEA, as had his success. Human nature again. There is nothing the mediocre and unsuccessful hate more than the dynamism and success of another human being.

Whatever the case, Dick had to go home. He'd learned to track and hunt, he'd taken command, maintained discipline and followed through, and he'd kept his nerve under fire and outwitted the enemy. He knew how to make tough decisions quickly and decisively, and he could stand his ground against all comers.

On boarding the French ship *Natal* on May 28, 1906, in Mombasa, the African coastline receding into the gathering gloom as the ship pushed out into the open sea, Dick's mind coursed back over these two tours of duty in Africa and concluded that they had indeed been "a good school for wars to come."[25]

Turkey

Mosul · Nineveh

Iran

Syria

Tekrit ·

EUPHRATES RIVER

Baghdad

Jordan

Mesopotamia

Kerbela ·

Babylon

TIGRIS RIVER

Saudi Arabia

Ur ·

Basra ·

Neutral Zone

Kuwait

Persian Gulf

N

MESOPOTAMIA (IRAQ)

Chapter 7

"Abird in the hand is worth two in the bush" must have had an absolutely farcical ring to it for Dick soon after his return to England. While awaiting further assignment, he was ordered to rejoin the battalion he had belonged to in Burma, the one commanded by the ridiculous Major Bird. Whom does Dick meet but Bird, now a colonel and commanding the battalion! Just proves the Peter principle—being promoted beyond one's true capacities.

Stationed at Bordon in his childhood county of Hampshire, southwest of London and close to the great British army base of Aldershot, Dick and a lady friend returned to the mess for dinner after attending a military tattoo. Now, the presence of ladies is supposed to tighten up behavior, not cause it to degenerate into a scene from vaudeville farce. Bird, the colonel, who was surely not in the same class as a true bird colonel, was well into his cups and flicked a piece of bread at one of the lady guests. It obviously hit her, because she then launched a chunk of ham at the ridiculous little man, hitting him smack in the chops. He then tossed a leg of chicken back at her, but it unfortunately hit Dick.

Dick, in cahoots with a junior officer, walked behind the colonel and was bumped so that he tipped a cup of cold soup down the commanding officer's neck. We are not told the sequel, but it must have been sufficiently gratifying for Dick to have remembered the incident at all in his *Army Diary*.

The foul-mouthed, drunken Bird was soon to be left behind once more. Dick had orders to ship out for South Africa and join the Third Battalion of the Royal Fusiliers.

I've always thought that Cape Town ranks with Rio de Janeiro and San Francisco as one of the most stunningly beautiful cities in the world. It certainly must have been so for Dick as his ship came into port in early February 1907, a midsummer's day with cloud spilling over the giant Table Mountain backdrop to the city like a tablecloth set for a visual feast.

Dick's published diary is rather thin on the ground concerning his two years in South Africa. What was obviously one of the most significant events of his years there (or here, as I am writing this at my home in South Africa) was his meeting in Pretoria, where I have lived for almost thirteen years, with the legendary Jan Smuts. I owned property not ten minutes' drive from the historic Smuts estate. One of the landmarks on my frequent drives to Johannesburg International Airport, formerly Jan Smuts Airport, is the *koppie* on the estate where a memorial has been erected and where Smuts' ashes were scattered.

Former commander of the Boer forces in the 1899–1902 Anglo-Boer War, this soldier politician was to go on to become a member of the British Imperial war cabinet during part of World War I, commanded the South African forces in the East African campaign during World War I, and eventually became premier of the country and led the South Africans into World War II on the side of the Allies. He became a field marshal in 1941 and enjoyed the respect and admiration of crowned heads and commoners alike.

In fact, Dick wrote that the two most remarkable people with whom he'd been associated in his life were Smuts and Chaim Weizmann, the first president of Israel.

Dick discovered that Smuts had met his mother at his Aunt Kate's residence. She was married to left-wing member of Parliament Leonard Courtney, who, with her, had condemned the British role in the Anglo-Boer War, hence the empathy with Smuts. Dick liked him immediately and was destined to cross spoor with him in British East Africa during World War I. Funny how Dick's life was to have these echoes.

Dick's battalion shipped out for the then British possession of Mauritius toward the end of 1909, and he had another spell of home leave, which saw him being drawn more closely into the world of military intelligence and man-hunting. While in England, Dick was obviously bored and looking for adventure, anything to get the blood racing in his veins and concentrate his energies. A man of action couldn't be happy in Edwardian salons sipping tea and listening to inanities. Not after his taste of life in the African bush and actual combat.

The Russian Section of the British War Office provided Dick with just what he needed: a mission in the Crimea.

Now what would the empire spooks at the War Office be wanting to know about that curious peninsula, a region of the Ukraine, jutting into the Black Sea? Plenty, it would seem. There is hardly a small boy alive who does not know about the legendary disaster of the Charge of the Light Brigade in 1854, when the British cavalry charged full tilt at entrenched Russian artillery just six miles southeast of the port of Sevastopol during the bloody Crimean War of 1853–1856. Well over a third of the British forces died that day and Dick, as a nipper in an upper-class British family, would have been raised on such feats of empire daring. And what kid hasn't heard of Florence Nightingale and her work under hor-rific conditions in the Crimean War as she battled terrible disease and, it seems, even worse, ignorance? With Britain, France, and Sardinia having declared war against Russia, bloody battles fol-lowed, and the year-long siege of Sevastopol eventually led to the Treaty of Paris and an end to this strange interlude in human affairs.

With history having a disconcerting way of repeating itself, countries with any smarts keep an eye on old foes, just in case. Well, news had filtered through to the War Office that the Russians were busy fortifying the northern entrance to Sevastopol Harbor, and, for obviously good reason, the Brits wanted to know what was up. The tsar had long since turned the first sod in the building operations, and all the efforts of the British naval attaché in St. Petersburg to penetrate the thick cloak of secrecy about the Se-vastopol fort were proving as difficult as obtaining permission for Salman Rushdie to take the air in downtown Teheran.

Enter Dick, a trained soldier, a man who'd cut his military intelligence-gathering teeth and who knew how to plan, follow through, and evaluate operations. His quick eye, retentive brain, and ability to think himself into a devious frame of mind made him ideal for this reconnaissance mission. He was told one icy fact be-fore setting out: If things went wrong on his intelligence mission, the War Office took no responsibility. In other words: If you're caught, you're on your own. We've never heard of you. That simply inspired the young officer to go all out in the Crimean mission.

Dick's cover? That of a military officer on vacation to study the Crimean theater of war—the battlefields where, no doubt, a dearly loved soldier relative died in glory for the Queen and em-pire. As the saying goes, the best place to hide a book is in a library. Before setting sail, Dick spent time, invited or otherwise, mostly otherwise and at night, at various harbor installations in Britain, familiarizing himself with naval guns, the layout of forts, and all relevant data, which he then sketched from memory once at a safe distance from the place just reconnoitered. He even devised a method of using detailed maps onto which he'd then add the new information in such a manner as not to attract attention from even the most neurotic of border guards.

Off to Sevastopol as a spy in the service of His Britannic Majesty. On a first stroll past the fort in question, Dick was actually starting to note matters of interest when two soldiers appeared out of the ether. Not only that, they were actually running toward him, clearly alarmed at the presence of an obvious foreigner so close to a sensitive installation.

Dick promptly had an attack of the tourist trots, dropped his pants, and squatted in full view of the fort and the soldiers, who, nonplussed, backed off. Dick's ablutions completed, they then approached him. Chatting in a tongue they could not comprehend, Dick was allowed to leave, proceeding at his own pace past the fort, no doubt making mental notes all the while. Rejoining his carriage, he drove on, his basic mission accomplished. The moral of the story: let nature take its course.

The Russian counterint boys, in the meantime, had become aware of Dick, and he was confronted by a fairly gruff elderly man back at the hotel wanting to know where he'd been. Dick, a rather restrained and distant man, as I discovered, promptly told the old codger he'd been to a brothel. When he was asked for the address (maybe the Russian was after a little R&R himself) and couldn't supply it, telling the old boy to pack it in, the Russian's antennae really started tuning in. In fact, after touching base with the British War Office's secret agent in Sevastopol the next evening, Dick discovered that someone had been tampering with his luggage back at the hotel. By no means a novice and forewarned about the tsar's secret police, Dick wasn't remotely concerned. He'd left nothing incriminating in his baggage, which was searched a second time when he was having lunch with the governor of the area. Chances are that the governor had purposely invited him out to give the int boys time to do their deed. Dick had already used the same tactic seen in the previous chapter.

But Dick's tenacity, one of his greatest assets, won the day. Despite these dangerous signals that he was being monitored, he went back to the fort, taking with him the young son of the secret agent as guide. Armed with a flower press and filling it with crocuses, the two made their way up a steep incline until they were just a couple of hundred yards from the structure.

Naturally, they were soon confronted by soldiers, who relieved Dick of his flower press and marched him and the boy into the fort to appear before the commandant. This was exactly what Dick wanted—to be inside the building itself. He and the commandant were able to converse in French, Dick explaining his great interest in botany and birds and the distant tragedy of the Crimean War. Joy of joys, the commandant insisted on taking the nice young Englishman and his little local guide on a tour of his installation—a critically important one at the entrance to the Russians' naval base in the Crimea—pointing out features as only an engineer could.

Dick's brain positively hummed with the amount of information he was noting for later use. He states that he felt a bit of a cad at abusing this officer's hospitality, but his is doubtful. Much of Dick's adult life was one of subterfuge, plots, and strategies. He thrived on intrigue. He loved a challenge. He had a thoroughly shrewd, sharp-witted streak in his makeup that made him ideal for intelligence work. He was a hunter in every sense, quick to spot an opening, even quicker to track his quarry and kill. In fact, his motto could well have been "One must never do an enemy minor injury!"

By the time Dick had steamed out of Odessa Harbor, he'd

come close to being shot by an agent who had been following him. The way Dick neutralized that sweetheart was to offer him a cigarette, immediately pat him down with both hands in search of a box of matches, only to discover that the Russian was armed. Dick confronted the man right away and threatened to knock him flying if he so much as saw his hand go to his right-hand coat pocket. Steering the man back from the fairly isolated spot where they had wandered, they parted. A close, close shave, one that prompted Dick to state on March 1, 1910, in *Army Diary*:

> Spying is dirty work, but most exciting. Never again shall I undertake such work, as it entails a complete abuse of all the laws of hospitality. The risks are, moreover, not worth it, and it involves too much mental strain. I feel a perfect wreck, tired out both morally and physically. It also requires too great a memory capacity for men of my calibre.[1]

This was just another example of the contradictions in Dick's character. He was to perform some quite extraordinary acts of espionage in later life, and only the tip of the Meinertzhagen iceberg is known from his published works. No doubt his decades of unpublished diaries would give greater insight, but, knowing Dick, even these works are unlikely to be too specific about his "other work," as he termed it. He remained something of an enigma to the end of his life, a strangely closed man.

The material Dick had managed to forage in Sevastopol earned him the praise of the director of naval intelligence, who wanted him to take on another mission on the North Frisian island of Helgoland under the guise of an ornithologist. Dick declined. Not four years after this, the British scored quite a naval victory there over the Germans. A curious fact of history reveals that the island had been ceded to the Germans in 1890 in exchange for Zanzibar.

In any case, Dick discovered that intelligence work had its stranger moments. While Dick was returning to England by train via Greece, the train jumped the tracks and was teetering on the edge of the Gulf of Corinth, actually sliding some 150 yards over the edge and, miraculously, not crashing into the ravine below. Not yet, that is.

Chaos reigned in the compartment where Dick was sandwiched between a huge German woman and her slightly less huge husband. A panicked Greek jumped out of the train and fell to his death on the rocky floor of the ravine while a young girl was dangling in the air, clutching onto a rail on the side of the train, which was destined to plunge to the bottom eventually. Dick grabbed the girl, kicking her fingers to make her let go of the rail. Throwing the poor kid out of the train onto the land, he had only just managed to scramble out of the carriage himself when the whole lot plummeted to its rocky grave.

The scene on the lip of the gulf was horrific. A horse, almost severed in two, lay among human body parts, the air rent with the anguished screams, the staring eyes of people half-crazed with the shock of it all as they wandered about in the black night trying to find out if their companions were safe, injured, or dead, the entire proceedings complicated by serious language barriers. Dick had a broken rib, was in great pain, and had been ill at the sight of the carnage.

By the time relief came and the remaining passengers could board a new train, Dick's real problems were only beginning. An Englishwoman went into labor in his compartment and before Dick knew it, he was helping deliver the baby with the aid of a nice-looking German. Using his penknife, Dick cut the umbilical cord of the baby boy, washed him in cold water in the lavatory, gave him the usual spank on the bottom, and handed him to his mother, wrapped in her petticoat. The child was promptly named Richard.

Turning to the German to thank him for his help, Dick asked him who he was. His already boggled brain was further boggled when he discovered that his fellow midwife was none other than the king of Saxony and would Dick be so kind as to accept his invitation to stay a few days at his palace on the island of Corfu!

As Dick put it: "If it was not for my broken rib I should roar with laughter."[2]

Dick briefly returned to Mauritius with his battalion, where he reveals his aversion for petty politics on an island that had no worthwhile hunting and where the people of mixed blood obviously rattled his sense of empire propriety. Before leaving for another spell of home leave, Dick became embroiled in a brawl when the local politicians and the mobs got out of hand. He clobbered a Frenchman full in the face with the hilt of his sword after capturing some forty-seven Frenchmen and a bunch of Creoles. Dick shows his clear imperial contempt for the non-British when he speaks of the French as "miserable curs"[3] after one tried to bribe him to be released.

This barely disguised dislike of the non-British appears on several occasions in Dick's writings, his aversion to the Latin-based races being very obvious. While he showed a fairly constant respect for and basic liking of the Germans, this soured to some extent once World War I got going, but he never really became a Germanophobe. This complex man whose early writings indicate an element of anti-Semitism or at least irritation with aspects of Jewish culture went on to become a staunch supporter of the Zionist cause and the Jews in the founding of the State of Israel in

1948. It was a burning loyalty to the end of his long life, and Israel acknowledged this multifaceted man's role. His attitude toward the Arabs was something else again, and we know he didn't have any great affection for the Indian people. Dick was his own, self-contained conundrum. It was at this juncture—September 1911—that Meinertzhagen married Armorel Le Roy Lewis, the daughter of a major in his former regiment, the Hampshire Yeomanry. A headstrong and unconventional woman, Armorel appeared to have little in common with her husband. The marriage, a disaster compounded by Armorel's blatant infidelity, was annulled in 1919. There were no children.

Like any ambitious British officer, Dick had started preparing for the Staff College entrance examination. Orders then came through sending him back to the Jewel in the Crown—India. After a brief spell in the crisp altitudes of over 7,000 feet at Chakrata, a hill station in the Himalayas of northern Uttar Pradesh State, Dick sat for the Staff College exams, came out on top, and was posted to Quetta in British Baluchistan, near the Afghani border in what is today's Pakistan. Quetta had a Staff College, and Dick joined it in February 1913, amid feet of snow.

Dick was attached to the Twenty-third Indian Cavalry, where he was very quick to discover that his previous fourteen years in regimental soldiering, especially in Africa, had been invaluable. Dick saw the function of the army in empire as being small, the driving inspiration being efficiency. With this sort of mind-set, Dick's disgust can be imagined at the truly pathetic display put on by the artillery at a practice camp he attended near Delhi just before proceeding to Quetta. Targets were missed by hundreds of yards, fire control "crude," as Dick put it, fire discipline poor, shells were badly fused—only one out of eighteen being effective—and a joint exercise with the cavalry was a shambles. Ranges were incorrectly gauged and, when found to be wrong, they remained uncorrected.

Ah, but Her Imperial Majesty's officers, their equipment and horses, were all turned out to spit-and-polish perfection. Appearances, old chap, appearances. One must keep up appearances. To blazes if you can't hit the proverbial barn with a baseball bat, as long as you look the part.

Dick was appalled at this military inefficiency. A very practical man, he would have chosen battlefield effectiveness over impeccable presence, although he believed you could be both well turned out and effective. Dick was not one to hide irritation, and he was to collide with the brass time and again in the years to come.

It was the scene of an incident that sickened me and that certainly sickened Dick. Lest anyone thinks that Capstick leaves out the bad bits on "hunting," listen up and read on. This incident reveals the steelly, fearless character of our man in Quetta. As a lifelong hunter, I am mentioning this incident in particular to point out something about Dick and about hunting as opposed to vicious slaughter.

The British officers of the Eighteenth Cavalry stationed there, all jolly good fellows, you understand, missed their traditional fox-hunting and had to make do with the local jackal. Being such sporting chaps, they would catch a jackal, roughly stitch up its mouth to leave it totally defenseless, and then let it go, only to pursue it on horseback with the inevitable end. No fair play, no fighting chance, no ability to strike back. The idea was to protect the hounds from "hydrophobia" if bitten by the jackal. If the poor bugger was not torn to shreds by the hounds it would starve to death or die of thirst, whichever happened first.

Dick, on hearing of this barbaric practice that went against the grain and goes against the grain of ethical hunting, raised ten kinds of hell. He began by firing off a letter of protest to the commanding officer of the Staff College. When that old codger did not react, he leapfrogged over him, military etiquette be damned, and wrote to the British boss of the entire Indian army. The cruelty stopped forthwith, and there were those who greatly resented the newly arrived Dick for his interference. But as he stated, "Whenever I come across cruelty my nature makes me fight it regardless of consequences."[4]

Not even a few months before that, Dick had caught his groom, or syce, brutally maltreating his two polo ponies. Dick thrashed the coolie very severely, finally thumping him on the head with a polo mallet, which eventually killed him. I defy any reader to drop me a line saying Dick was out of line in these two instances. Our world needs more of Dick's type, not less. We have become a conglomerate of hapless victims in a world awash with crime and cruelty on all fronts, people being afraid to stand their ground, speak up, and strike back. Dick would have freaked at the insipid stance of so much of our society today—the "Well, what can *I* do?" syndrome.

Dick was a killer. That was one of his trades, and he was good at it. But he was also a man who abhorred maltreatment, as already evidenced by what he did to put an end to the torture of the monkey by the drunken Germans aboard ship when he first went out to Africa. So whether it was rescuing little girls from brothels or terminating the ill treatment of animals, he struck back. He didn't just stand there, mouth agape, fearful of offending his superiors. Dick *was* the superior in most instances because of his sheer moral courage. The hogwash about spying being not very nice because it broke the rules of hospitality was just that—hogwash. Dick was a natural. He distinguished very clearly between legitimate targets in any conflict situation and the vicious maltreatment or exploitation of his fellow men or animals. The treatment he reserved for the Kikuyu who had tortured a fellow countryman to death in Kenya is a further case in point.

Unrest was in the air in India and elsewhere. Dick caught the whiff probably quicker than most other officers. There had already been several instances of sedition in India such as riots in Cawnpore, some 245 miles southeast of Delhi, when a small toilet belonging to a mosque in the city but quite separate from the sacred part was demolished to broaden a road. In the ensuing riots, people were shot, and this incident was like chili powder in a raw wound for the British. The story was being put about that the Brits had demolished the whole mosque in a strike against Islam. Sound vaguely familiar?

The British had suffered a horrendous episode in that same city during the Sepoy, or Indian, Mutiny on July 15, 1857, when British soldiers and European families were slaughtered like goats at a tribal feast. What triggered that epoch-making event was a rumor among the Muslim soldiers in the Raj that the cartridges they were using were smeared with pork fat. History is always repeating itself, and the observant, even in Dick's Quetta days, detected an embryonic renewed resentment against the Raj, a building up of forces that would culminate in 1947 and the British Imperial sun going to bed forever over India.

The Cawnpore incident still fresh, a bank in Lahore, in what was then northwest British India but is today's Pakistan, went under. The manager, a Muslim, was responsible, but he put out the story that the Brits had deliberately sunk the bank. This sowing of confusion, lies, and despondency is the classic stuff of nonconventional warfare, and Dick was getting the hang of things fast.

In southeast India, at the harbor town of Pondicherry, a French possession since 1674 and remaining so until 1954, the French were proving to be very difficult, and this compounded imperial woes. Britain was attempting to erect a wireless chain of communication throughout its empire, and the French were apparently trying to block this with a station of their own. Dick was an unashamed Francophobe, branding this behavior "typical."[5]

Yes, something was in the air. Dick learned from a General Hamilton Gordon during a lecture that the Russians had imperial ambitions of their own with plans for a railway through Persia to a place called Charbar on today's Gulf of Oman, outside the Persian Gulf proper and a camel snort away from the critical choke point of the Strait of Hormuz. If the Russians built up their presence through this railway, according to the general, then the Persian Gulf could be effectively sealed off.

This was said in December 1913, not on the eve of the Gulf War of 1991. Plus ça change . . . !

General Hamilton urged officers to travel to areas of the world likely to become embroiled in conflict, obviously to study, observe, and gather information for the benefit of the empire. Dick's request to travel to Mesopotamia—today's Iraq—had recently been turned down, but now it needed not one whit more encouragement. He approached the general, requested his intercession, and, quicker than you could say beautiful Baghdad in Babylon, he was on his way with a fellow officer, one Maitland. The assignment: to collect intelligence on behalf of the government of India about road and river transport and about the railway being built in Baghdad.

Dateline Baghdad, January 2, 1914, the Grand Tigris Hotel: When I entertained my wife, Fiona, with Dick's descriptions of the unutterable filth and squalor of the place, she dug out letters, terrifying stuff, from Baghdad. They'd been sent out by diplomatic pouch, of course, by a lifelong friend who had spent several years in Baghdad with her British engineer husband. They had survived the same filth and squalor of Baghdad's hotels, which damn nearly killed her infant son, the added touch being Saddam's horrendous persecution of the Kurdish people and the general tyranny of the regime. In the 1980s, that is.

Everything is relative in life. After the heat, stench, and discomfort of the steamer from Basra at the head of the Shatt-al-Arab waterway of eastern Iraq, the Grand Tigris was bliss for one night. But Meinerzthagen and Maitland admitted defeat within twenty-four hours. Apart from the ladies of the night who were obviously frequent guests of the hostelry, the "variety of vermin . . . half-starved cats, pariah dogs, rats, beetles and mosquitoes seemed to look on our room as theirs, and then in bed lurked the voracious tick, louse, flea and bug. We did not spend a happy night."[6]

The Arab manager was enraged that these mortals—infidels, after all—could question the cleanliness of his establishment. Dick and Maitland were the first to do so, which says everything about the clientele of the day. So it was off to the Grand Babylon Hotel. There is no mention whether it was any better, but the fact that Dick lived to an impressive old age indicates that he survived the bounties of Baghdad and that his constitution was tougher than even he suspected.

No doubt about it, there were worrying developments in the region. It was still part of the Turkish Ottoman Empire, but the Germans were forging ahead with plans for a railway from Baghdad down to Basra on the gulf and to the north as well. Basra was also the end point of the railway from Europe. India and the other British possessions in the east were threatened with increasing communications isolation as a result, but the Brits seemed unperturbed. Maybe this was the arrogance of empire, which could not contemplate any rising by the locals or anyone else, for that matter. The British seemed quite happy to rely on the waterways for transport, but Dick was already thinking strategically. What if Germany were to interfere with and dominate the means of communication through this proposed railway? What if the waterways were to be depleted through irrigation of the desert, rendering it impossible to use even flat-bottomed boats? Germany, Dick felt, had political intentions, not just mercantile objectives. She was gearing up for war. There is no doubt that Dick communicated all this to the military back in India. Clouds were starting to gather but toothache distracted Dick, who went in search of a dentist. Poor man.

Into the narrow, fetid streets, the din of guttural Arabic making heavy the still air, Dick being jostled as he made his way to the house of the only act in town, an Armenian dentist. He had his rooms at the top of the house, and, when Dick had finished thumping on the door, a dirty servant opened it saying the master was too ill to help him.

Dick never took no for an answer. From anyone. Least of all from an Armenian dentist's batman. The dentist eventually appeared, his face swaddled in bandages and looking really dreadfully ill. Dick pointed to the offending tooth, and it was yanked out. No mention in the diary of laughing gas or whatever they used in 1913. *That* would have been too much to ask! His tooth out, a relieved Dick asked the Armenian what, in fact, was wrong with him.

Smallpox!

Dick and Maitland went about their information gathering by paying a visit some fifty-five miles south of Baghdad, where they also saw the site of Babylon, the capital of ancient Babylonia on the Euphrates River. Slightly farther on and southwest, the two came upon the holy town of Kerbela, revered by Shiite Muslims, which is built on the site of a battlefield held sacred in their history. By now the two British officers were detribalized in their surroundings and impressions as they were transported into another reality entirely where British parade-ground precision and deadlines were alien concepts in this world of sand, thirst, and mystic beliefs.

A cart took the two adventurers to the far north of the country, to the town of Mosul, just on the edge of Khurdish lands. This gave the men time to study any changes to the infrastructure from the transport point of view and, no doubt, to study the people a little more closely. One does not necessarily have to speak the language to be able to gauge hostility and brewing rebellion or, on the other hand, contentment.

A curious thing happened just outside Mosul, amid the ruins of the ancient city of Nineveh, which was once the capital of the Assyrian Empire until it was destroyed in 612 B.C., as predicted by Jonah, the seventh-century Hebrew prophet. Dick and his friend visited the purported tomb of Jonah of swallowed-by-the-whale fame. The guide at the tomb proceeded to recount the story, but he got his history wires crossed and had Jonah swallowing the whale.

Dick and Maitland thought this amusing and started chuckling inside the tomb. Curses were flung at them for having behaved disrespectfully at the tomb, and this was to come back and haunt the two within days. I have always been very, very careful to respect beliefs in Africa, for example, where you simply do not deride the customs of the bush people. I've witnessed far too many weird events in my years in Africa that defy rational explanation. I am a free spirit on such matters and am careful to make it known that I do not *ever* scoff at beliefs I do not necessarily accept. My files are bursting with data on curses and spells that were effected in the mid-1990s. I'm a convert to the power of an alien culture's mind to exert influences, especially evil influences, we do not fully grasp. Not yet.

Dick and Maitland, having no doubt observed, absorbed, and perhaps taken some notes of the whole transport scene north and south of Baghdad as instructed to do so, now set sail from Mosul for Baghdad on a rickety river raft steered by two pretty unfriendly Arabs. To add to the growing scenario of things going wrong, the raft and the men were hammered by torrential rain, which left everything soaked and unusable. Nights were cold as they drifted on downstream, but winds buffeted them and their possessions so badly they were driven inshore to seek shelter on land in the dead of night among unknown people. A trip that should have taken between five and seven days or, if the river was in flood, a mere three days and nights dragged on for an interminable eight days, even though the river was in flood and the currents strong. Some 325 miles turned into an endless ordeal.

Arabic culture, especially that of the Bedouin of the deserts, is renowned for boundless hospitality, and Dick was to experience this firsthand. Forced ashore at some foresaken speck on the Mesopotamian map of the day, Dick and Maitland were given shelter by the sheikh of a nearby village. As I read the description of that night I couldn't help but agree with Dick's whole attitude concerning foreign intrusion into yet-to-be-contaminated cultures such as that of the desert or marsh Arabs at that time.

Imagining Dick in the desert night, sipping the aromatic coffee of his hosts, the air pleasantly perfumed with the smoke from their Turkish cigarettes, their parched, wise faces centered on the guest in their midst as he relaxed his worn-out body, I remembered the staggering brilliance of the stars in the blackness of the Namibian night, the arid conditions and lack of industrial pollution, which meant that you could see the heavens in a ball gown of brilliance such as no city folk can imagine. I recalled the heavenly softness of the night, all modern noise filtered out completely so that I could even hear a comb go through my thinning hair. And I knew Dick's surge of emotion as I read his words, sharply calling into question the wisdom of modern man barging in with his toys and all too often leaving behind a rubble heap of damaged lands and even more damaged people. I thought of the Bushmen of southern Africa and their lives now, compared with what they once knew in more balanced and distant times, times I had shared with them, however briefly. I understood Dick's emotions when his Arab hosts said, "Let us alone in our desert."[7] They resented the invasion of their way of life. They instinctively feared the creation of needs they did not yet feel through the introduction of goods quite alien to their spartan lifestyle. They dreaded the ruin of their essential freedom in every way.

A hilarious moment that night with the desert Arabs is reminiscent of Lawrence or of Wilfred Thesiger, the incredible desert explorer who is still alive. Dick had been sharing some of the marvels of modern transport such as cars and airplanes. When he said that his people had managed to make a ship that could stay completely underwater with people onboard who would survive the experience, his courteous Arab hosts told him in whatever way they could that *that* was going over the top and into space. Really! What did Dick take them for? Credulous fools?

Before eventually arriving in Baghdad on January 30, 1914, Dick and Maitland survived a string of situations that had my wife and me howling with laughter like a pair of hyenas on the hunt. For starters, their shifty Arab boatmen all but mutinied and the boat nearly didn't survive a series of rapids. This so terrified their Baghdadi interpreter that he wailed piteously to Allah to intervene and save them. That just fetched him a kick in the butt by Dick, who remained in charge throughout, always an in-charge type.

Even on a rickety raft raging along on a swollen river into the Mesopotamian wilderness, you have to eat. No sweat. Stopping once for food before changing the boatmen in Tekrit (spelled Tikrit today), roughly halfway between Mosul and Baghdad, Dick shot a teal "which was forthwith plucked and eaten."[8] It was a case of a bird on the boat being worth a couple on the wing.

No sooner had Dick and Maitland pulled ashore in Tekrit than they were surrounded by bullying hostile Arabs. They tried to keep

Richard Meinertzhagen in Iraq, 1914. (Courtesy of Ran Meinertzhagen and Rhodes House Library, Oxford)

the raft from leaving, pelting Dick and company with bricks and rocks and who knows what else. Not a man to sit around and do nothing, Dick let fly with number-four shot, which had the mob scattering like village curs after scraps.

Just out of Tekrit the Turkish governor had a soldier hail the raft from the shore, ordering Dick to come in that instant. He, of course, refused to come ashore and pay damages for peppering the rear parts of assorted Arab mobsters. In fact, Dick flew into a rage and got the Turk's attention to the extent that he promised Dick that he would have the previous boatmen arrested for inciting the mob and anyone else involved in the stoning.

The end was not nigh. In Baghdad the waters had risen seventeen feet. This meant that the raft careened through the town in an absolutely uncontrollable rush, eventually smacking into a trade steamer and all but breaking in two. Storms, floods, wrecks, riots, threats, a mutinous crew, and a belligerent Turk; it was all the stuff of a trashy novel, but it actually happened.

The bad luck after Nineveh and Jonah's tomb continued. After Baghdad, Dick and Maitland went back to Basra in the marshes, where really crazy storms ripped through the gulf, killing people. A British official committed suicide; there were riots in the nearby Abadan Island oilfields after the death of an Indian; a British captain of a trade steamer was murdered on his vessel; and, to top the lot, in Musqat, Oman, "the Arab who fires the signal-gun was transfixed by the ramrod and blown out to sea. It has indeed been a chapter of bad luck and I trust that by now the spirit of Jonah is appeased."[9]

Indeed. Makes whaling seem tame by comparison.

Dick's whole outlook on life was the opposite of that of the gray little men in the British Foreign Office who, as Dick saw things, were often too nervous to take a stand and make a decision, because decisions meant consequences and responsibilities for those consequences. So eager to be diplomatic and do what was correct, the gray little men would be guilty of what Dick detested—doing nothing. As he stated—and this would bring him into collision with nonmilitary and military types alike very soon—"To do nothing is to do something definitely harmful. An emergency requires immediate action and the Foreign Office training is not conducive to emergencies."[10]

Dick was very conscious of the difference between himself and the civil service types. He was a hunter, a warrior, a decisive and fearless man with a nose for intelligence activities. In fact, despite the near fiasco of the Mesopotamian trip, his intelligence report to the Quetta Staff College OC was forwarded to HQ in Simla, where the director of intelligence termed Dick's work as "first class and most valuable."[11] There is no doubt that this had a direct bearing on Dick's immediate future.

And the immediate future was beginning to look ominous, even in distant British Baluchistan. Dick sensed that a ghastly catastrophe was near, that Germany was intent on world domination, that the increasing tensions with the French and Russians masked Germany's real intent: the destruction of Britain's naval power. Dick felt war coming. His words in his *Army Diary* are most moving when he wonders if he'll be sucked into the horror he saw on the horizon. It's one thing to be brave and daring in noncombat conditions, and quite another to face bullets and stare at your own mortality day in, day out. But, as Dick says, "Wide horizons in thought and vision, freedom and always more freedom, fresh air and exercise and a contempt for Death—that is what I love. Those are the conditions I understand."[12]

Things had been spoiling for an all-out conflagration for a while. Germany's aggressive naval and economic policies, especially in the Near East, the German-Slav conflict in the Balkans in 1912–1913, and the arms race involving Germany, the Austro-Hungarian Empire, Italy, France, Great Britain, and Russia stirred the pot of tension to the point where it would take very little to have the whole mess boil over and burn the lives of millions throughout the world. Dick would get his chance to be contemptuous of death— over and over.

The fuse was the assassination by a Bosnian student in Sarajevo on June 28, 1914, of Franz Ferdinand, the heir to the Austrian throne. On July 28 the Austrians declared war on Serbia, and before you could think the next thought, Russia mobilized and Germany declared war on France and Russia, invading Belgium. On August 4, Britain declared war on Germany. The British Empire and, eventually, American troops were involved in a world war that saw over 10 million people annihilated and twice that many wounded. The English language enlarged its lexicon to include the expressions "trench warfare" and "mustard gas," and life would alter forever. Empires were set to crumble, and Germany would be dealt with in such a way that the seeds of the 1939–1945 holocaust were already sown.

Dick was tearing at the bit to get into all-out warfare. His urge to get into the thick of battle reminds me of a very close pal who had just retired as a colonel in the U.S. Army when the Gulf War erupted. He was our house guest at the time here in South Africa, and his desperation to re-enlist chilled me in the way it would have chilled anyone who has actually been in prolonged combat. We cannot understand what we do not know. We always yearn for what we have yet to experience. And often, once we have tasted what we longed for, we spend the rest of our lives trying to digest what we tasted, often with no success.

Orders came through. Dick was to report to General Aitken in Bombay before shipping out for Mombasa. He would be responsible for the general's intelligence section in the German East African campaign. The war games were over, and the real stuff was looming ever nearer. Accompanied by Indian cavalry and infantry, Dick set sail from Bombay on October 16, 1914. The ship was to be part of a convoy of twenty-one ships, including a battleship and two cruisers. Dick was part of "B Force," commanded by General Aitken.

The *Karmala* steamed into Mombasa Harbor on October 31, 1914. The boyish Dick who had first set eyes on Africa in May 1902 had grown into a teak-tough man of resolve and daring who would now be confronted with himself. Everything he had ever learned as a hunter and soldier would come into play: commanding troops and enforcing discipline, running an espionage network, skilled observation and intelligence gathering, tracking, the deadly accurate placing of the enemy in the sights of his rifle, the quick kill and withdrawal, gauging the ruses and risks, smothering cowardly behavior, bracing anyone over stupid decisions—and evaluating the aftermath.

The Big One had finally come.

Uganda

Lake
Victoria

Mwanza

Nairobi

BRITISH
EAST
AFRICA
Kenya

Serengeti
Plains

Kigoma

Tabora

Kilimanjaro
Moshi

Arusha

Ufiome

Kondoa Irangi

Kilimatinde

Usambara Railway

Dodoma

Northern
Railway

Tanga

Pemba I.

GERMAN
EAST
AFRICA

Bagomoyo
Morogoro

Zanzibar

Indian
Ocean

Belgian
Congo

Lake
Tanganyika

Tanzania

Dar es Salaam

N. Rhodesia

R. Rufiji

Mafia I.

Kilwa

N

r. Luvego

Lake
Nyasa

Nyasaland

River Rovuma

Portuguese
East
Africa

GERMAN EAST AFRICA

Chapter 8

World war was upon them. As the SS *Karmala* gathered speed and started pushing out into the Bombay roadstead, the scene of generations of arrivals and departures under the Union Jack, Dick turned back and gazed at the coastline, his mind a strange mixture of emotions—nostalgia and anticipation, relief and saber-edged excitement.

Dominating the horizon as Bombay slipped back into her silk sari of darkness punctuated by the lights of the villas and the small craft coming home to port were the Towers of Silence, the burial places of the ancient and exclusive Pharsee people who leave the corpses of the dead for the vultures inside the towers.

Dick was immersed in deep thought. Yes, this voyage back to Africa did not have that same buoyancy as did the trip out in 1902. Something had changed in him as he surveyed the various military groups onboard with whom he would be tackling the best of the kaiser's troops and elite bush-hardened Schutztruppe blacks under crack German command. And his stomach knotted. This was it! Funny how you do not rejoice with anticipation when once you have been under fire.

Dick was all but the only young officer in fighting trim who had had extensive experience of the East African bush—hence his usefulness for the intelligence branch. He knew the terrain and the climate, and the dangers posed by wild animals. He was a very experienced hunter and tracker, and he was utterly self-sufficient in the bush if he had to be.

He long knew the great danger, already detectable, where the Brits and their allies would start scoffing at the Germans and their askaris. First rule of the int game: never underestimate your enemy as you attend to the two overriding duties in that game: finding out what your enemy's strengths, dispositions, and intentions are, and preventing the enemy from knowing yours in return. Dick would surely have added a third: When you strike, strike first, strike hard, strike to terminate. Do it to them before they do it to you, and do it so that you need not do it a second time.

But what had Britannia dished up for the coming war that would make all other battles seem like a gentle afternoon of English high tea at Mottisfont? Dick's practiced eye studied the human material onboard. He had sure knowledge that some of the British officers were not up to speed for the bloody task ahead. As for the Indian troops, his trained ear listened to their chat. His gut felt out the morale as Mother India receded into the night. He sniffed out the will to fight, the ability to stay steady under fire and strike back under command. As the SS *Karmala* rode the swells and forged into the open seas, destination Mombasa, Dick's heart took a dip and he paled inwardly. This feeling worsened as the crowded vessel sailed into the tropical heat with its already disgruntled human cargo. He saw third-rate troops in fancy dress, with a goodly dash of outright cowards. History would prove him right. Apart from units drawn from Europe and the then Mesopotamia, there were three battalions drawn from India who had no martial background and had not seen action in the field for over a generation. Dick, already not exactly predisposed to Indians, was to discover many of them to be "chicken-hearted Hindus"[1] who were quite useless in combat.

What is now to follow is a glimpse at one of the most disgraceful routs in Britain's entire military history, as experienced firsthand by a real soldier of grit and daring—Dick Meinertzhagen. He was there. And the memory of that shambles rankled even after decades.

The Germans appeared to be keeping to their side of the border with British East Africa but had concentrated their troops in the Moshi region with an advanced post placed near Taveta to keep tabs on their adversaries. The Germans were smart. They had concentrated their efforts, whereas their enemies had spread themselves out all over the place with no strong, central reserves. The Germans had the power of the initiative.

Dick's commanding officer, General Aitken, planned on their landing at Tanga, the port just inside the border of German East Africa. The idea was to push up to the Moshi region, troops simultaneously moving in from Voi in the east to converge on Taveta under General Stewart. This would mean over 5,000 rifles and about twenty machine guns in all, the intention, according to General Aitken, being to "thrash the German before Xmas."[2]

Dick slammed the plan and did so in writing to warn his fellow Brits that this was madness. He was the only one with "B Force" who had had firsthand experience of the German East African bush and who knew the fighting fiber of the German-led askaris. He appeared to be alone in respecting the military clout of the Germans themselves. He certainly seemed to be the only man to understand the enormous psychological advantage of the askaris, who would be fighting on home turf, who were not remotely so vulnerable to diseases such as malaria, who knew bush warfare, and who, in classic guerrilla style, could pick the time and place to engage the enemy.

Dick urged his side not to just land in Tanga, but to occupy and fortify it, using it as a rear base, backed up by the British navy. The real strength would be concentrated up in the healthy highlands around Nairobi from where the British forces could fan out toward the German stronghold around Mount Kilimanjaro and Moshi in the southwest. The plan would be to defeat the Germans there and then push on southward, down the coast, to capture Dar es Salaam and rout the Germans once and for all in East Africa. There was even an offer to bring in Dick's old revered and bush-hardened battalion, the third King's African Rifles, to cover the British when they landed in Tanga. General Aitken refused.

Nobody listened to Dick Meinertzhagen. They would wish they had.

October 31, 1914, Mombasa: The SS *Karmala* heaved to off Mombasa, leaving the rest of the convoy out of sight of land. Dick was greeted with the curious news that the British navy had somehow arranged a truce with both Dar es Salaam and with Tanga in that the navy had agreed it would not attack either harbor, provided the Germans did not use these two locations for naval or any other military purposes. The British admiralty was unaware of this cozy little arrangement with the enemy, so it was unauthorized. In essence, because of this gentlemanly entente, the Brits would have to forewarn the Germans if they wished to attack Tanga!

This was such dangerous nonsense that Dick thought he was hallucinating. The news of his mother's death reached him that same day, deep sadness only momentarily distracting him from this crazy situation that was going to result in disaster.

HMS *Fox*, under Commander Caulfield, was at the outer anchorage of Tanga on November 2, the rest of the convoy out of sight off Tanga. The Germans were sent a message to surrender immediately. They ignored the demand, but they had been forewarned and were probably already bringing in reinforcements from Moshi. The decision was then made to land that night but, to Dick's horror, it would be in small strength on an unreconnoitered beach, in what looked like a mangrove swamp, there being no intelligence as to German forces in the landing area. And the element of surprise had vanished.

Dick saw this as criminal stupidity by the British. General Aitken positively paraded his contempt for the Germans but Dick quickly points out in his diary that the Germans "have created the finest military machine the world has ever seen,"[3] it being patent military madness not to respect the Germans on land and sea and to plan accordingly. There should have been a mass arrival at dawn by the whole British convoy, guns trained on the town while the British took control. None of this happened, of course.

Dawn, November 3, 1914: The British finally launched their attack on Tanga. A small force of Germans was entrenched just outside the town and had a proverbial field day as they picked off the Brits and the worse than useless Thirteenth Rajputs. The British suffered about 300 casualties in one morning as the Rajputs turned tail and scattered like bewildered rabbits. They had already been shaking with fear in the small craft used to bring them ashore. How could such people be expected to stand their ground under fire?

Dick witnessed the whole pathetic scene. By nightfall no patrols had been posted and no effort had been made to maintain contact with the enemy. An accidental discharge from one of the Rajput rifles sowed total panic at one stage, the Rajputs bolting back to the shore, it being a real struggle to force them to return to their temporary encampments. It's a fair bet that German intelligence scouts must have observed this entire episode. And it's clear what they must have concluded about the fighting morale of the enemy forces that day.

Dick went to sleep that night on a makeshift bed of ladies'

lingerie, taken from the house that had been requisitioned. His pillow consisted of palm leaves stuffed into a corset that obviously belonged to some large Brünnhilda, but the finishing touch was the blankets: a Union Jack and three German flags. A case of Deutschland über alles!

Good old Aitken decided to launch a fresh attack on Tanga the next day, but only after everyone had had a good breakfast. Not 600 yards out of Tanga, the Germans suddenly opened fire, and those Rajputs who were still operational immediately broke and bolted like traffic-shy horses. In a state of gibbering fear, rifle shots going off crazily in all directions, even from the rear, Dick literally had to kick butt and fire his pistol to regain some sort of control over the Rajput rabble. It got so bad at one stage that Dick killed a Rajput who threatened him with his rifle and he shot another Rajput native officer when he attempted to draw his sword on Dick. Nobody threatened Dick in wartime and lived.

Dick and some of his men got into the thick of things, surviving machine-gun and rifle fire as they indulged in a house-clearing exercise in downtown Tanga, mowing down a fair number of the enemy before being forced to retreat to the seafront. Holed up in the customs house with a couple of fellow soldiers, Dick took aim at a "tall man with a fine face"[4] but, most uncharacteristically, he missed.

He had come within a whisker of killing General Von Lettow-Vorbeck, commander of all German troops in German East Africa and who was to become a firm friend of Meinertzhagen after the war. As the German commander said, "This was my first social contact with my friend Meinertzhagen."[5] When it is realized that Vorbeck held out with a small crowd of askaris and almost no help at all from outside until after the Armistice, what the outcome of the East African campaign would have been had Dick found his mark that day in Tanga is an intriguing proposition.

The British forces in general were now demoralized and had little will left to fight on. The heat, the thirst, the easily communicated panic all infected the troops, who were also attacked at one stage by wild bees, Dick also being stung. The men's morale was further hit when it started sinking in that they had been thumped by mostly black troops. They felt disgraced.

They *were* disgraced, their empire arrogance in shreds.

Despite now knowing that Tanga was being defended, General Aitken did not order the sappers ashore, and he did not see to it that the mountain battery was deployed. Even the naval guns were left onboard. There was no liaison between the infantry and the artillery, and the bulk of the Indian army troops were "jibbering idiots, muttering prayers to their heathen gods, hiding behind bushes and palm trees and laying [sic] down face to earth in folds of the ground with their rifles lying useless beside them. I would never have believed that grown-up men of any race could have been reduced to such shamelessness."[6]

Dick blamed the Indian government for enlisting "such scum and placing them in the King's uniform."[7] The British did not capture a single enemy soldier. But they lost 800 killed and who knows how many wounded. The heat was hastening the putrefaction process as piles of corpses started rotting in the African sun. The stench of rotting human flesh cannot be described.

In between enciphering General Aitken's dispatch to the War Office, Dick went across enemy lines with a white flag to bring medical supplies to the wounded British and to deliver a letter for Von Lettow-Vorbeck. There was nothing that could be done for one youngster who was not only dead but mutilated. Dick now knew he was back in the East African bush. As he moved forward he saw a row of Indian soldiers, each with his own bayonet stuck into his back. Think about that one.

The Germans were courtesy itself to Dick, offering him breakfast and speaking of the war with him as if it were some normal event. But this cordiality soon changed when Dick, on his way back to his lines, was ambushed by an askari who fired at him. The bullet passed through Dick's helmet and grazed his hair! Not one to put up with such insolence, Dick promptly wrenched the rifle out of the askari's hands and impaled him with his own bayonet. The basic sense of decency toward the Germans turned to poisonous hate in a flash.

But more was to follow. On returning to the British camp, Dick was informed that orders had been given to embark forthwith. All the wounded were to be abandoned as well as all stores, weapons, ammunition, rations, and signaling equipment. The men looked like rats scuttling off one sinking ship and onto another. Dick was stunned at the disgrace of it all. He was all for blowing up the equipment rather than simply donating it to the enemy, but no such luck.

The mood among the troops had turned mutinous. Dick had then been ordered back to negotiate the removal of the wounded on condition that, once recovered, they would not serve again in this theater of the world war. Dick felt sick with shame. And a further meal with the Germans, consisting of "good beer, ice, plenty of eggs and cream and asparagus,"[8] surely increased his sense of humiliation. Even a chat with a German ornithology enthusiast about migration down the east coast of Africa could not have eased Dick's discomfort. The sheer discipline, correctness, and fighting trim of the Germans made a tremendous impact on Dick, who warned General Aitken that something other than the Indian army had better be used in order to beat the Germans. It is debatable whether Aitken even heard what Dick said.

Such was the magnanimity of the Germans that General Von Lettow-Vorbeck had Dick informed of the imminent arrival from Moshi of two field guns, which he would be compelled to use against the British vessels if they did not leave immediately. Talk about a tip-off—this was surely unique in anyone's naval history.

The British left Tanga, a routed force, all the most elementary rules of warfare having been broken and Dick's warnings ignored. Apart from the mountain of abandoned equipment, which included 600,000 rounds of ammunition, no less than 8,000 British troops and sixteen machine guns were beaten by about 1,000 Germans and their askaris, who had no machine guns or artillery. In fact, Tanga was able to resist until Armistice four solid years down the line!

Perhaps one of the most memorably offensive quotes of the war came from General Aitken himself when Dick warned him that, in the light of his own firsthand experience of the Germans in Africa, the German troops were better trained, better disciplined, and better led than even Dick's revered KAR. Aitken shot back in some irritation, "The Indian Army will make short work."[9]

The British committed four major tactical mistakes in Dick's opinion: they had inadequate reserves; General Aitken should have been stationed at the signal tower and not been on the ground with the troops, where the overall events so upset him as to affect his resolve and judgment; what little the British had in the way of reserves were used in the wrong place at the wrong time; and, finally, Aitken never landed his entire force with proper liaison between the artillery and the infantry.

Dick was so traumatized by these rudimentary blunders, by this criminal ignoring of the basic principles of war, which were dinned into the heads of every student at Staff College and which were emphasized in the Field Service Regulations, that he actually felt oddly grateful for the Tanga episode in his military career because he would never be able to forget such fundamental lessons for the rest of his life.

Aitken was replaced. Although he was exonerated for the

Tanga fiasco, he was destined not to work again. Dick blamed Simla for giving an already weak and unsuited man the flotsam of the Indian army for the East African campaign. His replacement, General Wapshare, "Wappy," was a nice old boy but "devoid of military knowledge"[10] and also not in the same league as a Von Lettow-Vorbeck. Nobody in East Africa was.

Meinertzhagen knew one thing in the wake of the Tanga tragedy: No military operations could succeed in the absence of information, of sifted intelligence for use in the field and in the ops room, where plans were made and men's lives laid on the line. Dick had seen useful information being ignored by his own commanders, resulting in the death of troops.

Dick was to devise his own intelligence system, which would change the game in East Africa.

When the war broke out, the Game Department in British East Africa was used as a basic intelligence department, which was in itself a bright move. The white settlers and hunters, aided by their locally born trackers and staff, knew the bush and the people intimately well and could report anything out of the ordinary when it came to strangers in the area. Dick tells us that, at first, the Game Department restricted its activities to Masai agents in the Kilimanjaro region. The coastal area was ignored, so enemy agents could come and go at will in a place like Mombasa, and the fact that the area covered was restricted to Masailand meant that the rest of BEA was a closed book.

At the outbreak of hostilities, the British didn't have quite 2,000 askaris, led by no more than a few dozen British officers. Round that out with a handful of not very reliable Maxim guns mounted on rickety Model T Fords, as Charles Miller states in *The Lunatic Express*, and the picture is clear. The Germans were infinitely better prepared and this included their intelligence service.

Their battle-tough black Schutztruppe quite frankly outclassed much of what His Britannic Majesty could throw at them. The command of the British forces was also complicated by the hugely diverse backgrounds, languages, customs, dietary habits, and physical endurance of the troops. They were drawn from today's Kenya, Uganda, and what was known as Nyasaland, now Malawi. They came from the Gold Coast—now Ghana—the then Belgian Congo, and Nigeria. There were also some Portuguese soldiers as well as troops from the West Indies, not counting the South Africans, Rhodesians, and Belgians. As for the Indian troops, they represented many languages, several religions, and separate cultures among themselves. The Germans, by comparison, had a more homogeneous force, which greatly aided command, control, and morale.

Dick saw and understood this very quickly. He also saw and understood even more quickly that the British had no coherent intelligence system. Yes, Lord Delamere and other such famous pioneer hunter/settler figures as Denys Finch-Hatton, Berkely Cole with his Somali Cole's Scouts, "Tich" Miles (D.S.O.M.C. no less after the war), Donald Seth-Smith, Ewart "Cape-to-Cairo" Grogan, William Judd, and Bror Blixen all did invaluable work for Queen and newfound country. There is a wonderful period photograph in a recent illustrated reprint of Karen Blixen's *Out of Africa* that shows Finch-Hatton court-martialing an askari for giving information to the Germans. Efforts were concentrated largely along the border with German East Africa in Masai country, but whole chunks of BEA were left wide open to enemy. The entire coastline was a sieve.

Morale was very low, especially after the Tanga disgrace. There seemed to be no offensive spirit, and intelligence reports appeared to be ignored. Dick's determination to "smash up this German organisation"[11] sustained him, no matter the apathy and stupidity surrounding him. General Wapshare proved to be a positive danger because he was so indecisive and downright useless as a commander. His pleasant nature saved him from outright rejection, but he was quickly replaced by General Tighe, and a whole new scene was now developing.

Dick and Tighe hit it off immediately, which was a good thing for the war in the end. They were getting to know each other while traveling on the train between Voi and Tsavo when there was a devil of an explosion as they neared Tsavo Station. Bullets smashed through their carriage, and it was incredible that nobody was killed in what was obviously an ambush.

Dick bolted out of the train into the surrounding murk, letting fly with his rifle at the bush, where enemy fire betrayed positions. Tighe brought up the rear wielding nothing more than a big stick and even bigger curses about all things Teuton. Only Dick seemed to have a rifle on a train "full of gibbering natives"[12] whom he had to guard while the slightly injured driver went off on foot to Tsavo to get help. The train had obviously jumped the tracks.

Despite this mess, Dick thoroughly appreciated the fight in Tighe and his will to follow through. As he says, "It was a comic sight to see the General Officer commanding with his intelligence officer, blown up on the Uganda Railway and guarding a train . . . with but one rifle and fifty rounds of ammunition. Tighe and I are now fast friends."[13]

Although the Germans constantly attacked the Uganda Railway, the British took poor precautions and Dick ranted at this ineptitude, telling of a so-called guard post on the Tsavo River, obviously a bridge, which the men deserted, claiming they had been attacked by a German patrol. This turned out to be a charge by a black rhino and her calf. The humans blew more than 200 rounds of ammo, never hitting her once and concocting a dumb story to cover up their uselessness. Dick fumed that the Germans could take these men, as they were "mere rubbish."[14]

Good old Wappy then left, en route for the Persian Gulf, but not before shooting a couple of ostriches on the way. Fellow passengers had to help him drag the two huge creatures back to the train, where the old chap proceeded to pluck them for the rest of the trip. Ever tried to pluck an ostrich? On a moving train? Maybe all those stories about the sun and mad dogs and Englishmen have a touch of the true about them. Some of the officers were often so wide of the mark as to be truly suspect in Dick's books. How about the *written* order that the sentry at the Tsavo post was not to shoulder arms during the day. Dick urged Tighe to court-martial the officer who inspected and approved the post at the Tsavo River but, as Tighe pointed out, if he were to do that, half the Indian army in BEA would not survive. Dick knew the seriousness of combat and stated, "We have got to win, win win."[15]

Nothing militarily worthwhile would be achieved without reliable information. Enter Dick. Now, he knew what a dirty game intelligence could be, but it was to become literally the pits under his direct orders. He devised a scheme whereby the ersatz toilet paper used by the Germans in their latrines would be retrieved by his network of agents and, after due washing off, would provide often excellent reports, even hard intelligence, of just what the enemy was planning.

How in heaven did Dick hit upon this idea?

The first thing Dick did was to organize a network of agents to cover the coastal areas. After all, this was where matériel would be arriving, and reinforcements, too. He worked through a local dignitary in Mombasa known as the Liwali. Clearly, you recruit from populations who are from the region you wish to cover, who speak the languages, especially the local dialects, who often have relatives in the area, and who can move about like fish in water—harmonizing with the whole as they go about their business.

Dick also roped in a selection of white hunters and a few Dutch immigrants from South Africa to boost his embryonic intelligence service. It wasn't long before he was receiving a steady stream of data, which then had to be sifted and evaluated before it could be passed up the chain of command for action. Britain's official war history gave high praise to Meinertzhagen for his accomplishments in all but unmapped country where, had it not been for advance information, the movement of the allied troops would have been infinitely more difficult if not impossible at times. As with anyone associated with Dick under such circumstances, there were tales of incredible feats as his agents went all out against the Germans and their formidable black troops.

Dick used mainly Swahili-speaking blacks in his network. He obviously worked out that two-ply tissue was not exactly abundant in wartime German East Africa so, with some courage, he set his men the task of foraging about in the enemy's latrines for used paper. And he was spot on. Quite apart from private correspondence, which can be very useful when keeping someone under surveillance, Dick's team brought in enciphering and deciphering codes, messages, notes, and the signatures and posts held by pretty well the

The author with one of P. J. Pretorius's rifles. South Africa, July 1987. (Courtesy of Fiona Capstick)

entire German strength in East
Africa. This helped Dick au-
thenticate subsequent intercepted documents.

One alarming fact comes
out as Dick talks of his DPM
method—I presume this to
mean "Dirty Paper Method":
It is clear that apart from Jan
Smuts of South Africa, the English commanders tended to ignore the intelligence reports
supplied by Dick. Smuts not
only listened, but often acted
on Dick's information.

*The author with one of P. J. Pretorius's rifles.
South Africa, July 1987. (Courtesy of Fiona
Capstick)*

In speaking about his
agents, Dick states quite bluntly
that most whites in the bush
would have been too obvious except for P. J. Pretorius, Smuts'
legendary scout. Dick speaks of that swarthy, wiry little man of the
bush as "a magnificent exception."[16] I wrote extensively about
"Jungle Man" Pretorius and his one-man war against the Germans
in the African bush in *Death in the Silent Places* (New York: St.
Martin's Press, 1981). The campaign peaked with his location and
sinking of the *Königsberg* battle cruiser in the mangrove maze of the
Rufiji River delta, opposite the island of Mafia, an ancient Arab
slaving center. P. J. had lived on the banks of the Rufiji for years
after leaving South Africa at the end of the Anglo-Boer War in
1902. This equipped him ideally for quite positively one of the
most outrageously colorful and successful guerrilla warfare operations in any theater anywhere at any time, and Dick was perfectly
aware of just what an extraordinarily talented, unconventional war-

rior Pretorius was. His sixth sense was to save him time and again from ambush and death.

My links with Pretorius are both very personal and unusual. If you look at pages 196 and 197, there are photographs of me with one of P. J.'s rifles, taken by my wife on the family farm in 1987 some four hours' drive from our Pretoria home and a solid seventy-two years after the time with Dick in East Africa. P. J. was a direct descendant of the Voortrekker, or pioneer general, after whom Pretoria is named. I also had the privilege of meeting P. J.'s son and two of his daughters, who all told me stories from their childhood about their near-mythical father and his unique life. He was an elephant hunter, adventurer, poacher, chief scout to Smuts, spy, and explorer. He survived forays into cannibal country way north, mass attacks by unreconstructed tribesmen who had hardly seen a white man in their lives, and battles with the Germans that left him with a lifelong hatred of the Huns—a hatred put to good use as a spy later on. There's nothing like good old-fashioned hatred to motivate a spy.

In the years preceding the war, Pretorius became an ivory poacher second to none in German territory, recouping the small fortune the Germans confiscated from him when they took his farm and other earthly possessions after one major breakdown in communication. He ghosted in and out of German-held territory without detection and could reconnoiter for the white gold and anything else, for that matter, right under the collective snouts of the Huns without their being so much as aware that anything was amiss until it was way too late. But they all knew of the dark little man, the legendary tracker and killer. And they respected his stealth, brilliance, and fearlessness with a good dose of loathing. Nobody likes to appear foolish.

When war broke out the Germans were desperate to nab Pretorius, as they knew just what an incredible intelligence asset he would be to the British. They never got their collective paws on him, and the sinking of the *Königsberg* remains to the end of time proof of the South African's skills and the Germans' loss. It was, after all, the biggest and most threatening vessel in the entire Indian Ocean and one that the British had to neutralize if only they could locate her. Only one man came to mind: Pretorius.

Through one stroke of genius after another and endurance such as cannot be imagined, Pretorius located the deeply camouflaged cruiser in the malarial mangroves of the Rufiji, his old stamping grounds. His complexion yellow-swarthy from years in the scorching sun and after repeated bouts of malaria, Pretorius passed himself off as an Arab and went about his reconnaissance business to perfection. The rest is history. The cruiser was located and destroyed. As I wrote in *Death in the Silent Places,* "*Königsberg,* Prince of the Southern Fleet, came into sight, a fire-blackened tangle of Krupp steel, torn and eviscerated, covered with the burned and explosive-mutilated, fly-covered bodies of her crew. *Königsberg,* the Raider was dead, tracked, stalked and hunted to her den by a lean, quiet, dark-faced man who had learned not to like Germans."[17]

That was July 11, 1915.

It came as a shock to read that Dick, although intelligence officer to General Tighe, was not being briefed about the *Königsberg.* It was clear that the Allies, through Pretorius, were being fed first-rate hard intelligence on the cruiser and the efforts to locate and destroy her. Dick had very quickly pointed out the critical necessity of covering the coastal areas from an intelligence point of view, yet he was kept in the dark. Was this professional jealousy or just plain sloth on the part of some misfit pommie back at base? Probably a mixture of both.

On page 200 you will see me and a friend holding up a somewhat grubby flag with the imperial German eagle emblazoned on

The author (left) with a German Imperial flag and shell case seized in German East Africa during World War I. South Africa, April 1987. (Courtesy of Fiona Capstick)

it. This was photographed in the South African bush soon after I met the Pretorius family. I had been told of a man who had the flag from the *Königsberg* on his farm, a war relic from his father's military career. Fiona and I drove out to the farm, only to ascertain that the flag, although typical of the flags flown over German installations in German East Africa, was not the cruiser's ensign. It was nevertheless a great day to be alive, excited and convinced as I was that I was about to touch history, as it were.

Skirmish after bloody skirmish followed the sinking of the cruiser, Pretorius working mostly behind enemy lines until the end. There was a huge price tag on his head and the British were acutely aware of the danger he constantly ran of ambush and capture, but this was not his fate. He not only survived but went on to serve in World War II and was eventually awarded the C.M.G., D.S.O., and Bar. He died in hospital in 1945, just up the road from one of our properties in Pretoria.

My links do not stop there. When I was on a book tour of the States in August 1987, my wife was contacted early one morning with the horrific news that one of P. J.'s daughters whom we had met and her husband had been hacked to death and burned to ashes on the family farm—by terrorists who were passing through. Fiona attended the funeral in Pretoria, as did very senior police officers, P. J.'s remaining children, and several of his grandchildren, who all knew of their extraordinary grandfather. The coffins containing the remains were tiny caskets, like those used for children. What is more horrific is that not one word of the tragedy made the papers of the day, and we are unaware that anyone was ever apprehended.

As I thought back on Dick and his admiration of P. J., on the handwritten war notes by Pretorius I was privileged to study, I felt a strange sadness at the ignominious end to the child of such a courageous man. As Dick's story unfolds his name will crop up again, a name long since engraved in official war records as an unconventional warfare expert decades before it became the fashion.

A s Dick squared up to his formidable foe in East Africa, he had to devise ways to sow panic and confusion, to infect the fighting morale of the Germans and their askaris. This started with efforts to maintain discipline among his own people, which meant the odd court-martial and execution pour encourager les autres— to serve as a lesson to the others. Cowards, malingerers, and deserters were summarily dealt with, but Dick was to be much more devious and effective as he got at the enemy's psyche. How about the following little gem:

A fairly jacked-up Arab was in the employ of the Germans for the sole purpose of thwarting the Allied intelligence effort. He had already had the Uganda Railway sabotaged in places and came close to blowing up the harbor facilities at Kisumu on Lake Victoria.

The man was very definitely being effective, and Dick had had enough. He did not take kindly to being made to look a victim or a fool in the eyes of anyone, be it local Arab or distant German high command.

The identity of the Arab was known, so how was one to sabotage his credibility in the eyes of his Hun paymasters? Very simple, really. Dick wrote the man a letter of thanks for valuable information received, complimenting him on its accuracy and emphazing the Allied gratitude for all the information that had, in fact, come through via intercepted German wireless messages. The lucky chap was also given 1,500 rupees for services rendered to date. The money and accompanying letter were entrusted—if that is the right word under the circumstances—to an agent whom Dick picked because he was fairly useless and was all but certainly going to be captured as he tried to deliver the letter.

The German officer commanding at the port of Mwanza on the southern shores of Lake Victoria got hold of the letter, and the Arab was executed on the strength of Dick's letter. He speaks of his conscience bothering him about this incident, but this is doubtful. Dick thrived on intrigue, and a successful outcome like this just stoked his scheming brain to hatch other schemes.

Dick wasn't phased by rank. When he came across a British post where the sentry was off duty, the men wandering about unarmed, and the Indian OC bathing in a pool with five dead hippo floating in it and twenty-eight others lurking nearby, he wanted to know what in blazes was going on. The OC had shot the five hippo for the sheer hell of target practice and, as for the general dereliction of duty, the worthy Oriental gentleman had no reply but was impertinent to young Dick.

The result? Dick got word through to General Tighe himself, leapfrogging over the chain of command and General Malleson, who was most put out at being told of a slack post. Tighe ordered a court-martial and the Indian officer was cashiered—a searing and permanent disgrace for anyone. What propelled Tighe to that end was the report of a party of German saboteurs near the post stumbled across by Dick and his party, who shot four dead and wounded the rest. They were obviously on their way to blow up a section of the Uganda Railway. The word was getting about: Watch out for Meinertzhagen! He's trouble. He's fearless and he's usually right.

May 1915 saw the arrival in Mombasa of one of the most unusual groups of soldiers to assemble in any war theater: the Twenty-fifth Battalion of the Royal Fusiliers, known as the Legion of Frontiersmen. The battalion's oldest member was none other than Lieutenant Frederick Courteney Selous, the Selous of hunting/naturalist/literary fame on whom Rider Haggard modeled his character Allan Quartermain. Selous was already sixty-four years old but he was firing on all pistons like a man half his age. My book *The African Adventurers* (New York: St. Martin's Press, 1992) speaks at length of this unique man and the legion.

Of the forty-eight battalions comprising the Fusiliers, this was the most colorful of the lot. There were former circus clowns, acrobats, a couple of Texas cowpunchers, a general from the Honduran army, faded opera singers and musicians, a lighthouse keeper and erstwhile arctic explorers, hunters and bartenders, farmers and exiles from Siberia, a millionaire and an ornithologist, former members of the French foreign legion, a naval wireless operator, stockbrokers, a submarine commander, American soldiers, and a Buckingham Palace footman. What a crowd! They all had one thing in common: a hunger for adventure, anything to shake off the dust and cheat fate just one more time. They were deadly tough and had none of the illusions or vanities of youth left in their aging bones. As Lord Cranworth puts it in *Kenya Chronicles*, "The 25th Fusiliers went far to achieve the impossible. They were the last white unit left, and again and again I have seen their remnants marching forward to the attack, in rags, shaking with fever, emaciated and white beneath the tan, yet full of an invincible determination which never let themselves or their Commander down. . . . They covered a retirement against overwhelming odds and fought until they were cut to pieces. All honour to 'the Old and Bold.' "[18]

Colonel Daniel "Jerry" Driscoll, who had fought in Burma and in the 1899–1902 Anglo-Boer War, was a personal friend of Selous and had written to him, just before the war broke out, about the feasibility of establishing the legion to go out and fight in East Africa. Before the Tanga disgrace, the authorities brushed the idea off, but after Tanga they accepted all the help offered, and the legion was on its way.

About 1,100 men arrived in Mombasa. General Tighe and Dick were on hand to welcome the men at a parade, but the general didn't bargain on Dick and Selous renewing acquaintance in the middle of the parade, where they began discussing the virtues of the Nakuru hartebeest and the nesting habits of the harlequin duck in Iceland. Tighe became tetchy and reminded Dick he had come to inspect a battalion, not listen to debates on natural history.

The British and their allies were being pushed by the Germans, and there were plenty of skirmishes up and down the country where the legion saw action. Malaria and dysentery, however, cut the strength to a mere 450 combat-ready men after twelve months, and Selous was at the top, never ill and never down. In a solid year Selous had not taken a day off or been absent from duty for whatever reason. He went on to earn the Distinguished Service Order for "conspicuous gallantry" and took part in many a mission before being shot dead near the village of Behobeho, northwest of the Rufiji River delta, on January 4, 1917. He was buried in the shade of a tamarind tree, which is mentioned in the obituary pasted into one of Selous's autographed books and which is one of the great treasures in my personal collection.

The point about the campaign near Behobeho, which involved the legion, was that P. J. Pretorius was supposed to be on that particular mission in the place of Selous but there was a last-minute change of plan. Smuts changed the orders, substituting Selous for Pretorius to lead the Behobeho expedition. Pretorius escaped sure death on several occasions through such changes.

Selous's passing evoked immense sadness throughout the armed forces. Even the Germans, through Von Lettow-Vorbeck, expressed regret at the demise of a great gentleman and soldier and naturalist. But there were several memorable military clashes before this, and Dick was there to record them.

It was clear that the big push was in France and that the East African theater was a mere backwater. This distressed Dick, who wanted to get going in an all-out offensive against the Germans and not just adopt a largely defensive position to protect their side of the border. But this was out of the question with the troop strengths of the day. There was, however, still plenty to do. Activity was being stepped up right along the border with German East, and Meinertzhagen had the opportunity of engaging in psychological warfare, which had a pretty devastating impact on the enemy in one instance. It involved a place southwest of Mombasa called Kasigau where German patrols were being encountered. How to stop them dead in their tracks without resorting to actual combat?

Poison.

Water takes on a particular meaning in the African bush, where you can't just drop by the local store for bottled whatever. In parts of the East African theater, huge stretches of country were like cracked leather in the dry season and not much better with the rains. What water holes existed were focal points for man and the animals that shared their domain with him. It was an unwritten precursor to the bush Geneva Convention that water holes were sacrosanct and that you left them as you found them, pristine, even if dangerously low at times.

The old saw about love and war and all being fair comes to mind. Dick sprang into action to fetter the German patrols, sending out a shooting party to down birds and some plains game. The dead creatures were then scattered about a fairly major well in the Kasigau region and a notice reading POISONED was stuck in the ground next to the pool.

The effect was immediate. One German patrol not only turned back without drawing water, but one of the members actually died of thirst on the return journey, provoking an official complaint about respecting water resources in wartime. Dick, naturally, didn't bother to reply. His action secured well over eighty miles of Uganda Railway from German attacks because the enemy couldn't launch such attacks without having access to fresh water at Kasigau. There was nothing in the rules about not bamboozling the enemy. Hell, Dick was only getting into his stride.

Water, or lack of it, hampered communications. A wireless station on the western shores of Lake Victoria, at Bukoba, assured liaison with der Vaterland, and something had to be done to smash this conduit of information and orders. In the early hours of the morning of June 22, 1915, the Royal Fusiliers disembarked just north of Bukoba, other forces landing too, with a mountain battery in tow. The air was shivering with tension as the troops pushed forward to the ultimate target, the wireless station.

Dick was with the King's African Rifles, but not for long. The North Lancs under one Jourdain were supposed to be deflecting the enemy, but the commander was a shaking mass of nerves, terrified of casualties, paralyzed, immobile. Dick, a junior officer, lit into Jourdain and threatened to take over the command himself if he did not move. Still nothing. Then came an order from above that Dick would indeed take over if the commander didn't get his cowardly act together and proceed with his maneuver before nightfall. Jourdain moved. Dick watched, sickened no doubt at the sight of a grown man masquerading in the King's uniform.

Enemy fire rained down on the advancing Allies, who nevertheless managed to contain the Germans despite tactical blunders and sheer operational idiocy reminiscent of the Tanga disaster. Dusk fell and the Allies dug in, watching their German prey like a leopard about to spring on an impala lamb, eyes straining in the gloom, ears nervously alive for the slightest move to break out. It was quite cold that night, and everybody was very hungry because nobody had thought about rations for this situation. How the empire lasted as long as it did is a source of some amazement when it couldn't seem to get out of its own shadow, let alone organize a military assault. One would have thought that the Tanga disgrace of a mere seven months previous would have made the commanders look sharp and get with it. Nothing doing. Jourdain had another attack of the jitters, which cost the Allies dearly, allowing some of the Germans to break out and take their guns and some portable wireless gear with them.

A bloody clash ensued, Dick killing a man at about five yards and winging another, going on to take another German soldier in classic sniper mode with his Mannlicher. The Allies' mountain guns boomed down on Bukoba from a rocky outcrop, making up for the lousy shooting by the naval guns. The Fusiliers took Bukoba, marching into the settlement, where they hauled down the German flag and hoisted the Union Jack to cheers and shouts. The wireless station was demolished in what was the first genuine success the British had had in the East African war so far.

Then the fun started.

General Stewart, a man Dick quietly despised, gave permission for Bukoba to be looted "provided there was no violence or drinking."[19] That's like letting a lion into an enclosure with a juicy young buffalo calf and expecting it not to start snacking. Dick was appalled. The Fusiliers got roaring drunk, women were being raped, troops were abusive to their officers, and all semblance of military control vanished. What sober Lancs there were had to be called in to restore order as Dick's stomach turned at the sight of part of his own regiment behaving like a bunch of Visigoths gone mad on the spoils of war.

The scene was straight out of a bush bacchanalia as British officers cavorted in German helmets, African porters sported the latest in German ladies' lingerie, puffing all the while on imported cigars, quaffing champagne, and throwing stones at a larger-than-life picture of the kaiser. Stone the crows with a difference.

There was a lighter moment, though. A certain Major Turner with a terrible stutter looted a tame parrot with the intention of teaching it proper English. As the bird was taken away all it could squawk continuously was "Ach, du Schwein!"

Chapter 9

Whether you are hunting man or beast, you will get nowhere without accurate information. That is what pro hunters and trackers are for. That is what intelligence officers are for—to provide the forces with sufficient information so that when an assault is planned it can have the maximum effect with the minimum loss of manpower and matériel.

General Malleson, a not very talented man, jeered at Meinertzhagen's information in July 1915 on the eve of an assault on the Germans at Mbuyuni just north of Voi on the Uganda Railway. He branded Dick an amateur whose work was not worth considering. Dick had warned the general that if he tried to attack the Germans entrenched there he would be overwhelmed by a force of over 3,000 men and some twenty machine guns, the extra forces coming in from surrounding areas, Dick giving the breakdown as to strengths and armament.

Malleson and 1,100 men moved out in broad daylight from Maktau, just fourteen miles away from the target. Of course the German patrols spotted the activity and reported back to their superiors, but not before actually firing on the Brits and their allies. The next day, after a frontal assault on an enemy vastly superior in numbers and, as seems likely, in training and morale too, Malleson was thumped. His poor judgment and arrogance cost 170 lives, a machine gun, and, according to Dick, 40,000 rounds of ammunition.

It says something about Dick's iron resolve and sense of duty that he did not buckle under the stupidity of his so-called superiors. He had seen intelligence warnings ignored at Tanga the previous year. He had seen intelligence reports brushed off concerning enemy strengths at Jasin on the coast north of Tanga in January of 1915 where the British were given a hiding. His warnings about Salaita, just east of Taveta, were disbelieved and the British were really thrashed there. Dick's caveat about the Bukoba operation on Lake Victoria was not heeded, and valuable time was lost. To feed his prejudices and anger, thirty or so men of the Twenty-ninth Punjabis suddenly manifested wounds to the left hand during the Mbuyuni circus—self-inflicted wounds. Dick had long since doubted this bunch, and he had seen General Stewart hushing up the poor discipline after disastrous military encounters in 1914. Instead of coming clean, reporting the truth to the War Office, and getting rid of the flotsam for the sake of the lives of the real soldiers, the commanding officers covered up. In anger, Dick writes; "Heavens, what a lot of trash we have out here. Why is it that the Indian Army is so bad? I imagine we should not now be in India if it were as good as we are."[1]

Well, Dick was never accused of being short on opinions. He sometimes comes across as a typically arrogant colonial of empire times but for a decisive man such as he was, being subordinated to fools and cowards was a particular punishment. It simply fed his scheming brain.

Take the incident at Mansa Bay. Lying just to the north of Tanga and opposite Pemba Island, it provided the history books with an example of what Dick termed "criminal folly."[2]

In April 1915 a German supply ship arrived off the coast. It was sighted by the British, who opened fire at long range and scored what they thought was a hit. The next thing the British saw was flames on the deck as the steamer appeared to run aground at Mansa Bay despite a so-called blockade. Several explosions ripped into the air, and everyone was satisfied the steamer had actually blown up and, consequently, destroyed whatever supplies were onboard.

Wrong.

Rule number one in the intelligence world and in warfare: never underestimate your enemy or presume one solitary thing until you have solid proof. The British navy, under one Admiral King Hall, who made a royal mess of this incident, presumed the German vessel was wrecked and, therefore, that there was no need to investigate further. Not only that, but the admiral saw no reason to brief Dick and other relevant personnel as to the entire episode.

Dick's agents put him straight, and he approached the admiral, who was at first not even willing to talk to a mere army officer, what. Second rule: do not underestimate the abilities of your own forces, even if they are in a different arm of the service and not one of the "annointed." The naval fossil was up against Meinertzhagen and would eventually learn what *that* meant.

Proof was coming in that the Germans and their askaris were using "1915" ammunition and that there was even an example of pretty liberal use of ammunition that did not fit the pattern. It was known that the Germans were short of rifle ammo, and now this extravagance. Something didn't add up. Several sources in Dick's network then reported back that the enemy had, in fact, managed to salvage a veritable armory from the so-called wrecked vessel in Mansa Bay—like hundreds of cases containing rifles, thousands of rounds of ammo, machine guns, and who knows what else given the German bent for thoroughness. When they resupplied, they really resupplied. One of Dick's agents even helped the enemy unload so the information was corroborated right and left.

Dick was told of the salvage operation while it was in progress and wanted the ship blown up because if the resupply went ahead, this could actually prolong the war in East Africa indefinitely. Everything Dick suggested was vetoed. Nobody wanted to "have a row with the Navy,"[3] as General Tighe put it. Despite being confronted with hard evidence of the most serious kind, the British did nothing, and Dick had to stand by and see the enemy rearm to such a degree that they even had six new field guns where previously the Germans had no such matériel. The picture had altered quite dramatically, and Dick was impotent in the face of the cringing, craven behavior of people like Tighe and King Hall. As he said, "This 'scratch-my-back' policy is ruining us out here. Everyone tried to screen his pal or smooth over instances of criminal folly, with the result that hundreds of lives and millions of money (sic) are sacrificed."[4]

There was little to no cooperation with the navy who, if they passed on any intelligence at all, did so once it was stale. Dick's constant requesting of intelligence reports was ignored, and every effort of his to gather information on the coast was thwarted. The whole scene was a stagnant, passive pool of incompetence. Dick seethed.

He smoldered all the more when he learned exactly what the Germans had done in Mansa Bay. They had purposely poured petrol on the deck and set it alight to give the impression to the British that the ship had caught fire. Certain explosives were then detonated to really cement the belief that the steamer was a goner. The complacent pommies believed what they heard and what they thought they had seen but had never followed up. The enemy then moved in and emptied the vessel so that they could *really* start making a noise—brilliant camouflage tactics. Dick was on to them, but nobody would listen to his warnings and advice. When one of the British patrols, composed of Muslims, broke off a pursuit operation against the enemy in order to observe the mandatory sunset prayers and the enemy got away, Dick thought he'd heard it all.

He understood unconventional warfare but he was pretty well alone in this. When seeing the Uganda Railway being blown up in places every week, the British not making a single successful capture or strike in this respect, Dick bluntly stated that any village in the neighborhood of such an attack should be burned to the ground and the headman strung up because the enemy was quite obviously getting cooperation from the locals and this was clearly a case where savage and swift action had to be taken to get the tribal people to report German movements. Dick had already adopted this tactic with success elsewhere.

For those who have experienced guerrilla warfare, there are no rules. Initiative and undaunting flexibility are the name of the game. It's useless mouthing words like Geneva Convention in such situations. As of this writing, there are dozens of guerrilla conflicts going on in many areas of the world where ditherers are goners, whatever cause they are defending.

Dick had his chance to brace the admiral, whom he found to be "a quite mediocre, stupid, vain little brain devoid of humour and lacking intelligence and initiative."[5] He packed it out to the admiral who, irritated, doubtless admired Dick's fearlessness and invited him to dinner. This did not remove the anger and shock later on when Dick discovered that the admiral had withheld information about another German supply ship that had broken through the supposed blockade near Tanga, and that a wealth of detail about the *Königsberg* had not been passed on to him. The impasse with the navy continued, and it is no accident that it was Pretorius, a South African under the command of Smuts, who eventually located the battle cruiser and organized her demise. Had it been left entirely to the British navy of the day, they would still be bumbling about the Rufiji Delta trying to figure out which end was up.

Dick was in the depths of gloom at what he knew was a loss of initiative on the part of the British, who could now no longer dream of invading German East Africa when they were barely holding on to their side of the border. But there was always something to laugh at—like the postcard General Malleson received, supposedly from General Von Lettow-Vorbeck, with just two words on it: "Thank you." That said it all.

Dick, sometimes impetuous, always fearless, especially in the face of fools, cowards, and incompetents, had the interesting experience of being branded a spy by implication when the editor of the local newspaper in Nairobi cast aspersions in August 1915 about his German surname. He had the fat, boozed pen pusher arrested and arraigned to appear before a court-martial the next day, and had the paper suspended. Dick was decisive and not many people could match him, including the generals under whom he served. Whether it was the foul-mouthed bully Malleson or the inept Sheppard and Tighe, this didn't matter to Dick. He had a job of work to do and was being hamstrung by the very people who should have been listening up for all they were worth. He was not about to put up with the slander of the local hack.

Another factor that bugged Dick and the military was the apathy and generally poor relations with the civilians in the embryonic Kenya Colony. Something had to be done about this, and Dick was the man. He and Ewart Grogan, the man whose story of his epic walk from the Cape to Cairo is another of the gems in my library, organized a mass meeting in Nairobi to ginger up the population. Everybody pitched—hunters, soldiers, traders, British officials, assorted settlers and Indians—to hear Grogan. His fame and the fame of his elephant-hunter brother, Quentin, drew in the people, who passed a resolution demanding compulsory military service. The response by the locals was excellent. They now realized the seriousness of the situation with the kaiser on their doorstep and were prepared to join in and go all out to hammer the Huns and send them packing.

But animals were never far out of the picture, even if it was a lion hunt with a difference. Malleson, whose bumbling ineptitude even got the attention of Tighe when he wasn't in the tight embrace of Dame Wampo, had been summoned to Nairobi, where Tighe was about to tell him of his intention to send him back to India. Malleson, not a total fool, had a day to play with in order to scheme. He organized a lion hunt—just outside Nairobi, where there had been no lions sighted in the past two decades!

The driver was told to pick him up again that afternoon after the lion hunt. But that afternoon there was no Malleson. A search party was sent out to scour the countryside that night. Hopes were starting to rise that maybe, just maybe, a lion had wandered in and eaten the general. The next day, in comes the man on a mule, disheveled and worn out, with an elaborate tale of being "treed" by a "troupe" of lions all night and into the next day.

It was rubbish, of course. Malleson was manipulating Tighe, who felt sorry for the old boy and, far from firing him via the War Office, took care of him and sent him off to bed after being overcome with pity. Dick's intelligence scouts were soon able to discount the nonsensical story. There was open rebellion in the ranks against Malleson, who saw fit to let it be known publicly that he was out to get Dick and his intelligence section. He had quarreled with everyone, but Dick remained resolute in his task.

The "old and the bold" certainly weren't slacking. The man who was once commander in chief of the Honduran army had a bright idea about making a long-distance gun, which would launch "dynamite bombs." Comes the day of the field test overlooking the Athi Plain outside Nairobi and, with much pomp and pride, a

The "dynamite" gun during World War I, outside Nairobi, 1916. Just before firing. (Courtesy of Ran Meinertzhagen and Rhodes House Library, Oxford)

target is set up at about 1,500 yards, and a hush descends over the soldiers and ordnance department observers as the lanyard is pulled. Santo Dios if the damn thing doesn't blow up in the barrel, letting loose a foul stench of gases and smoke amid a terrific explosion. The pictures on page say it all. Exit the Honduran. On with the war.

Sedition, always a part of any war and the target of any intelligence officer's activities, took on an interesting aspect in East Africa. Floods of pamphlets and such like were coming in from the States, inciting the Indians to rise up against the Brits, thus undermining the Indian army in its task. Dick got hold of such literature and trapped the main distributor in Nairobi. He gives no details except to say that he had the man sent to jail for ten years. Dick didn't fool around. He was devastatingly effective when not crossed by his own people.

In between the mail train being blown up on the Uganda Railway, despite advanced warning from Dick's intelligence network,

The "dynamite" gun during World War I, outside Nairobi, 1916. Just after firing. (Courtesy of Ran Meinertzhagen and Rhodes House Library, Oxford)

old Tighe was now showing signs of advanced alcoholism. His gout made him like a lion with hyenas hanging on to its buttocks and Dick couldn't understand how the man could be surely killing himself with booze "in the middle of the greatest war in history."[6] Distinct signs of delirium tremens set in, the old chap convinced not only that the boat they were traveling in on Lake Victoria was going backwards but that it was on fire, and being furious when contradicted.

German East Africa, a vast land of malarial swamps, rivers, mountains, thick forest, and vicious thornbush country, was starting to get the attention of the people back home. World War I was a war of rival empires, the British and the German, two of the European powers who had agreed to carve up Africa at the 1884–1885 conference in Berlin and then again in Brussels in 1890. The history books tell us that the Germans resorted to the utmost brutality in their efforts to subjugate their part of East Africa. They were not about to go quietly now, and Meinertzhagen says bluntly in his diaries that "civilised warfare in tropical Africa is quite off the picture. . . . Modern warfare cannot be waged in the tropics, in thick bush and against a determined enemy."[7] He foresaw a drawn-out war of attrition and horrendous expenditure in terms of money and lives. He was right, of course.

Tighe had to go. In his place came Sir Horace Smith-Dorrien, one of a mere handful of British officers to have survived the bloody and terrible defeat at Isandhlawana in Zululand, South Africa, in 1879, where the Zulus rose up against everything the British Empire could throw at them, leaving the corpses of almost 1,000 redcoats strewn about the battlefield. But fate played a strange card. Smith-Dorrien was taken seriously ill by the time the ship reached Cape Town, and he was replaced by Jan Christian Smuts as head of the huge colonial army pitted against the Germans. Almost 20,000 South Africans, all volunteers, left for British East Africa in what was now to be a full-scale, all-out attempt to crush the Germans and end the war. The South Africans set sail in December 1915 for East Africa.

Meinertzhagen already knew what lay ahead of the new forces: heat, periods of torrential rain, thirst, lack of food, dangerously long communication lines, malaria, dysentery, diarrhea, the scourge of horse sickness and tsetse fly, jigger fleas, and army ants. Marauding wild animals such as lions, leopards, hyenas, and jackals were a further hazard. In what sounds like the script of a B-rated horror movie, even Meinertzhagen could not have foreseen the level of suffering among the Allied troops and their animals, once they invaded German-held territory. There were to be outbreaks of smallpox and typhus as well, resulting in high death rates and the loss of huge numbers of troops. It has been said that not since the Crimean War had there been disease and suffering on such a scale. But everyone thinks of Europe when they speak of this world war. The East African theater was forgotten in a peculiar way. That did not lessen the drama that was unfolding, Dick being in the front ranks as he observed the horror and the defeats before the arrival of fresh forces and a new spirit under Smuts.

Just before Christmas 1915, Dick was out scouting water holes in the Voi district where he sniped at and killed three Germans with great precision. All his hunting skills were brought into play time and again as he stalked, reconnoitered, and, occasionally, killed. A belated Christmas party with a difference awaited Dick, his fellow officer by the name of Drought, and fifteen of his intelligence scouts up in the Lake Victoria region when they crossed the border into German territory in the Karungu area, traveling light and fast, with only their rucksacks.

An enemy patrol was spotted at dusk on Christmas Day, numbering some fourteen men and a German officer. This bunch were so damn sure of themselves that they had no sentries posted and were lounging about the camp, their weapons in their tents. The officer in command, who was supposed to be responsible for maintaining a militarily and mentally alert force at all times, was in his tent, feeding his fleshy face with all sorts of delicacies from Deutschland, no doubt. He was the "duke" or, more correctly, the count met at the beginning of this literary adventure who, stupid enough to attempt to draw a firearm on Dick, was shot dead in an instant. Dick and his officer pal Drought then sat down to "one of the best though most gruesome dinners I have ever had, including an excellent Xmas pudding."[8] The cooling corpse in the same tent didn't put the two men off one bit. Duly refreshed, Dick, Drought, their forces, and some prisoners headed for British territory, arriving back in Karungu on December 26.

A new year had dawned, and the South Africans had arrived in force to finish off the war, as they thought, in a few months. It is curious for me to be reading Dick's thoughts on the South Africans now, in 1995, after the tumultuous changes in South Africa, which have seen the dominant Afrikaner people reduced to a very much second-class political profile in every way. Then they were clamoring for their independence from Britain and told Dick that they were taking part in the East African campaign to help Britain and, essentially, to win points and push for complete independence. As one Boer said, "If you don't give it, we shall take it."[9]

Back then, in becoming better acquainted with the South Africans, Dick blows hot and cold and is full of contradictions when he writes of them. One minute they are splendid soldiers, steady under fire and disciplined, the next they have no discipline, are cowardly, do not understand bush warfare, are guilty of looting, and "hospitals are full to overflowing with strong healthy men suffering from cold feet."[10] He had the highest regard for Smuts yet accused him of not listening to the advice of his British staff officers, "although he gulps down and digests any disconnected trash from a Boer scout."[11] Was he taking a prejudiced swipe at the legendary "Jungle Man" Pretorius, the very man he thought truly exceptional? We'll never know.

Dick slams the racist attitudes of some of the South Africans and their underestimation of the black enemy troops for whom he had a very healthy respect. Yet Dick's diaries reveal on more than one occasion a dislike of black people and indeed of anyone not of his class and race, as already noted. But on with the battle. This complex man's psychological makeup is not the point of this book. His glorious adventures and cunning bravery are.

Sowing confusion is one of the prime tasks in undermining enemy morale. Dick hit on the idea of using counterfeit money when he took a German prisoner and laid hands on some wartime twenty-rupee notes. These were sent back to Britain so that a similar paper could be matched and a few million twenty-rupee notes printed for distribution in German East Africa. It would not be long before the soldiers and traders realized that they were dealing with worthless bits of paper and that all their combined efforts and hardships were in vain. Dick went to great lengths to have the newly printed notes bleached and baked in the sun, grubbied up, and rumpled to look authentic. There must have been untold numbers of scenes among the soldiers and with anonymous traders scattered thither and yon, yelling and threatening one another as the awful truth sank into their collective skulls that someone, somewhere, had caught them and caught them thoroughly. Nothing erodes fighting morale quicker than a sense of being defeated and cheated, of being conned by a faceless foe and of not being able to do a damn thing about it.

Dick was to be engaged in many battles under Smuts and against the Germans, but he was also up against chronic incompetence and prevarication by his own people. Take the fresh attempt to conquer the Germans at Salaita Hill in the shadow of Kilimanjaro. Dick urged decisive, bold action especially in this area, as this could shorten the entire war. But Smuts, nervous of casualties, preferred to engage in a series of "maneuvers." Dick tried to drum it into Smuts and the general staff that, with fresh, eager forces and with firsthand knowledge of the terrain, now was the time to strike in strength and with total determination.

Nothing doing. When the attack against Salaita Hill eventually took place, it was all but deserted. The Huns had set heading that morning. Foot-dragging, lack of dynamic leadership and decisions, incompetence by Malleson and company, and a drunken Tighe resulted in Smuts exploding and stating to Dick one evening, "Meinertzhagen, I am now beginning to understand how it was that we always outwitted your leaders in South Africa [referring to the Anglo-Boer War of 1899–1902]. Are they all like this?"[12]

That night, Dick rode back east to Mbuyuni, about twenty miles or so, but not before being fired on by one of his own patrols and having clearly hungry lions roar all about him as he cantered through the bush with a not-too-reliable compass. He says of that night that "it is nerve-wracking work."[13]

Smuts started cleaning house after that, getting rid of the has-been General Stewart, if he'd ever been up to speed in the first place. Tighe and Malleson soon followed, but not before the latter actually deserted the battlefield in the Taveta region, which the Allies had managed to take and from where they were launching attacks. Dick could scarcely believe his eyes on March 12, 1916, when he saw Malleson leaning back on a cushion and puffing a cigarette as his car and driver headed for Voi—in the opposite direction of the battle. The general wasn't feeling well. Smuts called the man a coward, which jangled several raw nerves in Dick, who writes, "I dislike a Dutchman calling an English general a coward."[14]

Here, the word "Dutchman" is used more as a term of abuse than to denote country of origin. By 1916, the Afrikaans-speaking people of South Africa, the Boers, were no more Dutch than I am Irish, although they were descended from seventeenth-century Dutch/Flemish stock, as I am descended from very early nineteenth-century Irish stock on my mother's side. In fact, as I soon learned, there is no love lost between the Afrikaners and the Dutch people. Time and again over the years I would hear jibes against the Dutch, and the few Dutch people I have met had a superior attitude toward their African cousins and their "kitchen-Dutch" language.

In between dealing with dallying generals and wasted opportunity, Dick also had the task of getting rid of two local mission-educated blacks who were caught cutting ground cables used by the artillery to connect them to their forward observation posts. Dick, who could never just stand about doing nothing, summoned a firing squad and shot both men after hard evidence was found. News of this event no doubt traveled through the bush Internet faster than a modern computer signal, reaching the ears of any other troops thinking of swopping loyalties. Dick could be a persuasive man.

His reconnaissance reached new heights, quite literally, when he went up in an airplane for the first time on March 11, 1916. His pilot, a young South African, took off with him from Mbuyuni for the purpose of scouting the enemy's position at Latema–Reata, southeast of Taveta and Kilimanjaro, on German-held territory. Dick's emotions surged as he saw herds of hartebeest, oryx, and giraffe rippling beneath him over the dawn-washed plains, their shadows chasing them as the roar of the plane skimmed over them like some demented creature from another world. Up and up the tiny aircraft climbed as it reached for the snow-capped crater of Africa's highest mountain. Dick flew close to the snow as bitterly cold wind knifed through his clothing, his horizon filled with the hazy distant plains of bush and sky.

Descending, Dick flew over Taveta, Moshi, and part of the deserted Usambara Railway before spotting Germans at a railway bridge over the Lumi River, which fed into a much larger-looking Lake Jipe. Suddenly shrapnel burst around Dick and the pilot, but they were not hit as their engines drowned out the noise, bringing them into Mbuyuni to land. Dick's head felt like jelly and his ears seemed plugged with wads of cotton wool, his mind in overdrive as he tried to get back to work. What a start to a new day!

A few days later, at a place called Kahe, southeast of Moshi in enemy territory, Dick decided to undertake a personal reconnaissance patrol of the German position. Slipping out toward dusk,

Dick followed the railway line for a while before penetrating the bush where he was guided by a "decent moon,"[15] as he put it, and managed to sneak up to within a few yards of an encampment of enemy soldiers. With incredible luck, he had not bumped into any pickets on the way in.

Funny how the things learned along the way in life suddenly come in use. Take Dick's excellent knowledge of the German language. As he blended with the shadows next to the enemy camp, he was able to eavesdrop on quite loud conversations, all informing him of the general trend of things back at the main German camp farther away at the Pangani Road Bridge. The patrols were so close at one stage, that Dick could have reached out and touched them. The blood drummed in his temples, his heart thickening his throat with floating anxiety at one point when a patrol would stare right at his very position. Again, only those who have been into deep reconnaissance work, well behind enemy lines, can know the mad surges of emotion that attack you. You want to open up and kill the lot. Then you want the ground to swallow you. You have an urge to shout your presence, then to slip back into the gloom and get going before you are detected, captured, or worse.

Dick stayed long enough to estimate the enemy strength at the main camp before melting into the bush and heading back to base at Old Moshi. With thoughts hammering in his head as he memorized details, his clothing damp with sweat, Dick had to swim the crocodile-infested Rau River as he made his way back as fast as he could travel. Thinking he was outside the enemy picket line, he slackened off a little.

It was then that it happened. Suddenly, the moon-punctuated blackness was broken by a voice not six paces from him; Dick was challenged. Knowing that it was too dark for his clothing to be made out properly, Dick answered back in Swahili and strode up to the man, clearly an askari. Lowering his rifle and before the sentry could even think to raise the alarm, Dick drove his bayonet right through him, tugging it out again as he accelerated his pace to get out of the hot area. He was back at base by midmorning, worn out with that strange exhilaration you feel when your life has been threatened but you have survived.

Smuts was briefed on the reconnaissance and given the information. On hearing the details he blurted out, "Meinertzhagen, you're mad, stark, staring. It's not your business to undertake this sort of risk, so please do not do so again."[16] Dick tried to explain to the boss that he actually enjoyed this sort of work and that, in any case, he was the best qualified of all his team to undertake such a mission. Smuts still thought him touched.

The Allies launched their attack but failed to go all the way, as Van Deventer of the South Africans feared casualties. It was a great opportunity flushed away and an example of the sort of tactics Dick would see time and again. He felt that, with a little more effort, the enemy could have been cleaned out of the area and the campaign finished right there. Dick was disappointed in the South Africans, who were very quick to talk contemptuously of the black troops but not so quick to face them in battle. Dick had a high opinion of the askaris, who were disciplined and tenacious fighters. They could take a great deal of punishment and were unafraid to face up to fire. Von Lettow-Vorbeck's leadership, of course, had everything to do with the morale of the men. This was in searing contrast to the British commanders so far.

In the meantime, Smuts had cleaned house concerning his inept generals. The Allies had managed to secure the Kilimanjaro region and could take a break as the torrential rains set in, making it impossible to move about, let alone conduct campaigns. Dick and a couple of other members of the headquarters staff battled through to a place called Kondoa Irangi, southwest of Arusha, "amid torrential rain, deep mud, voracious mosquitos, the roar of lions, clouds of tse-tse fly and the loss of all our mules."[17] In fact, horse sickness slaughtered the mounts of the troops. The South Africans resorted to the much more hardy Abyssinian mule at a certain stage, but even these creatures didn't always make it.

The battle of Kondoa Irangi was to prove to be a turning point in East Africa. The troops, with their spine protectors, puttees, and mosquito shirts, were wide open to the dangers of disease, much more so than were the locals. They survived on salted bully beef and, despite the lushness of the countryside in many areas, never saw fresh fruit and vegetables. Tracks just disintegrated into deep muddy troughs as the mule teams, spans of oxen, and positive battalions of porters battled through the thornbush in searing heat. The soldiers suffered also from blistered feet, blood poisoning, and sunburn. Despite the torrents of rain, the muddy pools were undrinkable, and the soldiers, now under ever-increasing pressure, were afraid of being wounded and of being simply left for the lions.

The troops pushed forward into what was to become a march of about 200 miles in three weeks for the South Africans. The idea was to keep Von Lettow-Vorbeck busy in the east while the South Africans swept around to the southwest of Moshi and the Germans up to the German military station of Kondoa Irangi. Smuts intended to come down hard on the Germans' railway line and stop them from pushing west to Tabora. Smuts knew the Germans could not just abandon their lifeline.

The putrid stench of rotting animals lined the way. The carcasses drew wild animals, which had to be kept at bay at night by fires and thorny bomas. The men, now in a state of exhaustion and emaciation, kept on, ever on. Bridges over rivers had been swept away and giraffes had broken the telegraph lines, disrupting what communication there was. Jigger fleas would burrow under toenails, and there was always the danger of red ants and the voracious black soldier ant, the siafu, whose bite was like a white-hot needle jabbed into your skin. Thick mists shrouded the mornings as the soldiers and their retinues struggled through dank vegetation. Smuts, in a letter home, speaks of a croc attacking three tethered mules. It grabbed one by the muzzle and dragged the rest into the river, drowning all three for a feast of vast proportions later on.

As the morning wore on, the sky would turn into a furnace of unspeakable heat that grabbed the earth and the pathetic humans in an ever tighter and more suffocating embrace as the day passed. What vehicle transport existed was frequently out of commission because of a lack of spares. And the Germans were turning more to the sniper mode as they also stepped up ambushes and the mining of roads. Soap was a luxury, and food was becoming all the more scarce. Filthy rations of rice and fly-blown meat, for starters. Forget about fresh clothing or extra boots. The situation was now so chronic that the convalescent had all but no chance of ever really recovering sufficiently to resume active service. The actual terrain and climate, disease, and terrifying privation were turning into the real enemy. Morale was taking a knock. It was May 1916; the war had been going on for nearly two years. As fate would have it, Von Lettow-Vorbeck seemed not to truly know about the terrible state in which the enemy's forces found themselves. Malaria, dysentery, tick fever, blackwater fever, suppurating jungle sores, sandfly fever—all this in an age where antibiotics were unknown and communications often nonexistent.

Dick was out front, on scouting patrols, alarmed that the South Africans had not reinforced themselves in that critical situation. He kept urging Smuts to strengthen his presence at Kondoa Irangi. Dick's intelligence network clearly indicated that Von Lettow-Vorbeck had pumped in all the troops he could spare from his eastern forces and an attack was imminent. The Germans were planning to overwhelm the South Africans. As Dick wrote in his diary, "It is the Germans' only chance and von Lettow is no fool. . . . Kondoa is now the decisive point and the present is the decisive time. . . . Attack it he must and before the rains finish."[18]

A bursting shell in the early hours of the morning of May 9 changed all that. Trenches were dug, some wire barricades went up, and everyone was now on double alert as the smell of a final showdown made the whole atmosphere oppressive. Rifle and machine-gun fire erupted on the eastern flank in a moonless night, bullets whining and pinging as they went their deadly way. Two German assaults were repulsed before Dick plunged into a bayonet charge of a German machine-gun position. With that streak of ferocity that made up Dick's character, he ended up using his rifle as a club, smashing his stock on human skulls. With only his fists and boots as weapons in the sooty night, Dick took on what he thought was an askari, wrenching his knobkerrie from him and bludgeoning him until he fell silent, permanently silent. The victim turned out to be a German officer by the name of Kornatsky.

Dick kept the "beautifully balanced"[19] knobkerrie and carried it with him to the end of his days. It is now on display at the Royal Regiment of Fusiliers at the Tower of London, together with all Dick's honors, awards, and medals. But first he was to use it again— and again.

Dick was impressed with the South Africans, who "behaved splendidly. . . . Their fire discipline was perfect."[20] This was Von Lettow-Vorbeck's first real hiding and, as Dick said, "My God, I should have liked to have caught old von Lettow instead of poor Kornatsky."[21]

The operation was extraordinarily successful largely because, as Dick found out, the Germans had faulty intelligence and did not know that they were attacking the strongest link in the enemy chain. Dick's intelligence department was habitually accurate in its estimations of opposition strengths and organization, but, as already

stated, this information was often as not ignored by the commanders higher up the chain of command, except for Smuts, who respected the accuracy of Dick's work. In fact, now that the Allies
were close to German lines, Dick's intelligence methods were
proving so effective that he often knew the orders before the
German officers did.

All wars offer the chance of booty of one sort or another. Dick,
a class unto his own, laid an ambush with the help of 160 of his
top intelligence scouts and managed to capture the ensign from the
destoyed *Königsberg* battle cruiser in dense bush west of Ufiome.
All the Germans died in the clash, and Dick shared his only bottle
of champagne with the South African who brought in the treasure.
The flag hung in his London residence to the end of his life, "probably the only German naval ensign captured during the whole
war."[22] It now hangs in the Naval Museum at Greenwich.

Dick's scathing prejudice of the non-British surges to the sur-
face when he speaks of Portugal having "the effrontery to declare
war on Germany."[23] He roasts these Latins for their sheer nerve at
speaking of invading German East Africa. After a fiasco of an invasion at the mouth of the Rovuma River, the Portuguese had sent
for more troops, much to Dick's ire. He blasts this "miserable effete
and decadent nation"[24] and lambastes them for the way they ran
their colonies, fuming that "except for introducing every European
vice and withholding every European virtue, they have done nothing."[25]

Strange man, Dick. I wonder what he would have had to say
for himself had I been able to sit him down with a number of my
Portuguese refugee friends from Angola and Mozambique, among
them the founder of the devastatingly effective Flechas guerrilla
group, men who had stood their ground and looked death in the
eye, never flinching, people who had lost a whole way of life, often
under conditions of unspeakable savagery. This is an aspect of

Dick's makeup that disturbs me, that empire arrogance that colors his writing as he dismisses whole nations. I find this prejudice alarming in its crudity for a man so keen-witted and far seeing. It makes his later passion for Israel and the Jews all the more strange as, if ever there were a people who have been the convenient scapegoats of hate and prejudice through the ages, it has to be the Jews. Perhaps the nascent Israeli tenacity and fight got his attention. Meinertzhagen respected strength and, obviously, sniffed out corruption or weakness, perceived or real, and reacted accordingly. All I know is that life is not just black and white, right or wrong. It is often a sea of shades of gray, of nuances where there can be no clear-cut condemnation or approval. Dick and I would have had difficulty with this one. This fierce and solitary man exhibited flashes of xenophobia amid an undercurrent of contradictory attitudes on many issues. Maybe even he did not understand his mood swings.

The sweet taste of success after the Kondoa engagement lingered. Meinertzhagen had been scouting far behind enemy lines at one stage and, true to his makeup, when he and his party came across cases of schnapps he set fire to them all—no "Schnapp" debate about this one allowed! The enemy was being gradually contained on all sides and Dick's special intelligence system was in full operation, giving quick and surprisingly accurate information. Not that the upper echelons always listened, but Dick was used to that by then.

The Germans, feeling the mounting pressure, evacuated Tanga in June 1916. This had a very particular significance for the British after their disgraceful nonperformance in November 1914. Tanga was occupied by July 7 that same year, and general headquarters was established there in September. The navy, however, was in no position to take full advantage of this evacuation, for reasons that remained a pure mystery to Dick. The navy still refused to cooperate fully on intelligence matters. Dick simply kept going and, by that time, had trained 2,500 black scouts and several hundred agents. He had access to British Secret Service funds for payment of these people. One of the perks of the job was that Dick did not have to report casualties. Did that mean that if he lost any of his agents or scouts he simply wiped them from the list as if they had never existed? The thought bothered me when I read of this. But then I quickly remembered one of the tarnished golden rules of espionage: If you get into difficulties, we've never heard of you.

Dick came across a particularly dangerous form of professional jealousy as an intelligence officer. Commanders sometimes kept vital facts to themselves for fear that a fellow commander would get hold of them and make use of them. Dick even learned that information was being withheld from Smuts himself. The commander in chief confronted his subordinates on this, and Dick had his backing to do the same. But the politicking continued, and this added to the general stress of Dick's job.

The stress was multiplied by the apparent unwillingness of the South Africans to go on the offensive. Despite this situation, which resulted in many lost opportunities for the Allies, the Germans were eventually driven south of their Central Railway. It wasn't a question of defeating the Germans, but rather of outmaneuvering them. This withdrawal now a fact, the Allies moved in to occupy Morogoro, west of Dar es Salaam. They were now playing a cat-and-mouse game with Von Lettow-Vorbeck who, with his askaris, could live off the land in classic guerrilla fashion, Dick talking of the possibility of Smuts eventually rounding him up "somewhere near Pretoria."[26]

With the gradual flushing of the Germans southward, GHQ transferred to Dar es Salaam itself, where Dick reported on a pretty undignified scramble by the senior officers to grab the best accommodation and loot along the way. Having the SS *Professor* as their base off Dar es Salaam, the senior officers would go ashore on their house-hunting cum pillaging expeditions. One day the tables were nicely turned when their servants, who remained onboard, climbed in and helped themselves to everything of value from silk pajamas to shaving brushes. Dick was spared simply because he hadn't gone ashore.

The past two years had been years of singular stress for Dick. Not only was it a question of climate and disease; it was also a question of mental strain in dealing with senior but incompetent officers. It was the pressure of organizing from scratch and running an intelligence network, only to see much of the information misused or ignored. It was the accumulated frustration of seeing opportunity after battle opportunity evaporate for lack of decisive action and offensive thrust. Dick was cracking up, and, by the time October 1916 rolled around, he was showing the classic symptoms of a nervous collapse: inability to sleep, lack of appetite, periods of gloomy brooding, and working himself to a standstill on crazy plans.

It was decided to send Dick back to England for a desperately needed break. The Germans were now on the Rufiji River border with Portuguese East Africa, but there was still no indication of an actual surrender by the Germans. In fact, a captured German officer told Dick straight that the Germans couldn't surrender without a good fight and the enemy kept maneuvering instead of outright confrontation with the Germans. As he said to Dick, "Give us a good fight and if you win we may surrender, but surrender is impossible without a battle."[27] Dick launches into a tirade against the South Africans, accusing them of incompetence and worse. He was becoming increasingly cranky and contradictory, so it was a mercy when he was ordered home, accompanied by complimentary observations by Smuts, who knew his chief intelligence officer's value.

Dick sailed for Mombasa from Dar es Salaam and then traveled up to Nairobi with Fred Selous. I can think of no more wonderful companion than that legendary man. I have a particularly fine portrait of Selous hanging in our home in Pretoria, and I have so often wished that I could have known the man and his times. He and Dick obviously chewed the fat into the wee hours as they reviewed the East African campaign, a campaign that was eventually to cost 6,000 lives as a result of wounds and disease. Over 2,000 of the lives lost were South African. Of the original 1,100 "old and bold" Legion of Frontiersmen, only some 200 were still able to shoulder arms by July 1916. Come the end of the East African campaign, soon after the armistice on November 11, 1918, over 3,000 imperial soldiers had died, including the unique Fred Courteney Selous.

As Dick closes off this chapter of his extraordinary life, he speaks of the gallantry of the King's African Rifles and the fine soldiering by the Rhodesians. We all know what he thought of the bulk of the Indian regiments, but he speaks highly of the Beluchis and the Kashmiris. What I found touching was Dick's special mention of the African porters, without whom the entire war would have been impossible to conduct. Dick's hunting and general safari experiences gave him a particular insight into the value of these robust, tough men. Drawn mainly from the Kavirondo tribe, the porters were the logistics backbone of the campaign, and Dick rightly says, "The Kavirondo, as a tribe, have rendered distinguished service to our cause and I doubt whether it will ever be recognised."[28]

Before sailing for Plymouth from Mombasa in December 1916, Dick summed up the errors of the East African experience and stated that had the imperial forces had a man of Von Lettow-Vorbeck's caliber and, by contrast, if the Germans had had any of a bunch of British generals such as Malleson and company—even someone like Smuts—the war in East Africa would have been over

by the end of 1914. Dick blamed the Indian army and the British
War Office for the people chosen and the strategies adopted. The
cost in lives was staggering, and the cost in crass financial terms
equally so.

But the wheel turns, often mercifully so, and Dick's intelligence star was on the rise once more after a good rest in England.
Destination? Egypt and Palestine. Designation? Chief of intelligence to the Egyptian Expeditionary Force. The hunt was on again.

Mediterranean Sea

Haifa

Jaffa

Alexandria

Port Said

Gaza

Jerusalem

Beersheba

Palestine

Egypt

Cairo

Sinai Pen.

Nile

Red Sea

N

EGYPT, THE SINAI PENINSULA, AND PALESTINE

Chapter 10

Meinertzhagen was on the point of entering one of the most inspiring periods of his life: his time in Palestine. He was to strengthen an emotional bond with the Jewish people that reached back to his eccentric great-grandmother, who once was obsessed with helping return the Jews to their ancestral home. Such was the compulsion that she got on a white donkey with a group of Jews gathered about her and set off for Calais and Jerusalem straight after the Napoleonic Wars ended in 1815. She reached Calais, but the group had thought otherwise and her husband had to act out the earlier equivalent of 911 and rescue her and the donkey from France and bring them home.

Dick's passion for the Zionist cause would last until he died and would see him playing a very meaningful role in the founding of the modern State of Israel. Long before it was fashionable or politically correct to back the Jews in anything, let alone their quest for a return to their ancient homeland, Dick was out there beating up a Russian lout in the streets of Odessa in 1910 during a de facto pogrom where he rescued a little girl from a fate that cannot be imagined. He was recruiting young Palestinian Jews into his intelligence network out of Cairo during World War I. He, a Gentile, was to tackle anti-Zionists belonging to none other than the

Rothschild family as he pleaded the cause with a conviction not easily found today in this age of disposable relationships and switch-on/switch-off cultures. He was to get to know Chaim Weizmann, the eventual first president of Israel, very well and the mercurial revolutionary Vladimir Jabotinsky, among others.

Dick was also fated to spend many an anguished time before September 1939, sometimes in Germany itself where he even pleaded the cause of the Jews with none other than the Führer himself in July 1935, by which time vicious discrimination and persecution of German Jews was the new credo in high places. He also met Ribbentrop and Hess. He foresaw decades in advance the massive problems that Jewish and Arab nationalisms would create in the Middle East, and he never wavered in his pleadings and warnings about a national home for the Jewish people. As the Jew-baiting stories from Berlin reached Dick's ears, he doubled his efforts to warn of what was coming. He had already heard dark and terrible tales of concentration camps in operation well before the war was declared. And he was met with disbelief as he tried to convey the enormity of the tragedy that was unfolding before his intelligence-seeking eyes and ears.

But Dick first had a special road to travel in the Middle East before bracing the masters of the Third Reich. It was to have bumps, craters, and slippery patches as he got his bearings as chief intelligence officer to his new boss, the bull-like man of legendary name, Henry Hynman, First Viscount Allenby. This blue blood became Field Marshal Allenby and commander of the British forces in the Middle East and the man chiefly responsible for defeating the Turks in Palestine, resulting in the capitulation of Turkey herself. Dick's intelligence activities played a pivotal role in this drama.

But all such extraordinary events often have rather strange and dramatic beginnings of their own. Take Dick's embarkation in

Marseilles on the SS *Transylvania* on May 3, 1917. He had fully recuperated and had recently been released from the stifling atmosphere of the War Office in London, where the toadying and self-glorification among the officials so sickened him that he decided he would no longer wear the decorations he had already been awarded. This stubborn streak could infuriate others, but it was the sort of grit that was needed in a theater of war.

Nearly 3,500 troops were aboard ship with Dick, including about fifty horses, all bound for Egypt. They were escorted out of Marseilles Harbor by two Japanese destroyers, and the voyage started off reasonably enough, despite the danger of German submarines.

Then it happened. The troop carrier was struck late at night on the second day out and it sank within half an hour, just off the Ligurian coast of Italy at Savona or "Savogna," as Dick incorrectly calls it. Two hundred troops drowned, as well as twenty-five officers and an unrecorded number of horses. In the wet blackness of the night, his ears filled with the shouts of shocked men and the terrified whinnying of panicked horses, Dick found the bar, which was empty under the circumstances, and helped himself to two bottles of brandy. He figured that with a decent life jacket he may as well be half-seas over for the sinking. His by then trademark knobkerrie clutched tightly, he walked off the crazily sloping deck into the sea and alcoholic oblivion. But not before knocking a couple of horses on the head that were thrashing about wildly in the sea, one fetching Dick a terrific kick in his stomach. When he next came to, he found that he had been scooped up in a net by a Japanese destroyer, undressed by the sailors, taken below to dry out in both senses and to sleep. Two empty brandy bottles bore testimony to the night's events.

Dick had to spend some time in hospital where he heard the actual story of how a few people had seen a dark object coming

Richard Meinertzhagen at Advanced Intelligence Headquarters in Sinai, 1917. (Courtesy of Ran Meinertzhagen and Rhodes House Library, Oxford)

toward the ship and shouted, "Look at the porpoise!"[1] The "porpoise" was a torpedo, and a second followed it very quickly after that. And yet others. A collection of small boats helped rescue the troops in addition to the two Japanese destroyers but scenes of carnage told the rest of the story.

With a shipwreck to set him on his way, Dick eventually arrived in Cairo a few days late and made straight for the Savoy Hotel, which served as the general headquarters. Having got his bearings, Dick was posted out as chief of advanced intelligence in the northern Sinai at a place called Deir el Belah, south of Gaza on a beautiful stretch of coastline. His mission was effectively to take charge of intelligence for General Allenby.

Camped out on the beach at Deir el Belah, Dick had time to digest the task at hand. He was in charge of field intelligence, the other arm of Allenby's operation being political intelligence. Dick soon discovered that there was no really front-line intelligence network in operation and that the actual security at Dick's advanced HQ was absent, with no agents being deployed from there. This fired his engines and he soon had the troops on alert, a couple of Arabs being caught very quickly.

After what must have been a persuasive little chat with the Arabs, Dick soon had the name of the Arab in Beersheba to the east who was "running" these agents. History had a weird way of repeating itself in Dick's espionage activities. As he had done in East Africa, Dick wrote a flowery letter of thanks to the Arab in Beersheba, enclosing a dollop of Turkish money to sweeten the deal, expressing his appreciation for the info made available. A dull-witted agent was used to convey the letter. He was caught, the Beersheba Arab arrested and executed, thereby smashing the entire Sinai espionage ring. I noted with some interest that, this time round, Dick expressed no remorse at the outcome, no pangs of conscious, no soul-searching monologues with his diary as was the case with the East African spy who was killed by his German masters on the strength of a letter and money from Dick.

There was now a need to have agents in the field. Dick got together a group of Arabs and Jews, the latter all being refugees from Palestine led by a man by the name of Aaron Aaronsshon who, in Dick's books, was the equal of "Jungle Man" Pretorius when it came to scouting skills. He was the man who introduced Dick to the heart of Zionism.

His special "DPM" method was up and running, and soon Dick had the inside track on enemy strengths, dispositions, and plans. The added touch was a wireless receiving station placed on the Great Pyramid of Egypt used to decode enemy wireless traffic. What chutzpah! What panache!

By December 1917 Dick had developed some understanding of the Zionist ideal, and his diaries make for strange reading eighty years later, with the Arab/Israeli stop-go peace talks. Some of his observations about the Arabs and the Jews all those decades ago would strike many an observer today as still valid, Dick's comments showing from the outset that he admired the Jews. He was impressed by their belief in themselves, by their tenacity, and by their rock-solid sense of purpose after centuries of dispersion and suffering.

After his first meeting in July 1918 with Chaim Weizmann, who impressed him, Dick quite plainly stated that he would be prepared to back the Jews at any time, as they represented progress, although perhaps upsetting a few governments in the process. For Dick, the Arabs of the day meant stagnation and corrupt, dishonest society. It was not long before Dick was championing the cause of Zionism, of resettling the Jews in their ancient land because he regarded the homelessness of a great people a rampant injustice. Not entirely altruistic, Dick believed that a strong Jewish presence in the Middle East would be good for the British Empire, too. Dick would soon be exerting influence on men such as Smuts to back the Zionist vision.

With these early pro-Zionist stirrings now taking root, Dick had to turn his attention to the work in hand, namely the tracking down of a Scarlet Pimpernel–type German spy known as "Franks" who was believed to be crossing the lines as an Australian. Dick had an elaborate story concocted about this man's supposed feats, which so stoked the mental boiler rooms of the troops that they were arresting people at random, even Dick, in their search for Herr Franks. The upshot was that this increased vigilance meant it was that much harder for an enemy agent to cross the lines.

What followed was an extraordinary series of events. Dick happened to be visiting a prisoner-of-war camp in Alexandria where he was asked by the camp commander to see a prisoner who claimed to be a Greek who had deserted from the Turkish army and had actually worked with the elusive Franks. Until that meeting, Dick thought the whole Franks story a figment of somebody's distorted imagination, but now he had to revise his original attitude. He decided to take the Greek back to Cairo with him, where the Greek consul himself testified to the man's "Greekness." And the Greeks were neutral in the conflict.

The former prisoner was given certain pretty harmless but obviously authentic information to carry with him back across the Turkish lines, where he said he would be able to persuade Franks to accompany him back to Dick's side of the fence where he could be arrested. It all seemed too smooth to be true, and, as life teaches, when things appear to be too good to be real, that is usually the case.

Dick was to meet Franks and his Greek pal in an isolated dry watercourse. The day dawned and, indeed, there was the Greek but sans Franks. He mentioned that Franks would be along shortly. He also asked Dick if he was armed. Dick's brain whirred into alarm mode, no doubt about that. What a strange question to ask of an officer in a wartime entrapment scenario! But before he could develop this line of thought, along came an orderly on horseback in the late desert twilight, the Greek saying that this was Franks's orderly. A strange story followed, given by the orderly in German, that Franks had been chased off at some point back into Turkish lines. The Greek said he'd probably only show up on the same day the following week at the same meeting point.

Dick, his instinctive antennae now picking up disturbing signals, of course had to arrest the orderly, who was now some way off. Franks agreed and asked Dick if he'd mind riding up "to the side of the gully and see if the coast is clear for me and we'll then hold up the orderly."[2]

Not ten yards away, as Dick was mounting his horse, two rounds whizzed past him. Flashing around, his hand on his revolver, Dick was stunned to see the Greek and the orderly firing at him! His horse bolted in the madness that followed, and Dick emptied his automatic pistol, hitting the orderly in the neck while the Greek galloped off, leaving his agonized body thrashing about just in front of him, screaming in a high-pitched voice.

It was a woman. She died a few minutes later as Dick stood momentarily frozen with disbelief.

The woman had been dressed in British uniform but was a German. Her exact connection to Franks was a huge, stunned question mark as Dick roughly gouged out a hole in the bed of the dry watercourse, rolling the body into the improvised grave and covering it with sand and rocks.

That was July 13, 1917. In December of that same year, while Dick was conducting a search of Franks's house in Jaffa, he came across a photograph of the man and realized in retrospective horror that the man who had been authenticated as a Greek was none other than Franks, whose astounding knowledge of Greek got him released from the POW camp in Alexandria. Dick not only had traveled to Cairo with him but had had the man in his office, a de facto German agent. The next shock was to discover that the woman Dick had killed was his wife.

A new twist to the saying, Beware of Greeks bearing gifts.

Dick finally met Allenby and was struck by the man's dynamism and his determination to kick life into the Egyptian Expeditionary Force and be in Jerusalem by Christmas. GHQ moved into Palestine itself, to a place near Rafa, south of Gaza, by mid-August 1917. Australian and New Zealand troops boosted the forces as they prepared for an offensive toward the end of October.

Aircraft, though still in their infancy, were being used in reconnaissance flights over enemy lines, and Dick was in the air most mornings just after dawn. He even had a few basic flying lessons as he went about his actual business of observation and photography. On October 6 it happened. A German aircraft tailed them and plastered the aircraft with bullets, hitting the pilot, who lost consciousness, sending the aircraft out of control.

Dick forced his way into the pilot's seat, on top of the pilot, as the plane whirled and spun like a sick bird, looking for all the world like an aircraft about to crash. Dick managed to level the aircraft out, thanks to his couple of lessons, and to drop a message below asking how to land—the stuff of nightmares or lousy movies.

Dick came over the airfield, which was now a madhouse of people and fire engines, a message being spelled out on the ground with bits of calico cloth that he was to land AT 80. How do you land an aircraft if you have never done so before? Dick found out in a hurry as he bumped to the ground, slewing off the runway into rough terrain before coming to a nerve-wracking halt against a small palm tree. Fire engines and ambulances appeared out of the ectoplasm as Dick was helped down and the pilot evacuated to Cairo. Dick had a megadose of whatever as his nerves reacted to the ordeal. As he said in his diary, "I was very frightened and cannot work this evening."[3]

All the while Dick was observing the whole Palestine-Arab-Jew scene, developing his regard for the Jews and the Zionist cause and consolidating his attitudes about the Arabs and the effects of their religion on their outlook. These were not complimentary attitudes but, in reading Dick's thoughts on the issue, they strike one as those of a man who has had time to weigh up the situation, not those of an impetuous outsider quick to draw conclusions. The foundations Dick was laying now were to hold a lifetime of strong beliefs and take him into many a fray, often at the highest levels, as he fought for the Zionist cause and a home for the Jewish people. This cannot be done if the foundations of convictions are a mere veneer. And there was nothing shallow about Dick. Love him or loathe him, people just knew that Dick was a deep and complex man of strong persuasions. He was not to be trifled with.

Dick would use certain impressive strategies to confuse and deceive the enemy. He concocted a staff officer's notebook with supposed military plans to mislead the other side and then went off into the desert northwest of Beersheba with the idea of attracting the attention of a Turkish patrol. Spotted, Dick galloped off before pulling up, dismounting, and taking a couple of shots at the pursuing Turks.

Now for the crunch. Dick, being chased by the Turks, purposely dropped his knapsack, field glasses, and that most precious of objects in a desert, his water bottle, as well as his rifle. The expert touch was the bloodstain on the weapon that gave the impression that Dick had been hit. It was, in fact, horse blood Dick had obtained by nicking his mount in the interests of king and country. The whole idea was to confuse the enemy into thinking that this was the panicked withdrawal of an injured man who had dropped pretty well all his possessions in his anxiety to get away. The bogus officer's notebook was dropped, including maps.

The notebook contained information to persuade the enemy into believing that no offensive could take place before the middle of November and that when such an offensive did occur, it would be in the west, at Gaza.

To complete this picture of trickery and ruse, the Desert Corps orders published a notice asking that the finder of the notebook lost on patrol kindly return it forthwith to GHQ. A patrol was even dispatched the next day to search for the notebook. Talk about a needle in a haystack. Very few people were actually in the know as to the true situation, so Dick was regarded as an inexperienced officer when it came to reconnaissance work. Of course, the order from the Desert Corps found its way into enemy hands, confirming for them the authenticity of the notebook and its contents.

This ruse was backed up by wireless messages to strengthen the enemy's conviction that Beersheba was not the target. This tangled plot worked like a charm when the Allies attacked Beersheba on October 31, 1917. There were no reserves to withstand the attack, enemy forces having been concentrated in the west around Gaza. In an incident that reminded me of the Israeli blitz on Egyptian aircraft on the ground during the six-day war in 1967, a solid sixty years later, the Allies were able to destroy or capture all of the fifty aircraft sent down to the scene by the enemy before they could even be removed from their packing cases and be assembled.

Beersheba was a singular victory and the curtain raiser to Jerusalem.

Of course, Dick's imagination and creative impulses had a field day with intelligence work when he dreamed up yet another way to undermine the actual physical strength of the enemy.

Opium.

The Turks loved tobacco, so Dick arranged for small consignments of genuine cigarettes to be airlifted to them at regular intervals, starting in August of 1917. Dick's POW intelligence had informed him that there was a shortage of cigarettes in the Turkish army, so this daily sunset airlift was the proverbial manna from above for the troops. They'd scramble out of their trenches when the aircraft droned into view with its fragrant cargo.

They were hooked on very nice cigarettes and became even more so when the cigarettes changed character and were laced with opium on November 5, 1917. The result? On November 6, when the Allies launched a major attack on Gaza, the Turks were befuddled and some, later captured, were barely coherent. Their fighting strength had vanished, and the Allies notched up another victory as they pushed north, ever north, to Jerusalem. Maybe Dick had learned the eon's-old prophetic Hebrew prayer that had sustained the Jews in exile all over the world when it rang: Next year in Jerusalem!

It's interesting to note that Allenby had actually vetoed the idea of doped cigarettes but Dick secretly pursued the plan, believing that anything that limited casualties was justified. Years later, when Dick and Allenby were lunching together in London and he offered Dick a cigarette, which was declined, he said, "They are not doped."[4]

Clearly, Dick had had a puff at his toys and found the effect quite sublime, the ability to think and act gone. He managed to filch a few and bring them back to England, where he'd hand them out to the odd talkative passenger on train journeys so that he could have some peace.

Jerusalem was now the prize, one charged with emotive symbolism, and it fell to the Allies in January 1918. General Allenby strode through the gates of that great and ancient city that had seen the Roman legions come and go, followed by Crusaders and, ultimately, the Ottoman Empire, which held sway until that cold January day when the Allies claimed it back. What few realized was that General Allenby's surname sounded very similar to El Neby in Arabic, meaning "the Prophet." This mere linguistic accident leant a mystical perspective to raw soldiering and elevated Allenby's prestige to a status of quasi-veneration by some locals.

My wife, who was in Jerusalem not long after it was recaptured in the six-day war in 1967, told me of the powerful emotions conveyed to her by a sabra paratrooper and his wife whom she met while a student in France. They took her on a tour of the city, pointing out significant places, the husband having actually been in the Jerusalem operation. I could feel something of Allenby's elation as Fiona told of that other time just under fifty years later when this same city was the subject of overwhelmingly emotional scenes.

Soon after this unique day in Dick's life, he was ordered back to the War Office in England, but not before Allenby wrote officially that "this officer has been largely responsible for my successes in Palestine."[5] Coming as this did from Allenby, it was praise of the highest kind.

The War Office. After the challenges and exhilaration of field operations, after becoming inspired with the Zionist ideal, and after having lived for a while in that ancient part of the world, Dick came back to earth and mundane realities with a thud one morning when he was abruptly asked by an officer in one of the War Office's murky passages why he wasn't wearing the regulation socks. Half out of disbelief at the sheer banality of the question, half out of good old Meinertzhagen ire, Dick replied to the senior officer, "Damned if I know."[6] A verbal scrap followed, and Dick had to accept that he was back in another world, a world he would not be able to inhabit for much longer. He was a fighter, an action man, the original individual, and there was no way he could fit the mold of these humorless gray little men who helped run the empire.

Not three months before Dick was back in London, the British foreign secretary, A. J. Balfour, wrote to Lord Rothschild, chairman of the British Zionist Federation, stating that His Majesty's Government was in favor of the establishment of a national home in Palestine for the Jewish people. This Balfour Declaration, as it came to be known, was to be the cornerstone of the eventual founding of the State of Israel in 1948, and Dick was immediately aware of the problems of Arab and Jewish aspirations competing in that narrow neck of land that had been the crossroads of millennia of strife.

Dick gave weekly lectures at the War Office on Palestine, Mesopotamia, and the East African theater. His meeting with Chaim Weizmann on July 10, 1918, in London gave altogether another perspective to the Jews' fight for a national home, and this must have influenced his work at the War Office, which was known to harbor anti-Semites.

In the meantime, as the war dragged on, Dick was accorded the privilege and no doubt a pretty onerous duty, of going to Buckingham Palace at regular intervals to brief the King on the three areas of his expertise. At one such briefing, the King spoke of the "final crusade" concerning Palestine, it being clear His Majesty was thinking in terms of extending the empire and not of according the Jews a completely independent country. Blighty was in for a surprise. It would take time, but the Jews, who had been forced into waiting for a couple of thousand years, could bide their time for a while longer.

At this juncture Dick was rescued from the stifling atmosphere of the War Office with the news that he was to be posted to France where he would be responsible for security and camouflage. The prospect of getting "mixed up in some fighting"[7] thrilled him. So out he went, where, one glorious early August day, he was in on an attack east of Amiens. There was Dick, his trusty knobkerrie in hand, chasing Germans in mature cornfields as low-flying aircraft swooped overhead. Dick personally diminished the German population by twenty-three, courtesy of a Hotchkiss gun, and he was about to lay into a German with his knobkerrie when a fellow officer finished him off with a bullet. Dick expressed genuine anger at "being baulked of my prey."[8] Before the day was over, Dick was actually back at the War Office in London!

Dick's hours were long and often strained, with no days off. When he did get some leave, he spent it salmon fishing in Scotland, where he roamed over 40,000 acres of grouse moor, no doubt wondering where all the years had suddenly gone since his magical childhood and youth, since his big-game days in Africa and the far-off Indian adventures. There's nothing like a fishing trip for going into retrospective gear and reviewing life.

Promoted to full colonel, Dick was just getting the hang of things as boss of security at GHQ France when the Armistice came.

On the fateful day of November 11, 1918, he was around to see the signing of the Armistice at General Foch's headquarters.

A chilling scene took place when the German delegation arrived to "discuss" the terms of the Armistice. They were bluntly slammed back into place and told there would be no discussion, that war was war, and that the threat of Germans starving was their concern. In fact, when the document was signed, Foch turned on his heel and, refusing to shake hands with the Germans, told them in icy terms, "Eh bien, messieurs, c'est fini, allez."[9] Meaning: "Well then, gentlemen, it's over, go."

But it was not quite over for Dick, who, that very morning, rode out with the copy of the Armistice for General Haig, the original "poster man" of "Your Country Needs You" fame, who was some way off at Advanced GHQ. As his vehicle drove to the east, a sudden explosion ripped at the car, killing the driver, a piece of shrapnel hitting Dick in the stomach, though not puncturing it. He eventually straggled in, and, a stiff shot of brandy down his gullet, he saw the general, who promptly recognized him as being the youngster in the Hampshire Yeomanry who had jumped over him with his horse twenty years previously at a place called Farley Down. General Haig was commander in chief of the British forces in the war.

Dick found himself surrounded by delirious French troops, tricolor flags waving. Searchlights that night splashed the dark heavens and antiaircraft fire deafened the air as rockets whizzed past and star shells exploded. There were huge bonfires burning as people deliberately set fire to small ammunition dumps. Trails of fire snaked across the countryside as gunpowder-drenched gun cotton was set ablaze. With an hour to go before the Armistice came into force at 11 A.M. on that day, the British forces took off in aircraft loaded with bombs for one last sortie, one final thrashing of the Hun.

Richard Meinertzhagen (front row, extreme left) with the British Military Section at the Paris Peace Conference, 1919. (Courtesy of Ran Meinertzhagen and Rhodes House Library, Oxford)

Machine guns chattered incessantly as the Germans were caught totally unawares, suffering heavy losses.

Dick had spent just over two years in East Africa, nine months in Palestine, and a year at the War Office with the French interlude in between. After an operation on his stomach, Dick was then accorded the honor of being included in the British delegation to that most significant of events, the Paris Peace Conference. He hobbled into Paris on crutches on January 25, 1919, once again a direct witness of events that would have repercussions for decades to come.

Paris: The Peace Conference turned the city into a modern Tower of Babel as Dick witnessed the most important gathering of the politically powerful, the famous, the rich, and the influential like so many hyenas around a carcass, each tearing at its favorite bit, each with its own designs. The world was about to be carved up, and millions of lives would be affected. Dick became quickly disillusioned as he saw the politicians flock to the feast, ideas being spouted as to who should have what.

After his long experience in East Africa, Dick was stunned to hear talk of making India the mandatory power of German East Africa. Never an enthusiast for things Indian, Dick's diary reveals his antipathy for the Indian soldier in general and for the Indians as people in Africa. He bluntly states, "Every disaster we suffered during the first twelve months of the East African campaign was attributable to the unreliable soldierly qualities of the Indian soldier."[10] His comment that the Indian experience in Africa had been an unhappy one still held true over fifty years later when Idi Amin launched his persecution of the Ugandan Indians. But Dick speaks quite plainly of the "vice, crime, unrest"[11] he accuses the Indian of bringing to Africa. The air positively ignited when Dick launched into the Indians-in-Africa idea. His thoughts were conveyed right to the top with the idea of quashing the India Office ambition. The fact that nothing came of the project must have had something to do with Dick's intervention.

In Paris the scenes of bloated excess and luxury sickened Dick. He wanted action, decisions based on justice, and the banishment of intrigue and immoral political games. As he said, "Here we are, at the end of the most fearful war the world has ever seen, when whole peoples are starving . . . and governments all bankrupt . . . here we are spending money like water . . . and quite incapable of making peace. By heavens, how sad and depressing."[12]

And depressing it was. Turkey and Germany were being tempted not to sign the peace pact the longer matters dragged on. Revolution was on the boil in Egypt, and parts of Eastern Europe were being targeted by the Bolsheviks. Countries such as Bulgaria, Italy, and Greece were refusing to demobilize, there was industrial unrest in England, and the Irish question was becoming more ominous by the month. The world's economy had ground to a virtual halt, the collective psyche exhausted. But the politicians continued to toy with peace as if it didn't really matter whether the pact was signed that year or the next.

In the middle of all this, Dick did not lose touch with his Zionist thoughts. In fact, what he considers to be the most important letter he ever wrote was dated March 25, 1919, Paris. It is addressed to the British prime minister, Lloyd George, and it contains Dick's thoughts on the whole Middle East scenario and Jewish/Arab sovereignty clashes. Over seventy-six years afterwards, Dick's words ring eerily true, uncannily current.

With much wrangling and delay, the peace treaty was eventually signed on June 28, 1919, in the fabulous Hall of Mirrors at the Palace of Versailles. Dick was there. As the British delegation entered the hall, the French soldiers came to attention with swords drawn. When the Germans entered, the French soldiers sheathed their swords, spat on the floor, and lounged against the walls. Dick found that unworthy behavior under the circumstances. The Germans would not forget.

Whole libraries have been written about the Versailles Treaty. The virus of a new and even more terrible war had already been spawned, and Dick was destined to meet the principal architect, Adolf Hitler. He contemplated what he considered to be a "disgraceful peace."[13]

Much of Dick's energy and time were devoted to the Zionist cause while he was in Paris, where he was joined by T. E. Lawrence, whose complex and tortured life was immortalized by Peter O'Toole in one of Hollywood's epics. Lawrence had paid Dick a visit in Palestine, where he shared his dream of the eventual creation of an Arab empire, his friend gently reminding him of the Zionist cause. Lawrence quickly assured Dick that Palestine and the

Jews would enjoyed self-governing status under Arab sovereignty! Although Dick obviously didn't have the benefit of our hindsight in the 1990s, he scoffed at the very idea of Arabs calling the shots to Jews. He knew enough about the Jewish people to dismiss Lawrence's thought. That the two peoples would clash over competing nationalisms was as sure as the gathering of vultures over a carcass in the African bush. It was only a question of when and for how long. As Dick said, the peace conference had laid two eggs, namely Jewish and Arab nationalism, and these eggs were to hatch into two very troublesome chickens.

Dick lobbied Smuts and other leaders in Paris to support the idea of Jewish sovereignty in Palestine. He wrote numerous notes and memoranda to the decision-makers, urging clarification on the Balfour Declaration, fighting anti-Semitic sentiment in official circles, and promoting the cause of Jewish sovereignty. This was a path from which he would not stray until he died, despite hostility, ignorance, and ages-old prejudice.

Chaim Weizmann told Dick of a meeting with the French prime minister, Georges Clemenceau, who also presided over the Paris Peace Conference. The Frenchman was unsympathetic to the whole Jewish national-home concept, telling Weizmann that Christians could never forgive the Jews for crucifying Christ. Weizmann shot back, "Monsieur Clemenceau, you know perfectly well that if Jesus of Nazareth were to apply for a visa to enter France, it would be refused on the grounds that he was a political agitator."[14] Touché.

While in Paris, Dick was appointed chief political officer for Palestine, Syria, and the then Transjordan on the staff of General Allenby, and this was a position he would use to champion the cause of the Jews. His whole working day was immersed in Middle Eastern issues, which brought him into contact with the decision-makers, the people who were gathering about them the clout to decide the destiny of whole nations. Dick was for a decisive stance, not a series of appeasing comprises. Ever the determined warrior, the goal-directed hunter, Dick knew that malevolent forces would be waiting to exploit any lack of resolve on this Palestine issue.

Based in Cairo from September 1919, Dick had a split loyalty: He was on General Allenby's staff but also had to report to the British Foreign Office. But all was not gloom. As he was out of Cairo two weeks out of the four, Dick had the comfort of two Rolls-Royces, one fitted with a bed so that he could snooze in comfort in the desert night, hotels being very few.

He raised the Zionism issue with, among others, Feisal of Transjordan, who accepted it, rejecting the French, whom he accused of slavery, their administration of Syria being damned as corrupt and oppressive. Dick, like it or not, was plunged into political intrigue, but the Zionist cause always stayed anchored in his mind. Hence his quoting of an incident I wrote of in my introduction to the reprint from my library of J. H. Patterson's *Man-eaters of Tsavo* (New York: St. Martin's Press, 1986). Colonel Patterson commanded the Jewish Battalion in Palestine in 1919 and came up against a notorious hebraphobe brigadier who insulted one of the Jewish soldiers. Patterson immediately barked an order for the men to fix bayonets and form a square around the offensive officer, demanding an apology and refusing to let him out of the square of steel until he did so.

Dick was ordered to investigate this incident, which resulted in the brigadier being shipped back to India, the battalion disbanding. Patterson, as the world knows, gained fame for his stalking and slaying of man-eating lions that paralyzed the construction of the Uganda Railway in the Tsavo region in 1898, eating over a hundred people. In fact, an American film crew was in South Africa filming the Tsavo story, and I spent time with the scriptwriter and director. It is a story whose horror grips generation after generation of readers, and now, with film, a whole new dimension is involved for fresh generations.

Dick's life was not without its lighter moments. Take his trip from Beirut or "Beyrouth," as he spelled it, down to Haifa via Tyre, Sidon, and Acre. Approaching Sidon in early November 1919, he saw something bobbing up and down in the surf about 400 yards off and concluded it was a rare Mediterranean seal. His thoughts were nearing conviction as he drew his firearm and was about to put a bullet through the creature, no doubt intending it for a British museum, if not *the* British Museum.

Suddenly, Dick froze. His eyes traveled to the beach, where he saw a pile of clothes and his friend, Waters-Taylor, the financial adviser to the Palestine administration, puffing at an enormous cigar. Dick then realized that he had not seen a seal. He had seen his pal's extremely eccentric wife bobbing about in the shallows, nude. The mind boggles at the note verbale to the Foreign Office trying to explain the death of madame who had been mistaken for a seal!

This was the same Waters-Taylor Dick discovered as being very chummy with various Arab leaders in Jerusalem, one of the most pernicious being a certain Haj Amin al Husseini, who became the mufti of Jerusalem, a sort of Muslim legal expert. Dick was up to his old espionage tricks and, via his network in the ancient city, he discovered that Madame Waters-Taylor would visit Haj Amin disguised as an Arab and that her husband was actively encouraging anti-Jew riots in Jerusalem. This no doubt played a role in the Arab mobs eventually exploding into the Jewish quarter of Jerusalem in April 1920 where they conducted an old-style pogrom in which many Jews were slaughtered.

Dick, in dispatches to George Nathaniel, First Marquis Curzon of Kedleston, the foreign secretary and former viceroy to India, turned up the heat, reporting Waters-Taylor's seditious behavior and stating that the Zionists were the only ones now in Palestine "with the necessary brains, energy and resources to institute a commencement to progress."[15] In a letter sent just two months before this, Dick tells My Lord that he does not "approach Zionism in Palestine with an open mind, but as one strongly prejudiced in its favour."[16]

It was an uphill slog all the way. Dick speaks of the intrigue, the ignorance, and the prejudice. He tells of the suspicion and antagonism against Jewish intelligence and wealth, of being a lone voice among Gentiles in fighting for the Zionist ideal. He shares the fatigue and his own conflicting emotions where he wishes that Zionism could be separated from the Jewish nationality. He faces the fact that Jewish immigration into Palestine would inevitably mean eventual dispossession of Arabs by Jews and that a Jewish state must follow. Arab fears were not entirely groundless. But Dick asks his diary if it is fair that Palestine's resources should remain undeveloped or that no progress should be made because the inhabitants, that is, the Arabs, were unwilling or incapable of undertaking such development. Two worlds, two peoples, despite being racial cousins.

Dick concluded that intelligence was a Jewish virtue and intrigue an Arab vice.

Dick's total singleness of purpose led to a shake-up in the British administration and a confrontation with Allenby. The anti-Zionists were dealt a blow, but it did mean Dick's having to move on after the Foreign Office rejected certain of Allenby's policies concerning the Arabs. When Dick called to take his leave of Allenby, the latter asked him to stay to lunch and congratulated him on his straight dealing. The two men had a good laugh when Dick told the general that he gave less notice than one usually gives a housemaid! They parted as friends and kept in touch. The director of military intelligence noted that "Meinertzhagen has loyally carried out the policy of H.M.G. and the present situation has occurred owing to the impossible situation in which he is placed by the present system. He is in no way to blame."[17]

Dick had indeed been in an impossible situation. He had to represent the Foreign Office on Allenby's staff, keep his government informed about the whole Palestine issue, and ensure that British policy, that is, pro-Zionist policy, was carried out. His work made him into a sort of spy on Allenby's staff, and the parting of ways was inevitable. But, as Dick stated in his diary, he believed that Zionism was destined to be a world force that would "outlive its lawless cousin—Bolshevism."[18]

Dick found in his posting as chief political officer that he was alone in the Zionist cause and that he was the target of hostility. He stood up to the general staff on this issue and fought the anti-Zionists. It cost him his posting and perhaps made him fresh enemies in the "old boys club" of the British military caste. Dick resented the turn of events, but he knew it was a consequence of remaining true to himself.

With that, Dick took six months' leave and went off to Crete, where he was the guest of the island's most notorious bandit, a giant of a fellow who spoke only Greek and who was the Robin Hood–type idol of the simple mountain folk. Glorying in the name of George Nikolokakis, he regaled Dick with his incomprehensible humor as the two imbibed life, Cretan-style, the British Foreign Office, War Office, and Colonial Office belonging to another planet.

After a mere two weeks of peace, the Foreign Office tracked Dick down better than a leopard after a wounded buck and ordered him "home," where he was offered the post of heading the Palestine section of the office's Middle East section. But Dick's horror of His Majesty's bureaucratic drudgery outweighed all else and he declined the offer, demanding instead that he be accorded six months' leave.

Rested, Dick then accepted to work for Winston Churchill as military adviser to the Middle East Department in the Colonial Office. T. E. Lawrence was "Arab adviser," and Dick had other good friends about him as he was warned about Churchill who gave the impression he was a fresh edition of his famous ancestor, the Duke of Marleborough. Churchill had obviously inherited something of the duke's bulldog spirit.

Dick was soon crossing swords with the hebraphobes who inhabited the Colonial Office. He confronted Churchill in a rage when it became apparent that the land earmaked for a Jewish national home was now going to be reduced to one-third of what was originally intended when Transjordan was severed from Palestine. The pro-Arab lobby was out in force but that didn't faze Dick, who accused the Colonial Office of dishonoring the Balfour Declaration and sabotaging H.M.G.'s official policy—strong stuff indeed. Churchill listened and said he would think things over.

It was against the backdrop of these events concerning Palestine that Meinertzhagen married Anne Constance Jackson, in 1921. She was the daughter of a military officer, Major Randle Jackson, and had studied zoology at the Imperial College in London, an unusual achievement for women of her generation. She became a noted ornithologist, contributing to learned journals of the day.

Anne and Dick seemed very happy, she giving him three children, a daughter and two sons, the firstborn son being named Daniel according to family tradition. The marriage was hardly seven years old when tragedy struck. Anne had been handling her husband's revolver when a shot rang out and a bullet went through her head.

After this tragedy Meinertzhagen went into a steep mental decline and eventually had to be hospitalized for nervous depression. He did not marry again.

Weizmann, back from a visit to America, spoke to Dick of his fears that the British government was chipping away at the Balfour Declaration. Immigration to Palestine had pretty well come to a halt, and the British officials posted there were unsympathetic to the Zionist cause. Dick tried to make his fellow countrymen understand that the Arab and his religion would not be threatened by Zionism but would, if anything, benefit. He wrote to Smuts on the issue to lobby support before a major meeting with Churchill, Lloyd George, Balfour, and Weizmann in July 1921.

With the British foot-dragging and vacillation, the Palestine Zionists eventually did what all threatened communities will do in the end: They took matters into their own hands. The Zionists started smuggling guns. They had had enough of talk, of succumbing to Arab threats. If there was no constitutional way of obtaining their homeland, they would resort to force. They were not about to be led to any more slaughters. Enough was enough, and Dick fired off memoranda in support of greater protection by the British of the Palestine Jews in the early stages of Zionism and an end to the go-slow policies. He made enemies in the process. But Dick never looked back when he was convinced of a cause. He even stated that the illegally armed Jews should be recognized as a police reserve. Weapons were coming in so they might as well be given legal status. Dick stated that British officials themselves were guilty of political sabotage in working against the Zionist policy of H.M.G., and his solitude in this crusade was intensified when the likes of Churchill showed no real interest. The head of the Middle East Department, for God's sake, was a rampant anti-Semite by the name of Shurkburgh who set rumors going that Meinertzhagen was responsible for leaks from the Colonial Office, leading to suspicion and tension.

Clearly, Dick's days as a full-time servant of His Majesty's Government were numbered. He was far too much of an individualist to toe the line like a good boy and accept what he knew to be manifestly wrong. But before he set course for another direction in his amazing life, he would have the satisfaction of seeing the Palestine Mandate approved by the League of Nations in July 1922 in London, this significant act clearly imposing a moral responsibility on the cautious Brits to get with it and adopt a firmer stance in their Palestine policies.

Three months later, Dick visited Palestine and Mesopotamia for an extended military tour, during which time the British government had changed hands, Churchill going with it, the new secretary of the Colonial Office being the Duke of Devonshire. During his six-month absence, Dick revisited Jerusalem, where Zionism was now well-rooted. He then went by desert track to Baghdad, where he dined with King Feisal before going down to the marshy gulf region where he lived for a couple of weeks with the Marsh Arabs immortalized by that great explorer, Wilfred Thesiger. He visited a British battalion in Kurdistan and the Yemen Infantry just north of Aden, fitting in a visit to the unique and awesome beauty of the reddish ruins of the ancient city of Petra in Transjordan, south of the Dead Sea. A quick visit to Egypt and the Sinai region followed before Dick returned to the dun-colored dullness and petty politics of the Colonial Office.

This could not go on. Dick was in his midforties now and had retained his rank as colonel. With no more ado he left the Colonial Office in March 1924 and returned to regimental soldiering after an absence of about twelve years. As two battalions of his regiment, the Royal Fusiliers, had been disbanded, he was transferred as second-in-command of the Duke of Cornwall's Light Infantry. Anyone who knows anything about the intense loyalties and traditions attached to British regiments will appreciate the emotional impact of this change on Dick's life.

He shipped out to Cologne, Germany, where he became aware

of the intense hatred between the Germans and French and the Germans' tendency, as Dick saw it in September 1924, to be "easily led and influenced."[19] The hardships imposed after the Versailles Treaty and the Depression later were warm, fertile incubation spots for the hypnotic madman who would emerge to terrorize the world. Dick could already sense the trouble. He was already speaking of "the next war."[20]

Life was coming full circle as Dick was ordered out to Lucknow, India, in December 1924. As the ship headed for the east, Dick had time to reassess his life. He had had the chance of becoming British military attaché to Japan; he could have accepted the post as chief of Irish intelligence; he was also offered the chance of becoming governor of the Falkland Islands. Had he accepted any of these positions, Dick's career would have been guaranteed, but he chose, instead, to stick with soldiering, and it was in that arena that he butted heads on too many issues too often—a fact that would block his path forward. Lloyd George, in his 1936 *War Memoirs*, spoke of Dick as being "one of the ablest and most successful brains I had met in any Army. That was quite sufficient to make him suspect and to hinder his promotion to the higher ranks of his profession."[21]

Dick was forty-seven and tired of the regimental rut and the pecking-order squabbles. He wanted out. His overwhelming interest in ornithology and the wilderness areas meant that he wanted to be free to travel and collect specimens. He felt the wrench of not being with his old battalion and states quite clearly that it would have meant a great deal to him if he had been given command of a Royal Fusiliers battalion. Most of his old army friends had died in the war, and the prospect of unfamiliar faces and the heat of India simply added to the foregoing, and he decided to resign his commission. Life, for Dick, was not about staying in a groove. It was about personal freedom.

While making plans to visit Tibet and the Kashmir region,

Dick resigned, and the relief was intense. Dick found himself in what is today's northwestern Pakistan, near the legendary Khyber Pass. It was here that he ran out of the sort of notepaper than an officer and a gentleman was expected to use. Rather than ignore correspondence, Dick wound up his affairs on toilet paper, called "bromo," including a receipt for back pay demanded by the command paymaster in Meerut.

The response was immediate and humorlessly predictable. Dick was verbally smacked for using "shameful paper" for official correspondence, and GHQ in Simla got in on the act with a letter of reprimand from the adjutant-general. Using a fresh sheet of "shameful paper," Dick replied to the adjutant-general, an old friend from Palestine days:

> I have exceedingly little "Bromo" left and must request that
> this correspondence now ceases [sic]. Having recently
> contracted cholera, both my supply of "shameful paper"
> and my wish to conduct tiresome correspondence are as
> exhausted as appears to be the sense of humour in the non-
> combatant services of the Army in India.[22]

With that, Dick took his leave of military life. He was now entering a phase where he was without any doubt connected to the British intelligence services and where he would fight on for the cause of Zionism and the future of the Jewish people. Even he had no idea of the horrors ahead. But this mature lion had a long way to go before sheathing his claws and calling it a day.

Chapter 11

"I am as optimistic as ever about the future of Zionism and consider it will be judged to be the greatest constructive work which has emerged from the wreckage of the Great War, and long after memories of that struggle have become dimmed by time, Zionism will stand out as a landmark of civilization and progress."[1]

London, November 1927: Dick was entering a period of his life during which he would be serving the interests of the British Secret Service and of British military intelligence, certainly until after World War II and who knows for how long after that. His uncle, Sidney Webb, had become secretary of state for the Colonies and a Zionist sympathizer, and Dick used this relationship to defend the cause. He conducted a public campaign of letters to the *Times* in which he stoutly denied that any Arab rights or privileges had in any way been curtailed by the Jews in Palestine. Zionism, in Dick's books, had come to stay, and any "attempt to interfere with Jewry is to interfere with history. . . . Enemies of Zionism can delay the ultimate destiny of Palestine, but they cannot prevent its ultimate fulfillment."[2]

Dick knew that an armed confrontation with the Arabs would inevitably be part of the price of establishing a Jewish national home. Palestine was already being threatened by a Pan-Arab confederation that intended to swallow it up. Dick, in writing up his diary in March 1933, thought that he would not live to see the actual establishment of the Jewish state. Not only did he live to witness it, but he survived for almost two decades beyond that momentous day in May 1948. But horrors would intervene before then.

Under the genuine cover of ornithological research, Dick went to Berlin, where he had lunch on October 17, 1934, with Ribbentrop, who was Hitler's foreign affairs adviser, German ambassador to Great Britain from 1936 to 1938, and foreign minister from 1938 to 1945. Nazism had been born, and Dick smelled disaster. He knew that Hitler was obsessed by the consequences of the Versailles Treaty, by Russian communism, and by the belief that the Jews were out to ruin Germany. Hitler also had imperial ambitions, which made him dangerous.

Ribbentrop suggested that Dick meet Hitler concerning an Anglo-German rapprochement. The meeting was arranged for that same day in the late afternoon. Dick entered a massive room where Hitler walked toward him, raising his hand and barking "Heil Hitler!" Dick obviously not having heard this soon to be all too familiar battle cry, responded with "Heil Meinertzhagen!"

Nobody cracked a smile.

With Ribbentrop as interpreter, although Dick spoke German, Hitler and Dick started conversing. Dick noted the hypnotic personality, the atmosphere of physical and mental power the German chancellor gave off, his ruthless truthfulness as he spoke of the German need for more "Lebensraum." Germany wanted back her colonies. She wanted peace, Hitler speaking of 500 years of peace with Britain. He denied any aggressive military intentions in the Nazi movement and reiterated his desire for peace with France.

Dick made various suggestions to Hitler to improve relations with Britain but he hit a raw nerve when it came to the Jews. Hitler bluntly admitted to being a fanatic and an anti-Semite. He ranted on about how the German Jews had amassed money during World War I, how they controlled finance and the medical and legal professions, and how they dominated the press. Hitler accused the Jews of imposing their politics and culture on millions of Germans and stated that they were the principal organizers of the German Communist Party.

At the time, Dick honestly believed that only communist-leaning Jews in Germany had been arrested or expelled. He truly thought the stories of persecution were isolated cases and that this did not form part of actual government policy.

By May 1935, Dick had an entirely different picture from Weizmann himself about the sustained and growing persecution of the German Jews. They were being increasingly barred from all avenues of life as normal citizens of Germany and were not allowed to emigrate with all their money and possessions to Palestine. Weizmann implored Dick to intervene in whatever way he could, and this indicates to us that Dick remained highly connected and influential.

Not two months later, Weizmann was back with Dick, this time with further information about the maltreatment of the Jews in Germany and the curtailing of their daily lives on every front. Dick left for Berlin where he met Hitler for a second time on July 15, 1935, together with Rudolf Hess, Hitler's deputy and head of the Nazi Party.

As soon as Dick mentioned the Jews, Hitler became enraged, ferociously shouting as he hammered the table with his fists, his eyes dancing with hate. The tirade stopped only when Hess arrived and the Führer had to leave the room. Dick continued the conversation with Ribbentrop.

Before Hitler lost control, he spoke to Dick about the need for a new ambassador to Britain. Dick had a brain wave and suggested Von Lettow-Vorbeck. He was a man of impeccable credentials, spoke reasonable English, and was honored in both countries. Hitler slapped his thigh and thought it a great idea. As history tells us, Von Lettow-Vorbeck would have nothing to do with the Nazis and declined the suggestion. He was persecuted because of this and, had it not been for food parcels from Meinertzhagen and Smuts, the old boy would have been in an even worse situation, an old warrior living in penury.

After the scene with Hitler, Dick returned to his hotel, where two Jews were waiting to see him. They accompanied Dick to his room, where they gave an anguished account of actual concentration camps that had been set up and where Jews were being subjected to torture, rape, and murder. They gave details of specific cases but were too terrified to put anything in writing for fear this would leak and that they would be rounded up and shipped off themselves.

Dick couldn't believe that the British Foreign Office didn't know about this and that the press would not have, by then, exposed such cruelty. Days later, Dick was able to establish that the Jews were like rats in a deadly trap in Germany. Most countries did not want them as immigrants and their way was barred for Palestine because they could not bring out money and did not have a craft or trade.

The word was out that Dick was in Berlin on behalf of the Jews, and his hotel was besieged by Jews and Zionists. The security implications were clear, and the Jew-baiting would only get worse as a result. The Germans told Dick that they would allow the Jews and their money to go if they headed for Palestine but they would not discuss the matter with any Jew! The Germans also relented at

Dick's insistence and allowed schools to be established where Jews could learn Hebrew as well as agriculture to ready them for emigration.

Dick, in a quite amazing statement at the time, said that the German government had a perfect right to treat the Jew as an alien, deny him citizenship, and expel him but "it must be done decently and with justice."[3]

This statement is, quite frankly, astounding, coming from a man who would literally take up arms for the Jewish/Zionist cause, a man who engaged in shuttle diplomacy on their behalf long before the phrase existed and who went to extremes to assist them in whatever way he could. Dick had an odd streak in his character that made him the complex and contradictory man he was.

June 28, 1939: Dick was back in Berlin, visiting his cousin and, no doubt at all, engaging in some intelligence work for the British. He was sixty-one years old when he was told that Herr Hitler wished to see him.

The appointment was for 11 A.M. Before Dick left for this third encounter with the Führer, he placed a loaded automatic pistol in his pocket "so that I could prove 'opportunity' to kill the man."[4] Dick had long since had a chance to sum up Hitler and was now convinced he was actively seeking war, one that would drag in the entire world just thirty-five years after the last world war.

Ribbentrop met him, unsmiling and gruff. He had since returned from his posting as ambassador to Britain, where he developed an intense loathing of the British. His uncouth behavior was such that his son was barred from enrolling at that shrine of shrines for the education of the elite, Eton College. This so infected Ribbentrop that he further poisoned Hitler's attitude toward the British from that day on.

Hitler subjected Dick to a lengthy harangue about British obstruction of German expansion to the east and rambled on about "encirclement," as Dick's diary puts it. After nearly an hour of this, Dick indicated he wished to leave, which he did. He couldn't figure out why Hitler had wanted to see him in the first place. Clearly, he knew of Dick's connections and was no doubt sure that certain of his rantings would be reported to the inner circles of British power. It was, after all, just over two months away from the invasion of Poland and the actual start of the war, and Hitler must have already had firm plans for that invasion by that late date.

Dick could have killed Hitler and Ribbentrop. He told his diary that if war came he'd feel he was to blame for not having finished the two off there and then. One can only wonder what would have happened had Dick assassinated Hitler and Ribbentrop. He would have been arrested and worse. He may have been branded a nut but maybe the course of that whole tragic and bloody period would have been different had the venom been removed from the heart of it all.

As it was, war erupted. Just a couple of weeks after it was declared, Dick had a visit from Zionist revolutionary Vladimir Jabotinsky, whom he had first met in Jerusalem in early 1920. Back then, Jabotinsky was accused, tried, and sentenced for training a private army of Jews, known as the Haganah, the forerunner of the formidable Israeli armed forces of today. Dick interceded and had the six-year sentence reduced to six weeks and a twelve-month deportation order.

The old jackal was back, this time pleading for Dick to help him obtain explosives, which he intended to use on German oil barges on the Danube. Jabotinsky had all the operatives in place, ready and waiting. Dick obliged, even organizing a demonstration of the jelly-like explosive. Some two hundred bombs were given to Jabotinsky and it wasn't long before reports started filtering through of German oil barges being blown up.

Something strange then happens in Dick's published diaries. He takes us up to the outbreak of the war, gives a few details, and falls silent for the duration of the war. He was involved in intelligence matters and this probably explains the silence, as much of value would still have been under official secrecy wraps when Dick started publishing some of his memoirs in the late 1950s. He served for a while in the War Office and was in the Dunkirk operation to rescue the remainder of the British forces. Dick was also in the Home Guard, which must have frustrated a man like him who, despite his age, was incomparably fitter and more alert than his contemporaries.

Tragedy struck when Dick's son, Daniel—the eighth such Meinertzhagen since 1657—was killed by mortar fire on October 2, 1944, at the age of nineteen in the Netherlands, just spitting distance from the German border. A member of the Coldstream Guards, Dan Jr. was backing up the Eighty-second American Airborne Division when he died.

Dick compiled a book of his son's letters, *The Life of a Boy* (Edinburgh: Oliver & Boyd, 1947), and, in leafing through it, the pride and the emotion Dick felt concerning his son is evident. Thoughts go back the Buddha statue and the Mottisfont curse and what happened to the statue, whether Dick still kept it in his London home or whether he got rid of it after his son's death.

The wheel turns and Dick was now immersed in Middle Eastern politics more than ever. With the liberation of the concentration camps, the full horror of the war and the special hell reserved for the European Jews now coming out in all its terror, the Palestine issue took on a fresh urgency. He saw a great deal of Weizmann and his wife in London during the war and continued after the war to lobby for the Zionist cause. He still found anti-Semitism and appeasement of the Arabs a problem, despite the war years and the revelation of the systematic atrocities against the Jews. Churchill had broken his word about giving the Jews sovereignty over Palestine for fear of stirring up the Arabs, and pro-Arab propaganda was making its appearance in Britain.

Dick advised Weizmann on strategies and arguments to be used in the endless fight for Palestine. He states that the "Arabs can never, owing to their backward state and low standards, their inherent laziness and dishonesty, their disunity and their lack of desire to improve, give us anything approaching prosperous stability in the Middle East. . . . The Jews, on the other hand, are a most progressive and enlightened nation, could give us prosperous stability in the Middle East and would constitute a strong bastion within the British Commonwealth."[5]

Acts of Jewish terrorism were now taking place in Palestine under the umbrella of a guerrilla group known as the Irgun, which claimed responsibility for the King David Hotel bomb in July 1946 in which ninety-one people died. Dick did not condone such acts, but he understood the rage behind them. With millions of their people dead at the hands of the Nazis and Nazi sympathizers, the Palestinian Jews wanted one thing known: Zionism was not dead. It would not go away quietly. The Jews would have their corner of the earth to call home. Dick said, "If I were a Jew, I should be a terrorist, a violent one, and I would aim at Whitehall."[6]

The British then referred the whole Palestine issue to the United Nations, and Dick took off for an extensive trip through Arabia to collect material for his book on the birds of Arabia. It remains the bible on the subject to this day. Just out of Mecca Dick received a telegram on March 7, 1948, from Weizmann stating that the United Nations had decided to grant Jewish sovereignty over a partitioned Palestine. In this moment of victory the telegram to Dick read:

TO YOU DEAR FRIEND WE OWE SO MUCH THAT I CAN
ONLY EXPRESS IT IN SIMPLE WORDS—MAY GOD
BLESS YOU.[7]

April 23, 1948, dawned as Dick came into Haifa Harbor, on his way back from his Arabia expedition. As luck would have it, a company of Coldstream Guards was onboard, his late son's regiment. There were those who remembered Dan, and this delighted Dick. What delighted him even more was the all-out battle between Arab and Jew that was raging along the seafront.

The Jews had the upper hand by late afternoon. The duty of the Coldstream Guards was to protect British government stores in the port area, so they walked right into the fighting. Dick, never a man to be left on the sidelines if he could possibly help it, knew that one of his late son's pals was sick onboard ship. So he went to see him, asked to borrow his uniform and full kit, put it on, joined a Coldstream detachment as it marched ashore, and then began his own private one-day war with the Haganah as backup! At seventy years of age, Dick was about to demonstrate that he had not lost his touch. Not at all.

Dick walked to where he could hear the firing and quickly found a group of Haganah soldiers in the front line. Sighting in his rifle at 200 yards, Dick finally managed to inch forward and take up position in the sand about 250 yards from Arab snipers. He and his Haganah companions then opened fire, and Dick killed an Arab, to the cheers of his Jewish friends. He shot a further two Arabs and, with the Haganah, got five more, capturing one. Another four Arabs went down before Dick's day came to a halt when a Coldstream officer loomed large and ordered Dick back to the ship.

Back onboard, Dick returned the kit and a cleaned rifle before cracking a bottle of champagne with his sick pal. His comment? "Altogether I had a glorious day. May Israel flourish!"[8]

And flourish she did with her declaration as an independent and sovereign state on May 14, 1948, with Chaim Weizmann as president. Few people could have appreciated the emotion Dick felt after all those long decades of struggle, after the intrigue, horror, and disappointment he had witnessed, after the sacrifices made, the risks run. It had been a lifetime.

Epilogue

Dick lived to see the triumph of Israel against staggering odds in the 1948 war, which erupted straight after independence. He would see the unraveling of the British Empire, starting with India in 1947; he witnessed the Mau-Mau uprising in Kenya and he lived through the cold war, traveling extensively to places as far apart as Yemen and South Africa, where he had a most nostalgic reunion with Smuts in 1949 at one of Africa's great hotels, the Mount Nelson in Cape Town.

Chaim Weizmann died on November 9, 1952, in Israel, and the news touched Dick's soul. He stated at the time, "Chaim was a great chemist, a great Jew, a great man and a Prince of Israel. He and Smuts are the two outstanding figures of my generation and I am proud to have worked with them. . . . I had no better or more loyal friend than Chaim Weizmann."[1] Losing friends of decades' standing reminded Dick of his own mortality as he continued to travel and cram into his remaining years as much as his health would allow.

He returned to Kenya in 1956 at seventy-eight years of age where he visited the scene of his encounter with Koitalel of the Nandi fifty-one years earlier. He saw gigantic trees in the place where he had planted blue gum seedlings, symbolizing that a part of his soul was forever rooted in Africa, in memories of youth, vigor, and war. As he shook hands with the elders and was introduced to new faces at the Nandi location of Kapsabet, Dick was presented to a fine-looking man who was told, "This is the gentleman who shot your grandfather."[2]

Dick revisited Israel where he met David Ben-Gurion, the prime minister of the day, and stayed on for the Independence Day celebrations in Haifa, the scene of Dick's "final stand" for Zionism. He also discovered that Ben-Gurion had been a member of his regiment, the Royal Fusiliers, during World War I.

The Suez Crisis followed, Dick cheering on the Israelis as vigorously as he denounced the policies of Anthony Eden, the British prime minister. Dick was never a man for compromise or appeasement. He also found his diary a great safety valve for his emotions as he surveyed world events and deplored what he saw as the incompetence of the United Nations and the poor example they were setting. He lived to witness the tragedy of the Hungarian uprising in 1956 and the barbarism of the Congo events of 1960, country after country in Africa throwing off the yoke of empire.

Dick's health declined quite sharply in his last few years. He could no longer travel and escape into the wild and solitary places, away from a world that had become alien to him. He, born into the Victorian era, raised with the Edwardians in a society of great taste and refinement where manners and character counted, now found in his last years that his world had vanished. It had shrunk, and the threat of nuclear war had grown. The Soviet Union loomed large, a distinct threat to the West, and the Middle East went on the boil again, erupting into the Six-Day War of early June 1967.

It is appropriate to recall here what Dick wrote as an old man:

I feel that I belong to a world that is dead. . . . Peace is but a dream—an interlude. . . . We are now entering a world of indecision, dishonesty, and irresponsibility, a world I shall not be sorry to leave.[3]

The old lion finally left his lair for the last time on June 17 of that year.

Go well, old friend. Your tracks through history will remain.

۝otes

INTRODUCTION

1. T. E. Lawrence. *Seven Pillars of Wisdom* (London: Jonathan Cape, 1935 edition, 4th impression), p. 384.

CHAPTER 1

1. R. Meinertzhagen. *Diary of a Black Sheep* (Edinburgh: Oliver & Boyd, 1964), p. 79.
2. *Ibid.*, p. 148.
3. *Ibid.*, p. 198.
4. R. Meinertzhagen. *Kenya Diary, 1902–1906* (Edinburgh: Oliver & Boyd, 1957), p. viii.
5. R. Meinertzhagen. *Diary of Black Sheep* (Edinburgh: Oliver & Boyd, 1964), p. 300.
6. *Ibid.*, p. 301.

CHAPTER 2

1. R. Meinertzhagen. *Diary of a Black Sheep* (Edinburgh: Oliver & Boyd, 1964), p. 314.
2. *Ibid.*, p. 328.
3. *Ibid.*, p. 334.
4. *Ibid.*, p. 342.
5. *Ibid.*, p. 343.
6. *Ibid.*, pp. 347–348.

7. *Ibid.*, p. 344.
8. *Ibid.*
9. *Ibid.*, p. 345.
10. R. Meinertzhagen. *Army Diary, 1899–1926* (Edinburgh: Oliver & Boyd, 1960), p. 14.
11. *Ibid.*, p. 14.
12. *Ibid.*, p. 15.
13. *Ibid.*
14. *Ibid.*
15. *Ibid.*
16. *Ibid.*
17. *Ibid.*
18. *Ibid.*, p. 20.
19. *Ibid.*, p. 19.

CHAPTER 3

1. R. Meinertzhagen. *Kenya Diary, 1902–1906* (London: Eland Books, 1984), p. 2.
2. *Ibid.*, p. 3.
3. *Ibid.*
4. *Ibid.*, p. 6.
5. *Ibid.*, p. 12.
6. *Ibid.*, p. 10.
7. *Ibid.*, p. 15.
8. *Ibid.*, p. 21.
9. *Ibid.*, p. 24.
10. *Ibid.*, p. 25.
11. *Ibid.*
12. *Ibid.*, p. 26.
13. *Ibid.*, p. 27.
14. *Ibid.*, pp. 32–33.
15. *Ibid.*, p. 34.
16. *Ibid.*, p. 41.
17. *Ibid.*, p. 40.
18. *Ibid.*
19. *Ibid.*

20. *Ibid.*, p. 51.

21. *Ibid.*,

22. *Ibid.*,

23. *Ibid.*, pp. 51–52.

24. *Ibid.*, p. 52.

CHAPTER 4

1. R. Meinertzhagen. *Kenya Diary, 1902–1906* (London: Eland Books, 1984), pp. 46–47.

2. *Ibid.*, p. 93.

3. *Ibid.*, p. 47.

4. *Ibid.*, p. 57.

5. *Ibid.*, p. 72.

6. *Ibid.*, p. 71.

7. *Ibid.*, p. 61.

8. *Ibid.*, p. 64.

9. *Ibid.*

10. *Ibid.*, p. 66.

11. *Ibid.*, p. 67.

12. *Ibid.*, p. 73.

13. *Ibid.*, p. 74.

14. *Ibid.*

15. *Ibid.*

16. *Ibid.*, p. 202.

17. *Ibid.*, p. 83.

18. *Ibid.*, p. 84.

19. *Ibid.*, pp. 84–85.

20. *Ibid.*, p. 96.

21. *Ibid.*, p. 97.

22. *Ibid.*

23. *Ibid.*

CHAPTER 5

1. R. Meinertzhagen. *Kenya Diary, 1902–1906* (London: Eland Books, 1984), p. 113.

2. *Ibid.*, p. 117.

3. R. Meinertzhagen. *Middle East Diary, 1917–1956* (London: The Cresset Press, 1959), p. 2.

4. R. Meinertzhagen. *Kenya Diary, 1902–1906* (London: Eland Books, 1984), p. 117.

5. *Ibid.*, p. 122.

6. *Ibid.*, p. 99.

7. *Ibid.*, p. 129.

8. *Ibid.*, p. 144.

9. *Ibid.*, p. 172.

10. *Ibid.*, p. 173.

11. *Ibid.*, p. 176.

12. *Ibid.*, pp. 178–179.

CHAPTER 6

1. R. Meinertzhagen. *Kenya Diary, 1902–1906* (London: Eland Books, 1984), p. 181.

2. Charles Miller. *The Lunatic Express* (New York: The Macmillan Company, 1971), p. 457.

3. R. Meinertzhagen. *Kenya Diary, 1902–1906* (London: Eland Books, 1984), p. 163.

4. *Ibid.*, p. 190.

5. *Ibid.*, p. 192.

6. *Ibid.*

7. *Ibid.*, p. 203.

8. *Ibid.*, p. 208.

9. *Ibid.*, p. 214.

10. *Ibid.*, p. 215.

11. *Ibid.*, p. 222.

12. *Ibid.*, pp. 229–230.

13. *Ibid.*, p. 243.

14. *Ibid.*, p. 257.

15. *Ibid.*, p. 293.

16. *Ibid.*, p. 298.

17. *Ibid.*

18. *Ibid.*, p. 311.

19. *Ibid.*

20. *Ibid.*, p. 315.

21. *Ibid.*, p. 318.

22. *Ibid.*, p. 323.

23. *Ibid.*, p. 324.

24. *Ibid.*, p. 327.

25. *Ibid.*, p. 334.

CHAPTER 7

1. R. Meinertzhagen. *Army Diary, 1899–1926* (Edinburgh: Oliver & Boyd, 1960), p. 40.

2. *Ibid.*, p. 43.

3. *Ibid.*, p. 48.

4. *Ibid.*, p. 75.

5. *Ibid.*, p. 56.

6. *Ibid.*, p. 58.

7. *Ibid.*, p. 62.

8. *Ibid.*, p. 63.

9. *Ibid.*, p. 68.

10. *Ibid.*

11. *Ibid.*, p. 69.

12. *Ibid.*, p. 78.

CHAPTER 8

1. R. Meinertzhagen. *Army Diary, 1899–1926* (Edinburgh: Oliver & Boyd, 1960), p. 89.

2. *Ibid.*, p. 84.

3. *Ibid.*, p. 88.

4. *Ibid.*, p. 92.

5. *Ibid.*, p. 93.

6. *Ibid.*, p. 96.

7. *Ibid.*

8. *Ibid.*, p. 101.

9. *Ibid.*, p. 105.

10. *Ibid.*, p. 109.

11. *Ibid.*, p. 121.

12. *Ibid.*, p. 123.

13. *Ibid.*

14. *Ibid.*, p. 124.

15. *Ibid.*, p. 126.

16. *Ibid.*, p. 127.

17. P. Capstick. *Death in the Silent Places* (New York: St. Martin's Press, 1981), p. 101.

18. Lord Cranworth. *Kenya Chronicles* (London: Macmillan & Co., Ltd., 1939), pp. 227–228.

19. R. Meinertzhagen. *Army Diary, 1899–1926* (Edinburgh: Oliver & Boyd, 1960), p. 136.

CHAPTER 9

1. R. Meinertzhagen. *Army Diary, 1899–1926* (Edinburgh: Oliver & Boyd, 1960), p. 139.

2. *Ibid.*, p. 141.

3. *Ibid.*

4. *Ibid.*

5. *Ibid.*, p. 143.

6. *Ibid.*, p. 159.

7. *Ibid.*, p. 160.

8. *Ibid.*, p. 163.

9. *Ibid.*, p. 164.

10. James Ambrose Brown. *They Fought for King and Kaiser* (Johannesburg: Ashanti Publishing (Pty) Limited, 1991) p. 213.

11. *Ibid.*

12. R. Meinertzhagen. *Army Diary, 1899–1926* (Edinburgh: Oliver & Boyd, 1960), p. 167.

13. *Ibid.*

14. *Ibid.*, p. 170.

15. *Ibid.*, p. 173.

16. *Ibid.*, p. 174.

17. *Ibid.*, p. 178.

18. *Ibid.*, p. 179.

19. *Ibid.*, p. 184.

20. *Ibid.*, p. 183.

21. *Ibid.*, p. 184.

22. *Ibid.*, p. 189.

23. *Ibid.*, p. 190.

24. *Ibid.*

25. *Ibid.*

26. *Ibid.*, p. 195.

27. *Ibid.*, p. 198.

28. *Ibid.*, p. 203.

CHAPTER 10

1. R. Meinertzhagen. *Army Diary, 1899–1926* (Edinburgh: Oliver & Boyd, 1960), p. 210.

2. *Ibid.*, p. 218.

3. *Ibid.*, p. 222.

4. *Ibid.*, p. 224.

5. *Ibid.*, p. 294.

6. *Ibid.*, p. 227.

7. *Ibid.*, p. 234.

8. *Ibid.*, p. 242.

9. *Ibid.*, p. 236.

10. *Ibid.*, p. 249.

11. *Ibid.*

12. *Ibid.*, p. 252.

13. *Ibid.*, p. 269.

14. R. Meinertzhagen. *Middle East Diary, 1917 to 1956* (London: The Cresset Press, 1959), p. 22.

15. *Ibid.*, p. 60.

16. *Ibid.*, p. 50.

17. *Ibid.*, p. 88.

18. *Ibid.*, pp. 87–88.

19. *Ibid.*, p. 275.

20. R. Meinertzhagen. *Army Diary, 1899–1926* (Edinburgh: Oliver & Boyd, 1960), p. 275.

21. *Ibid.*, p. 295.

22. *Ibid.*, p. 282.

CHAPTER 11

1. R. Meinertzhagen. *Middle East Diary 1917 to 1956* (London: The Cresset Press, 1959), p. 140.

2. *Ibid.*, p. 145.

3. *Ibid.*, p. 158.

4. *Ibid.*, p. 159.

5. *Ibid.*, pp. 208–209.

6. *Ibid.*, p. 219.

7. *Ibid.*, p. 221.

8. *Ibid.*, p. 223.

EPILOGUE

1. R. Meinertzhagen. *Middle East Diary, 1917 to 1956* (London: The Cresset Press, 1959), pp. 254–255.

2. R. Meinertzhagen. *Kenya Diary, 1902–1906* (London: Eland Books, 1984), p. 233.

3. R. Meinertzhagen. *Diary of a Black Sheep* (Edinburgh: Oliver & Boyd, 1964), pp. 358–359.

Index

description of the African warthog
in, 100–101
destruction of, 6
discussion of Koitalel's death in, 142
dislike of black people revealed in,
220
Kenya Diary, 5, 16, 45, 49, 53–79,
87
spying in, 149, 164
DPM (Dirty Paper Method), 197,
240
Driscoll, Daniel "Jerry," 204
Drought, J. J., 2, 3
Ducks Unlimited, 21

East Africa, 1–8, 45, 80–104, 183–
208, 252
East African Rifles, 50
Eastwood, Mr., 87–88
Ecotourism, 106
Eden, Anthony, 276
Egypt, 236, 243, 252, 261
Egyptian Expeditionary Force, 243
Eighteenth Cavalry, 168
*Elephant Hunting in East Equatorial
Africa* (Neumann), 100
Elephants, 99–100, 105–6, 107, 115,
143, 214
Eliot, Charles, 122
Embu country, 109–10
England. *See also* Britain
Meinertzhagen in, 128, 158, 160,
165, 234
and the Paris Peace Conference,
252
Ethiopia, 89, 101
Ethnic cleansing, 148
Eton College, 268
Euphrates River, 173
Explorers Club, 151

Falkland Islands, 262
Falkner, Dr., 88
Farley Down, 35, 250
Feisal of Transjordan, 255
Ferdinand, Franz, 179
Field Service Regulations, 191
Field tactics, 43–44

Finch-Hatton, Denys, 193
First Battalion, 39
First War of Independence (1881),
33
Foch, Ferdinand, 250
Foran, W. Robert, 64, 65
Foreign Office, 178, 255, 257–58,
267
Fort Hall, 62–63, 66–67, 70–74, 111,
115, 117, 121
France, 150, 179, 205
and India, 170
Roman Catholic missionaries from,
153
and Russia, 161
Franks story, 241–44
Fuzzy-Wuzzis, 33

Game Department, 192
Gaza, 243, 246
Gazelles, 107, 151, 155
Gcaleka, 133
Geneva Convention, 206, 213
George, Lloyd, 253, 260, 262
Germany, 11, 31, 47, 53, 172
and the Anglo-Boer civil war, 150–
51
Hanoverian forests of, 32
Nazism in, 265, 267, 271
and Palestine, 244
and World War I, 1–4, 149–50,
152–53, 155, 165–166, 179, 180,
182, 252–53
Ghana, 193
Gibbons affair, 109–10
Giraffe, 107, 112
God, 71, 108, 146
Gold Coast, 193
Gordon, Hamilton, 171
Grand Babylon Hotel, 172
Grand Tigris, 171, 172
Grand Tigris Hotel, 171
Greece, 20, 165, 252
Green People, 89
"Greening," 5
Grellman, Volker, 147
Grogan, Ewart, 193, 214
Gulf of Corinth, 165

and battle of Kondoa Irangi, 225–
    28, 230
character of, 4–8, 32–33, 128, 132,
    260–61
and Churchill, 12, 259, 260, 271
and death of his dog, 123–125
and death of his brother Dan, 31–
    32
delivery of a baby by, 165–66
dislike of non-British by, 166–67
DPM (Dirty Paper Method) of,
    197, 240
first exposure to military life, 33–34
and the Gibbons affair, 109–10
and the Hampshire Yeomanry, 32–
    34, 36, 167, 250
and Hitler, 265–66, 268–70
hospitalization of, for depression,
    259
hunting records, 48
illnesses of, 47, 80–81, 259
injury of, in a train wreck, 165
and the King's African Rifles, 50,
    130, 145, 186, 206–7, 233
and the Koitalel affair, 132–33, 136–
    44, 146, 150, 155–56, 275
and Lawrence, 4, 7, 95, 176, 253–
    54, 259
marriages of, 167, 259
and the Nandi campaign, 122–23,
    124, 128–56
photographs of, 32, 139, 177, 239,
    251
and the punt-gun incidents, 20–21,
    23–27
rebelliousness of, 32–33
and the Victorian era, 4, 8, 9–29,
    60, 72, 276
and Weizmann, 160, 237, 241,
    248, 254, 260, 266, 270–73, 275
and the wreck of the SS
    Transylvania, 238–39
Melksham, 34, 36
Mellon, James, 85
Meon Valley, 34
Mesopotamia, 157, 171, 172, 176,
    184, 261. See also Iraq
Mexico, 48

Middle East, map of, 52. See also
    specific countries
Miles, "Tich," 193
Mill, John Barker, 27
Miller, Charles, 130, 192
Missionaries, 122–24, 130, 153
"Mixed double," 117–18
Mombasa, 50, 53–54, 125, 128–30,
    155–56, 180–81, 184, 195, 204–
    5, 232–33
Mombasa Club, 54
Mondalay, 48
Mongolia, 15
Monte Carlo, 15
Montezuma, 39
Moshi, 153, 187, 226
Mosul, 173, 174
Mottisfont, 14–18, 23, 27–29, 37–38,
    184, 270
Mount Elgon, 64
Mount Kenya, 62, 83, 92, 105,
    119
Mount Kilimanjaro, 81, 83, 55, 151,
    186, 192, 221
Mount Kinangop, 83
Muslims, 92, 104, 170, 213, 256

Nairobi, 55–57, 59, 62, 68, 86–87,
    92, 101–2, 121, 125, 155, 186,
    214, 216, 233
Naivasha region, 108–9
Nakuru, 88
Namibia, 114, 116, 147, 175
Nandi Field Force, 133
Nandi Fort, 129–30, 137, 142, 146,
    149
Nandi tribe, 122–24, 130–33, 135–
    36, 140–44, 275–76. See also
    Nilotic Nandi tribe
Nansen, Fridtjof, 32
Napoleonic era, 44, 235
Nasirabad, 39, 40, 42–43, 45–46
Nasirabad Tent Club, 42
Natal (ship), 156
Nathaniel, George, 256
National Guard, 33
Natural History Museum, 137
Nazism, 265, 267, 271